TOTALXS

TOTALXS

RHETTHUTCHENCE

NEW
HOLLAND

First published in Australia in 2004 by
New Holland Publishers (Australia) Pty Ltd
Sydney • Auckland • London • Cape Town

14 Aquatic Drive Frenchs Forest NSW 2086 Australia
218 Lake Road Northcote Auckland New Zealand
86 Edgware Road London W2 2EA United Kingdom
80 McKenzie Street Cape Town 8001 South Africa

National Library of Australia Cataloguing-in-Publication Data:

Hutchence, Rhett.
Total XS.

ISBN 1 74110 077 1.

1. Hutchence, Michael. 2. Singers - Australia - Biography.
3. Rock musicians - Australia - Biography. I. Title.

782.42166092

Hardback edition published in the United Kingdom
ISBN 1 74110 182 4

Co-writer and Editor: Larry Buttrose
Managing Editor: Monica Berton
Project Editor: Liz Hardy
Designers: Karl Roper and Joanne Buckley
Production Controller: Kellie Matterson
Printed in Australia by Griffin Press, Adelaide

10 9 8 7 6 5 4 3 2 1

contents

dedication time

To my beautiful children, Zoe Angel, Sophia Rose, and Banjo, who were my inspiration to become and remain clean.

To my Dad, Kell, a true gentleman. I thank you for your patience and belief in me.

To my brother Michael, a loving, sensitive, soul, who brought an interesting aspect of the world into our lives. My people thank your people.

All my Angels, Andrew Farriss, Andy Patchett, Anmarie Myers, Astra, Arthur, Arthur Grogan, Auntie Croy, Baron Von Walters, Beaver, Brad & family, Byron Bay Post Office, Cameron, Cameron Bennell, Cathy Sneddon, Cassie, Charles & Luli, Charles and Marlene, Chris, Jack & Jali, Damian, Davina, Chris & Jed, Dee Mytton, Dean Agic, Desley White, Elaine, Fiona Schultz, Kate Richards, Liz Hardy and the rest of the team at New Holland, Garry Gary Beers, Greg Perano, Guru Adrian, Gus, Cosi, Ashanti and Emerson, James Corliss, Joan Poignonnec, Jane Chandler, Jenny Morris, Jon Farriss, Jo, Kay, Jai & Che Kennard, Kate & Jean Poole, Katy, Kayti, Hector, Severin and Bella, Kirk Pengilly, Kendall Casey, Lazy John, Lil Indy, Luka, Luke, Mandy & Russel, Margaret Helback, Mary Woods, Mark Hayning, Michele Bennet, Misti Bernard, Nick, Clare and Grace Morley, Nick & Jenni Donnelly, Nino, Paddy Door, Paul and Rebecca, Paul Hayes, Peter L, Phoebe and Rebecca Black, Plague, Putu, Terry & Ryder, Rachel Edwards, Rachel O'Dwyer, Sandy & Robbie, Sigi, Skate O'Neill, Steve Miller, Susie Hutchence, Tim Farriss, Troy, Mahogany & Epiphany Planet and all the others who have stuck by me or helped me with my journey.

the airport

What I do remember I remember perfectly. But there are gaps, some of which I only became aware of much later.

A month before my twelfth birthday I was walking home from school with my brother Michael to our house in Belrose, a leafy Northern Beaches suburb of Sydney. It was 1974, midwinter, a crisp chill in the air. Michael was two years older, already a serious teenager. I was having problems with maths and asked him to help me with my homework, as he sometimes did.

It had been a pretty humdrum day at school, nothing out of the ordinary. Also, as usual, my parents had been having 'troubles', but Michael and I didn't think too much about it. Dad was up in Maitland that day, running his clothing factory. I was wondering what we'd be having for dinner as we turned into our cul-de-sac. Manicured lawns, deep suburbia. Michael used to call the neighbourhood Sausage Hill because of all the barbecues and pool parties. Normal as far as the eye could see.

Or was it?

As we entered the driveway, there was a strange car parked there. When we went inside, in the living room I noticed things stacked up in cardboard boxes. Mum walked in with what looked like two airline tickets flapping in her hand, and introduced a stranger standing behind her. Hello Mrs So'n'so. In a hurried tone she told Michael to go upstairs and pack the suitcase she'd left on his bed. He did as he was told.

Mum then told me that she and Michael were going away to Los Angeles for a while, while Mrs So'n'so would be looking after me until Dad came back from Maitland. I was to remain there with Mrs So'n'so. I listened, nodded. I didn't know it then, but she was to be my first Dial-an-Angel, like dial a nanny. You call them after Dial-a-Crisis.

Then, no matter how much I cried, they were gone, off to the airport, and the City of Angels. And I was left with mine.

I phoned Dad and told him Mum and Michael had gone. He was dumbfounded. Shocked. Speechless. He took it so hard that he couldn't even do the three-hour drive down from Maitland to Sydney. Instead he called a friend in Sydney who drove up and brought him back.

It wasn't the first time Mum had run off. Once she took Michael and me to her mother's place in Melbourne. After Dad came home to an empty house, he jumped onto a plane to try to work things out and retrieve us. The cracks in a once healthy marriage were widening though. On that occasion Mum did come back. But this time she and Michael were gone for a year and a half, and things were never the same again. Our family life had changed forever. But the reality of that day was not to be revealed to me for many years.

Dad had to keep working, and was gone half of each week. I was left with the Angels. I don't remember the first, but I do remember they didn't last long. One by one they left, or, as a result of something they did to me or I did to them, were replaced. One of them accidentally sliced the top of my thumb when she swiped at me with a knife as I tried to grab a finger-full of chocolate cake-mix out of a mixing bowl. Bye bye Angel. Dad caught one shooting up with her bikie boyfriend in her bedroom. So long Angel. One of them got drunk and tried to come onto my dad. Seeya Angel.

I got the odd letter from LA, the odd package, the odd surprise. News and views from a world I had tasted myself on a short visit a few months before—so familiar, yet so different, so far. But all the T-shirts, bubble gum and candy in the world didn't make a difference.

With Michael gone, I soon got bored. I sold my bike and bought a second-hand drum kit. A friend showed me a few beats, making it look easy, but I honestly knew I wasn't improving with practice. The friend was Jon Farriss, who went on to fame in INXS, and is considered one of the best drummers in Australia. I guess I found it intimidating learning from such a talent. I never went back to it, although if anyone asks me now if I play anything, I say 'Drums'. Which I do, a bit.

The news from Michael was mixed. He was enjoying aspects of LA, but was missing the rest of us back in Australia.

Dear Rhett,
It's great to get a letter from you, it really is. I'm coming along pretty well, but miss you and Dad a lot.
*   Your drum set looks great, wish I could play it. Could you ask Dad to send me my guitar, by sea, but make sure it's packed really carefully. Yes, we've got a colour television set, it's borrowed, but works quite well. Say hello to Faz [Andrew Farriss] for me, and Robin or anyone else I know. That's too bad about your finger but that's what happens when you fight. (You must have hit him hard.) Mum says hello; she got your letter and you'll get one from her pretty soon I suppose. I went to that Universal Tour with Tina on Wednesday, it's really incredible but we didn't know it was four hours long. I've finished my bike and I'll send pictures of it as soon as I get some film. Also saw the Superbowl of Motocross, really fantastic. Have you seen it there? I hope you get good enough on your drums to get into a group, just keep at it until it bores you to death, then practise a little more and pretty soon you'll get the hang of it all, haven't got much more to say. Keep cool.*
Michael xx p.s. Hi Dad

I kept up the drumming for a few months, annoying the neighbours, before I got bored with that too and sold the drums for a new surfboard. Bad move. It was a Shane pop-out, el cheapo, mass-produced. After I got bored of boarding, Shane sat in the garage collecting dust.

Before too long Dad was forced to sell the house for a lot less than it was worth as his business needed the cash. My current Angel and I moved into another house Dad had rented, a cream brick bungalow in nearby Frenchs Forest.

My Angels were not memorable women—that is, until Sigi, the last Angel Dad dialled. Sigi was German, twenty-something, a hip hippie who wore a splinter from the Cross of Jesus enclosed in a silver-meshed crucifix around her very alternative neck. She was the great great great great great great (or thereabouts) grand-daughter of the late great Johann Sebastian Bach, a true free spirit, a lovely lovely lady, who introduced me to cheesecloth, herbal tea, incense, and 'pot' as my mum used to call it. I used to think that term was so uncool, though it's kind of in vogue again. To Dad, 'pot' was always 'that marijuana stuff'.

One cold night in the Blue Mountains, while visiting an old hippie friend, Sigi gave me my first joint. We were in an old wooden barn, full of some old pianos and some old sofas and some old joint. It came from a bag bigger than me, though if you remember mid-seventies pot, it wasn't much to rave about. If it hadn't been my first joint I wouldn't have remembered it either. It was Sigi's friends who had rolled it, and to be fair to Sigi, in her professional capacity as an Angel she didn't really want me to have any. Yet I insisted, and being thirteen years old and hard to resist, I wangled a toke. I laughed and laughed and loved it. I had also started getting drunk on the week-ends, as abandoned teenagers do, and found in these releases ways to be funny, to laugh, to forget.

hong kong

Our family life hadn't always been so difficult. We had eight good years in Hong Kong. Good for Michael and me—I don't know about the folks. I suppose their first problems were already appearing even while we were still in nappies.

We had an older half-sister called Tina. Mum had her in 1948 when she was just nineteen years old. At the time it was very much frowned upon to be a single mother, and Tina grew up in Melbourne with Mum's mother. Mum had been a model before deciding to make her living on the other side of the lens. Being more professionally minded than maternal, when Michael was born Mum felt she needed assistance and brought Tina back into the family to help raise him, and later, me. In all fairness, Tina really played more of a mother-role with us.

In 1964 Dad was offered a job working for an international liquor company in Hong Kong, and went on ahead to find us a place to live. I was two when we arrived there. The five of us lived in the Hilton Hotel for six weeks, until we moved into a spacious apartment on Old Peak Road on Hong Kong Island.

Those years were swinging times for my parents, lots of cocktail parties, a social whirl. Mum was working on commercials and movies as a make-up artist and she and Dad met everyone on the circuit. Movie stars, famous people. The singer Frankie Avalon and actor Klaus Kinski and his young daughter Nastassja were among others we entertained. The apartment was always busy with people popping in, lots of dinners and parties.

Dad was forever looking for ways to make more cash. During the 1950s he'd helped introduce louvre windows to the east coast of Australia. After arriving in Hong Kong, during the early days of the Vietnam conflict he got himself a meat gig. He rented an old

DC-3, fitted it with a ten ton freezer, loaded it up with prime Aussie beef and did beef runs into Vietnam. They'd fly in, as dad used to joke, with 'wheels, flaps and underpants down'.

The Americans were always after the freshest beef, and it all went well for a while until Dad decided to go bigger and rented a ship with a twenty-ton freezer. He flew in to Saigon from Hong Kong to meet it, only to read in the paper over his morning coffee that it had been hit by mortar shells and sunk in the Mekong River, with the loss of the captain's life, and all the cargo.

Our family had a Chinese amah, Ah Chang, who was with us most of the time we lived in Hong Kong. I started at a Chinese kindergarten, and learned Cantonese. These days all that's left of my Cantonese is the ability to speak to taxi drivers and count to ten. We moved back to the mainland to Kowloon Tong at the bottom of Lion Mountain and Michael and I both started attending Beacon Hill Primary School.

Neither of us was particularly turned on by school, but we loved getting into the pool afterwards. We were both promising swimmers, even once being picked to race against the Philippines in an international event. But Michael's swimming career came to an abrupt halt when he broke his arm chasing girls around our backyard. It wasn't set properly, and he never quite recovered the full use of it.

Luckily the hospital was just across the road, as I also spent a lot of time there. I was always spraining, cracking or breaking something. The doctors and nurses knew me on a first name basis, and I can still hear Dad groaning exasperatedly, 'What have you done now Rhett?'

One memorable incident occurred when, at the age of seven, I climbed on top of the fridge and ate a whole bottle of tasty Fred Flintstone vitamin pills. Back in the hospital again, having my stomach pumped. Early signs of compulsive behaviour—and my first OD.

I loved Hong Kong. I enjoyed its colours and cultural contrasts. I also loved all the parties, with lots of creative types about. It was where Michael started taking an interest in music, buying records. The first record he ever bought was Jethro Tull's 'Aqualung'. Mine was The Carpenters' 'Close To You'. I had a thing about The Carpenters. Dad took Michael and me to see them when they played in Hong Kong. I still like them today. No, really.

Just before we left Hong Kong, Tina got a job as a nanny with a man in Burbank, Los Angeles, whom she later married and with whom she had her son Brent.

On the way back to Sydney we had a family holiday stopover in Bali, staying at the La Taverna Hotel in Sanur. At the time it was the only hotel on the beach.

It was a magical time for us all. Two weeks on the beach, in temples, playing with monkeys. *Kecak* and *Legong* dances, gamelan music. Tropical fruits. The sun, the sand, the sea.

It was my last memory of us as an intact family unit, without a care in the world. I suppose that's one reason why Bali has always been so special to me.

4 skene place

Returning from Hong Kong to Sydney in the early seventies, it wasn't too long before we moved into Mum and Dad's dream house, in Belrose—a two-storey, orange brick, faux Tudor mansion with four bedrooms, two bathrooms, a dining room and large rumpus room. The address was 4 Skene Place: I was surprised no-one else got the joke.

Michael and I settled back into school, not necessarily the work, just the fringe benefits: making friends, mucking about, mischief and mayhem. Well, I did anyway. Before returning to Australia, we had been very buddy-buddy, doing most things together. Mainly this was because foreigners living in Hong Kong were close-knit. We shared friends, good times, everything.

But Australia was different, and we started to make friends with our classmates, kids of our own age. The first time my big brother told me I couldn't go somewhere with him, it hurt. But that's life, I got over it, although I was jealous he got to do things that I couldn't because of my age.

On our first Christmas in the new house, there was a sense of excitement and whispered hush-hush conversations. The folks had obviously organised something big, and were noticeably chuffed. Michael and I sensed it, but try as we might, we couldn't figure out what was in store. Previous Christmases in Hong Kong had never been a disappointment. Growing up in the middle of the world's biggest toy factory was a child's dream.

As per usual, Christmas morning we were up while it was still dark and off downstairs to the tree. There was a card on the branches for Michael and a big present under the tree for me. The card was attached to a red ribbon. Michael opened it and it said, 'Dear Michael, Happy Xmas '72. Follow the ribbon XX'. We followed the ribbon. It trailed out of the dining room, through the kitchen and off into the garage.

We opened the door and there was a brand spanking new shiny Honda XR-75 mini-bike. Fucking beautiful! A seventies adolescent's wet dream. Michael was beside himself, then on the bike, kicking it over, revving it up, and quickly waking up Mum and Dad. Dad came downstairs smiling, but telling Mike to knock it off till a bit later. I was feeling very jealous…but…wait…what was I getting? I left Michael beaming and followed the ribbon back to the tree.

My package was large yet intriguingly light, not your preferred combination for a kiddie Christmas present. I ripped off the wrapping to reveal…a punching bag. I was going to need one. Disappointed to say the least, nearly crying as I set it up. As far as punching bags went, it wasn't even a good one. I punched it, it fell over and that's where it stayed. I guess I must have been pretty angry that Michael got such a great present and I got such a crap one. Up until then we had both been treated fairly and equally by Mum and Dad so I really didn't understand their reasoning in giving us such different presents.

The following Christmas I got a Yamaha YZ-80, and promptly ran over my old punching bag. From then on, most afternoons and weekends Michael and I blazed through Belrose, tore along Terrey Hills fire trails, glazed the brick pits and dusted Oxford Falls. Some nights we would meet up with friends and cruise over to the old Skyline drive-in to see what we could watch from the outside for free.

Michael took riding more seriously than I did, having more balls. He upgraded his bike and got fully decked out. Dad built a special trailer and even got full leathers stitched for us both in Hong Kong.

One school holidays Dad rented a holiday house near his factory in Maitland. After we had been there a few days riding around, we were out one evening when it started to get dark so Michael hitched up the trailer and we headed back towards where we were staying. I was sitting in the back of the car looking out the window when we went over a little bump and I saw our trailer cruise past, overtaking us, jump the gutter and smash into the corner of a newsagency. Both bikes shot out of their shackles and flew from the trailer through the air, eventually landing, then scraping and sliding, and finally stopping up the footpath. Dad screeched us to a halt and we all jumped out to inspect the damage. Considering the events, the bikes weren't too badly damaged. Only a couple of bends, mangles and dents to fix, and the newsagency had only lost a few bricks.

It was lucky the bikes hadn't gone through the window, lucky it was a Sunday, and lucky no-one was around. Dad hitched up the trailer and told us to get on our bikes and hurry home. The next day he went back to the newsagent to offer them some money, but they said it was okay. Seventies Australia…imagine that now.

Back at home, I was aware of troubles between my parents, but I never dreamed they would lead to what they did: Mum's escape to LA, and the ultimate break-up of our family. But that of course was what happened. Six months after our holiday in Maitland, Mum and Michael were gone.

frenchs forest

A year after Mum and Michael's departure, my Angel Sigi and I moved into the house in Frenchs Forest that Dad had rented. He came down on weekly visits from his factory, but we didn't see that much of him. He had to work hard to keep our heads above water.

When the first shopping centre was built in the area, being close to my house, it soon became my home away from home, a new place to get up to mischief. After school and during the night, the shopping centre was the local hang. Skateboards had just made a comeback and a bunch of us used to whittle away the hours on the sloping car park and slick new walkway through the mall. Pretty soon skateboards were prohibited and the centre had to employ a security guard to chase us around. But come nightfall, it was our domain.

On weekends, way past the closing of the fish and chip shop, we would hang out and get drunk on a bottle of the finest Brandivino or vintage Blackberry Nip that we'd all chip in for and get some-one over eighteen to buy for us. Early signs of the manipulation skills I later honed to perfection. Mum always told me I'd make a good used car salesman.

I must have been pretty angry or bored, and without much parental guidance I was becoming adventurous, reckless. I became friends with a guy down the street, Gazza, who was a couple of years older, and he became the main instigator of my early criminal career. Until I met him I'd been happy doing late night commando-style crawling up someone's lawn to lift their milk money, or making prank phone calls. But under his influence and guidance, I started doing break and enters. Only shops after hours. There is a kind of safety knowing you're the only ones inside, and are not going to awaken some irate owner. I would have been shit scared doing houses—I don't handle confrontation.

We got small change for the most part, petty cash, no safes or anything. Usually the most expensive items left out were the new-fangled calculators. Plus a guitar here, a complete set of dental tools and wax impression plates there—slim and weird pickings really.

I started looking further afield for kicks. A football field, to be exact. It was over the road from the oval where we played rugby on Saturday mornings when I first saw it—a portable tuck-shop, crammed full of meat pies, soft drinks, chips, cream buns…and lollies and lollies and lollies.

During the week, this Cecil B Demeals on wheels lived a quiet, stationary life in the car park of the service station next door to the shopping centre. I hatched the plan late one night after a joint brought on the munchies. Under the cover of darkness and the influence of mind-bending chemicals, I climbed onto the van's big silver roof, prised the air vent off its hinges, and dropped down inside.

The first thing I noticed was I couldn't notice anything. It was pitch black, and as I didn't have a light I groped my way to the door. I was pretty fucking scared, adrenaline pumping, but when I opened the door and saw my mates I felt relieved, and cracked the biggest cheesiest grin imaginable.

Someone found a shopping trolley and we loaded it up with boxes of licorice, musk sticks, redskins, cobbers, milk bottles, sherbet fountains, chocolate and caramel buttons, wild berries, snakes, and any other kiddie teeth rotters we could find. After we filled another trolley, it was time to leave the vault, seek refuge and stuff our faces. As we pushed and pulled the heavy trolleys away we eagerly sampled our spoils, leaving a trail of wrappers which the police had no difficulty following. They caught us red-handed, chocolate-mouthed and rainbow-tongued. We were taken down to the station and parents and minders called in.

We got off lightly. No charge, court or conviction. Just a stern warning from a well-meaning sergeant who thought a reprimand was all that was needed to save us from a life of crime. We each had to pay back around $18 for what we'd taken—a small fortune in those days.

I wasn't supposed to hang out with Gazza after that, but we managed to get together and hatch more mayhem before his family moved away.

After the great lolly heist came the supermarket. I told Gazza I'd noticed that about eight feet up the wall at the back of the store was a two-foot square hole in the bricks, which was an outlet for a large industrial fan. Every half hour or so the blades stopped spinning momentarily, and it was possible to crawl quickly between them before they started moving again, and hop down into the back of the supermarket. You'd have to plan your move precisely as it was extremely dangerous, but we did it.

The procedure became routine. Friday nights Gazza and I would enter through the vent while a mate kept watch out front. First stop Aisle Three, garbage bags. One of us would hit the confectionery section while the other would start in hardware and stationery, filling up with padlocks, batteries, pencils and whatever caught our imagination. The riskiest part was crawling up to the checkouts for the cigarettes, as they were in an exposed area. When we had enough of what we wanted, and the fan stopped and the coast was clear, we would toss out the bags, jump out and run.

We hit the supermarket every Friday for two months until they grated up our entrance. That was okay really because we still had heaps of stuff hidden in stockpiles in the bush. A good lurk while it lasted, especially as we didn't get caught.

One day, out of the blue, after an eighteen-month absence, Mum and Michael arrived back, bearing gifts. Mum had injured her back on a movie set, and had decided to return to recuperate. Just as when they left, I have few memories, though I do have a mental picture of Mum arriving back in a wheelchair.

So they had returned, and I was happy to see them, but not necessarily happy that Mum was back. I had less leeway with her than I did with Dad. At the same time I was resentful that she'd gone to Hollywood and not taken me.

But no-one ever spoke about them being away, or me staying behind. Communication between Mum and I sort of ceased, and hence we ceased to get on. I was angry with her, and now, fuelled by drugs, would start fights over anything. Dad, with his love of Asia had just moved to the Philippines.

Michael had left as a boy and came back a young man of sixteen. He'd become fashion-conscious and more confident. Being that much older, he also got on well with Sigi, almost as an equal, while I was still the kid being cared for by her. But with Mum back, there was no need for Sigi now. Sigi left, much to the disappointment of myself and of Michael, who had also managed to learn a thing or two from her. We hugged and said goodbye to her. Peace.

One of the strongest triggers of childhood for me is the smell of make-up. It comes from playing with the make-up kit Mum used for work. With the help of books and what she taught me, I perfected the art of fabricating stabs, bruises, first to third degree burns, rashes, slashes and bullet wounds. Armed with all the right tools, spirit gums, mortician's wax, latex and lots of theatrical blood, I was always scaring the fuck out of strangers or making the neighbours scream.

One rainy night I covered a mate's long-sleeved white school shirt with nearly a litre of fake blood. We walked up the road and stood in the middle waiting for a car to come by. When we saw headlights, I placed a machete under his arm. With the lights shining brightly on us, we acted our dramatic scene. I looked around shocked and surprised, pulled the knife theatrically from his body and bolted off into the bushes as he crumpled to the ground. The car screeched to a halt, a door opened—and then my mate jumped up, made a sweeping bow, and ran off after me into the bush.

When Mum got a job doing make-up on the long-running seventies soapie *The Young Doctors*, we moved yet again, this time to a flat in Neutral Bay, that definitely genteel suburb on Sydney Harbour's northern foreshore. Though it was closer to her work, for me it meant a new school, Mosman High.

Michael had already formed his life-long connection with the Farriss brothers in their new band, Doctor Dolphin, which soon became The Farriss Brothers, and was busy practising, writing songs, playing, and spending a lot of time out of the flat.

From their early gigs I knew they were going places. It wasn't just brotherly bias—they really did have something. Michael was a great front-man, and the band was tight, a sure-fire combination for success. At the time they were playing lots of covers, from Marley's 'I Shot the Sheriff', to Steely Dan's 'Kid Charlemagne', to 801's 'Miss Shapiro'. But soon they started adding some funky originals to their set-list.

When Mr and Mrs Farriss decided to make the move back to Western Australia, as Jon was yet to finish school, rather than lose a fantastic drummer the rest of the band decided to relocate with the Farrisses. They changed their name to INXS, and started to cut their teeth.

The day soon came when Kirk Pengilly, then the rhythm guitarist and backup singer, rocked over in his white panel van with the Christian fish sticker on the bumper. The sticker was a ploy to deflect suspicion from activities that occasionally went on in the van.

We all had a goodbye bong, Michael's stuff was loaded in, then Michael himself, and they drove off to cross the Nullarbor for Destiny, Western Australia. I cried a lot that afternoon, feeling abandoned again.

With Dad in the Philippines and Michael now gone, it was just Mum and me, and things couldn't help but get steadily worse. I decided I should go and try living with Dad. After making the necessary arrangements, all was set: I was off to finish high school in Manila.

I flew via Perth to visit Michael. He was living with most of the band in a big house in Subiaco. The interior showed all the makings and trappings of fast-approaching success. Messy with rubbish, dirty dishes in the sink, piles of clothes, girls in the rooms and instruments everywhere. There was even a bra hanging off the living room light.

They had a residency at a local pub and were touring to country towns. Things were really moving for them. It was hard work but they seemed to relish it. And there were the obvious fringe benefits of a sex, drugs and rock 'n roll lifestyle.

It was exhilarating for me to see the band up on stage, even if the act was still developing. And it was a fun time for me there too, getting high on hash, being smuggled into gigs, and drinking up their rider. I liked it so much I could have stayed on, but one morning Michael drove me to the airport and it was goodbye, yet again. I was sorry to be leaving but excited at the coming change.

My flight took me via Kuala Lumpur, where I overnighted in a hotel as part of the package. On the way to the hotel the taxi driver asked me if he should return that evening to take me to an opium den. Intrigued but scared, I declined, instead opting for dinner near the hotel. I had an early flight to Manila. I was fifteen years old and a whole new chapter was opening for me.

manila

Apart from extreme poverty, the first thing to hit you as you leave the plane at Manila International Airport is the heat and humidity and you know you're not in Kansas any more. Manila is a huge city, with massive contrasts in wealth. Shantytowns next door to mansions.

Dad was already well settled, living in an apartment in a nice neighbourhood, and was getting into women's shoes and hand-bags—manufacturing, not wearing. He was working hard as ever, and I usually only saw him late at night and on weekends.

The year 1977 was a strange time to live in Manila. Marcos was still in power, so martial law remained in effect. Everybody had to stay off the streets between midnight and 4 am, unless they had a permit—a signed, stamped and dated permission slip. A permit could also be a fifty-peso note, a couple of packets of Marlboros, or the house favourite, Johnnie Walker. If for some reason you were caught out during curfew and couldn't talk your way out or come to some amicable financial agreement, you would be detained overnight. In the morning, curfew breakers were ordered to start cutting the presidential lawn with nail scissors, throughout the heat and humidity of the day.

Dad wanted me to go to a government school, but I insisted on going to one with more foreign students. I didn't want to be the only non-Filipino at school. I also liked the idea of not having to wear a uniform, so the International School was perfect.

When I first arrived in March it was too late to enrol as the schools ran on the American semester system. I spent the days and weeks looking around my new city and hanging at amusement arcades. When the summer vacation finished, I enrolled at the International School. As I'd only attended the first few weeks of year nine back at Mosman High, rather than making me repeat a year Dad told the administration that my records had been burnt in a fire at my previous school.

School began early, at 7.15 am, and went until 12.45 pm, mainly because after midday the heat and humidity made it impossible to work. We took taxis to school. Except for curfew time, taxis were ridiculously cheap. Flag fall was 'Phive Phipty' (five-fifty), and it stayed like that for miles. Generally you could take taxis everywhere—the shop, next door, the toilet.

For a school with students of diplomats and other VIPs, bomb scares and kidnappings were not uncommon, hence the security. Walls fifteen feet high, with blades of broken glass cemented along the top, then rolls of razor wire, made it very difficult if not impossible to get in—and challenging to get out too. The only official way out during school hours was to have an absentee note, signed by the principal, which you would then have to hand in at one of the gates. Easier still was the ten-peso pass, which was a blank sheet of paper with ten pesos folded inside.

Most afternoons a brewery of us would go drinking. Talk about beer group pressure. Our favourite hangs included 'Hobbit House', a low-lit folk bar with large murals of wizards, elves and other creatures from *The Lord of the Rings* on the walls, and staffed entirely by midgets and dwarfs. The bouncers, waiters, bar staff— everybody who worked there was vertically challenged. It's strange to see a tray of beers float past you at knee height. Another favourite haunt was 'Daktari', an African-themed den, with a live tiger in a cage behind the bar. Anyone who got drunk enough could enter the cage and have their photo taken with the tiger. After doing the rounds of the drinking dens, our Liquid Lunch Club would retire to someone's place for more beer, food, joints, and the latest imported tunes.

It was in the Philippines that I started smoking pot every day. Australian weed at the time was stemmy and seedy. But in Manila the quality was astounding, from fluffy green buds to red-haired skunk, to manicured gold heads, to sticky, purple sensemilla that looked like it had been hand painted, and may very well have been. And it was cheap. On the whole we were a very high school.

I didn't have much contact with Mum and Michael back in Australia. Mostly limited to a couple of letters and birthday and Christmas calls. Michael did post me INXS' first single. I was really proud, and raced over to the American Embassy to blast it out over and over on the Youth Club's expensive sound system. I found 'Simon' hard to take seriously, and the flip side 'We Are The Vegetables' didn't explain a thing. But still they had a single out, and things were obviously moving ahead for them.

Dear Dad and Rhett,

Hello there, yes I am very sorry for not writing but I have not had much time and too many things on my mind. I've been working through the day to support myself as we are putting all our 'music money' back into the 'company'. Running costs are high, so is our publicity. Our PA will be finally put together in a month for our big push for the '80s. At the moment we're probably making around a grand or so a week which is a pittance but it covers the cost of hiring PA and lights, which is about $800 a week, the rest goes into an account for posters etc.

As far as the loan goes Dad, I've been a bit behind on the last couple of payments, but not out of carelessness. I just couldn't afford it at the time. But I've sold my microphones and that'll pay for 4–5 months in advance, soon as I can sell the rest I'll pay off the loan.

Do you remember Buffy, Tim's girlfriend? Well her father has some money he's been wanting to invest, he was going to buy some land, but we gave him a proposition. If he bought us a PA he'd be making $800–1000 a week from it which is a much better return than buying land. If I had the money I'd do it myself, those PA hire places must make a fortune. He's going to be putting in about $30–50,000 though just for one PA. It'll be good!!!

Mom's eye is much better now. Luckily for her as she might have gone blind but she is only fuzzy in one eye now. It should get better in the future—we can only hope.

The band's being lauded as one of the biggest things in the '80s—so it looks good—we went on 2JJ live to air last month and also we recorded at ABC studios and 3–4 of the songs are being played on 2JJ.

Last week a guy called Michael Browning came and saw us—he's AC/DC ex-manager. He sold out for millions last month, and is starting a new record label–company here. He was very interested in us and will probably sign us up—there are only 3 people in Aussie who can secure overseas contracts and he's one of them.

Ananda's [Michael's girlfriend at the time] back with me and we have moved once more!! But this time it's for a while. We've got an old style flat with shag carpets—dimmers on the lights, really nice antique furniture etc. etc. $85 a week—a guy called Ashley who is an actor is also living with us.

As far as a Xmas present goes for you guys well—I ain't got no money!! BUT I'll send you our first EP or a tape of it either over Xmas or Jan OK.

Hey Rhett, in Dad's last letter he says you've quit school. WHY? Write and tell me, OK. I know all the obvious factors like it's very boring at times—and it's a hassle to get out of bed and have to actually think all day. But put it this way—what it comes down to is this. Now that you have quit school you'll have no piece of paper saying you went. So nobody knows how smart you are, when you go for whatever you want to do. So that means that the next bastard that isn't as smart as you, considering your talent in many fields, will get the position. Or job, or higher salary because he finished school even if he got an average or below mark than what you could have got. I went through to 6th form but I never studied and generally I'm not the academic type so I got a lousy mark. But you're bloody intelligent and all I can say is that the harder you work now, the easier it will be for the rest of your life, that's no bullshit—it's a fact I've learnt the hard way. To support myself at the moment I'm working in factories and screwed jobs like that. I get up at 7 am and work my ass off for lousy pay and always feel thick in the head 'cause I can't get better jobs that use brains. So the moral is get a good pass in your exams. Go to another place and study or something and you'll be able to get up at 8 or 9 am, use your brain, get paid well, 'cause you finished high school. The only way to get anywhere unless you're a talented genius is to buck the system at its own game. Fuck you've only got till May '80 to finish then you can tell the school to stick it and laugh down at the teachers etc. in a few years when you drive by in your new car + 3 piece suit and say to 'em 'You couldn't bring this one down'. Believe me you're too smart to waste opportunities like good exam results. I screwed my exams up, now don't do it to yourself as well. PLEASE.

Sorry to lecture you but I care a lot for your future and even though you might be able to do it by yourself, the chances are like one million to one 'cause everybody is out to beat everyone else. Your best friend, will never be able to support you when you're out in the world—it'll be you against the rest of the world. Get a head start or be honestly prepared to work your ass off for the rest of your life, just to exist. (There I go again.)

Guess I better go now, Take care, both of you—and write back to me Rhett. I mean it this time. Don't you think I want to hear from you? Everything you do is important. I love you. So don't hurt yourself. Anything you want you can have, it's just a matter of knowing how to get it.

Lots of love to you both,
Michael

I hadn't actually quit school, as much as I might have liked to. But it was good for making friends, that's for sure. As most of my friends' parents held positions in the US government, I got to hang out at the embassy often. So much so that security at the front gate got lax, eventually stopped checking for passes and just waved my taxis through. This meant that when I bought greenbacks on the black market, I could get my friends to buy imported records, cigarettes or American groceries for me at the commissary. It was cheaper than buying the same food on the black market for three times the price. I also got to see the latest movies from the States, had access to the pool, and developed a taste for Mai Tais and Zombies from the bar at happy hour.

Some afternoons, a bunch of us would go up to a friend's eighth-storey apartment and sit on the balcony and smoke spliffs and drink beers. From up there you could see the airport's constant stream of aircraft on approach, or taxiing down the runway for take-off.

One day we were watching planes come and go when we saw black smoke rising from behind some buildings, so we jumped in the car to check it out. We knew where there was a hole in the airport fence, and we came to a Chinese 707 gutted out in the short grass off one of the runways. Surprisingly there were no security guards stopping the quickly assembled crowd from looting. There was a lot of booty strewn about, from half-burnt cartons of cigarettes to clothing and meal trays and cutlery. I even found the flame-singed flight manifest showing two hundred passengers on board. The plane must have been carrying a shipment of Oil of Olay beauty cream too, because the smell of it mixed in with the foam the fire crew had sprayed over the wreckage creating a familiar but pungent stench.

The next day the papers reported that a small fire had broken out in the tail section just before the plane had landed, and the pilot had gone into an emergency procedure. Everyone on board had exited down the escape chutes and no-one had been hurt beyond smoke inhalation, and minor burns to the hands of a stewardess who heroically helped people off until she was the last one on board.

The airport had long been a place of fun for us. Whenever we were bored on the weekends, we'd grab some beer and roll some spliffs up and drive along the service road beside the main runway. We'd make our way to the end near the red marker lights and sit and watch take-offs and landings, the planes barely fifteen metres above us, until security noticed and sent cars out.

One night we ventured even further down the tarmac, and a jumbo jet thundered towards us. I lay down on my stomach and cupped my hands around my ears, watching it get nearer and nearer, louder and louder. The wing tip passed about five metres above my head and the wheels left the tarmac right in front of me. It was so fucking loud, and I was pelted all over with little rocks and bits of twig and flying grass. Our esky broke up, flying away and losing all the beer and ice. We stopped going there when security chased us one night, firing shots at us as we ran back to our car.

A classmate, Brad, turned up at school one day with a bottle of Valium. I asked him where he got it and he reluctantly told me about the ambulance at the embassy. A few nights later I broke into the ambulance and found a black leather doctor's bag.

Among other things, we found more Valium, a vial of morphine and one of methedrine. I had never shot up before, but one of the others was happy to play nurse, and skin-popped mein butt. I didn't feel much, and soon fell asleep. Later we divvied up the loot, though we hardly knew what to do with most of it.

Brad also had an army issue smoke bomb. It was a drab, olive green, stubby aerosol can with a pin on top like a grenade. We were trying to think of some place to use it as a prank. I suggested the school, and Brad said, 'It's yours to do, if you do do it', and I said, 'Consider it do done did.'

I used it the following Friday in the cafeteria. I waited until the place was maximum students per square metre, holding the canister in my schoolbag, then pulled the pin and rolled the can across the floor.

For a moment I didn't think it was going to work, but then thick purple smoke started spewing out, billowing up until it hit the low ceiling and spread out like a bright purple mushroom cloud. It looked fantastic, and I would have loved to stay and watch the whole thing, but I hightailed it outta there. Soon smoke billowed from each doorway, followed by coughing students and kitchen staff. The guards ran up trying to figure out the problem, adding to the commotion. Eventually the police were called and the empty can was taken away to be examined.

A week later the principal called me in and angrily said he knew I had done it. I denied any involvement and left. He called my dad and told him, and though they never proved anything, I was given an early graduation, seven weeks before school finished. I still got my diploma, but missed out on the square hat ceremony. That was alright. I wasn't in school for academic reasons, it was purely social.

After three years of just scraping through high school, I left Manila to go back to Sydney. I'd had a nice connection there with

Dad, and was sad to leave him. The night before I left I decided to take some of that good Manila pot back with me. I took the inner soles out of my sneakers, that Dad manufactured, and started digging a deep gouge out of the rubber soles. Then I mulled the pot into a fine powder and put it into two airtight packets which I set into the gouges, and replaced the inner soles. Very professional. Voila, constant reminders that you're doing something illegal. Every step I took I felt the pot in my sneakers, 'pot pot pot pot pot pot', all the way home. Very stupid.

I acted naively on arrival in Sydney and declared a butterfly knife. Was it illegal? I wasn't sure, I wouldn't want to get in trouble by bringing anything illegal into the country. Sure, I told Mr Customs Man, you can keep it.

sydney

Michael picked me up at Sydney Airport. It had been three years since I'd seen him and he had turned from an adolescent into a young man. The band was recording its debut album, fittingly titled *INXS*, and playing gigs around the traps, still at the beginning of a very long road. They were touring relentlessly, as the rock cliché goes, and soon would be crisscrossing the country playing almost every night, living out of vans, coaches, and cruddy little motel rooms.

Being the elder brother, Michael wasn't very impressed with my pot smuggling from Manila, but after his lecture he was happy enough to have a joint with me. I decided against sharing any other dubious adventures with him.

He was living in Neutral Bay now with his current girlfriend, Vicky Kerridge, an artist who had her own flat overlooking the wharf. Vicky was an XTC freak in the days they were a band you were into, and not the drug. The flat was small, with one bedroom, and every night I'd fall asleep on the couch to the sound of them fucking. So it wasn't too long before I looked elsewhere, and moved into a run-down, four-bedroom share house in Mosman.

The Tivoli, the Tiv, or I LOV IT backwards, was one of the better venues in Sydney at the time, a place to see the best of local and overseas bands. The Oils, Cold Chisel, the Models, the Birthday Party, Mental As Anything, Jenny Morris, Hunters and Collectors, the Hoodoo Gurus, as well as INXS, all brought the house down numerous times with spectacular yet intimate gigs designed for the trash Eighties pseuds, the up-market Stolli and Bolli crowd that shunned the more down to earth venues like the Trade Union Club, or as we dubbed it, the Dried Onion.

I went to the Tiv one night to see Jo Jo Zep and The Falcons. When they took the stage and I went up closer to watch, I happened to glance down and saw what I thought was a ten-dollar note. It was dark, and as there was no-one near it, I slid over and put my foot on it. It felt odd, lumpy. I realised it wasn't just one note. I stood there transfixed, heart pounding. I forgot all about the band and looked around, expecting to see someone frantically searching for whatever was under my foot. Then, in a single orchestrated movement, I bent down, picked up the wad and shoved it under my shirt. Outside I counted it three times to be sure. It turned out to be eight fifty-dollar notes in a rubber band.

The amount happened to be the high-range price for an ounce of good coke. I hoped the poor bastard who lost it didn't end up paying too high a price for his mistake, headless and handless in a shallow grave out west. But what was I going to say? 'Oh, has any-one just lost a suspiciously large amount of cash?' Or hand it in to the police? It was better off with me than the NSW Constabulary.

I felt pretty chuffed, and bought two bottles of French champagne. Then, just like on acid, I got paranoid, started thinking people were watching me, or looking for a large sum of money, or both. Then a surge of relief as nothing happened, and it appeared I had gotten away with it.

The money didn't last long. I've never been good with money, and having lots of it made me ridiculous. I had a crush on a girl, and on her birthday a dozen of us spent $1600 at Pavilion on the Park restaurant, plus I gave her five grams of coke. But my little binge was nothing for the era. Entire waterfront mansions disappeared up noses in the bathrooms of Sydney nightclubs in those days.

Three weeks later I was broke and kicking myself for it, waiting for my dole cheque to arrive and nothing to show for my windfall but a $150 painting I bought from a friend, Wart, at her exhibition called 'Food Slut'.

I had recently started hanging out with The Models, the Melbourne band, and some of them were using smack. They had a gig at the leg-endary Manzil Room in Kings Cross and I was in their room at the Astoria Hotel as they got ready for the night. A couple of them had chipped in and bought a gram from a hail damaged hooker called Trixie. She made the deal, had her blast and punctually OD'd on the spot. The guys brought her back around by slapping her and then tossing her fully clothed into the shower. It fascinated me that Trixie's state, rather than turning them off, for some reason seemed to make them more eager than ever. They couldn't wait to try some. Funnily enough I did too. I bugged them into giving me a bit, plus hitting me up. I couldn't even watch, that first time. I made a vein stand out on my arm and looked the other way, felt the distinct prick of a needle and briefly thought, 'Is that it?' then smeared the drop of blood across my skin before it stained my shirt.

In seconds a thick, deep blanket rolled like a wave over my brain, over my head, and slid down my body. I rose to go to the bathroom and reaching vertical was instantly sick, leaving my lunch on the lounge. It seemed the most normal thing to do, and no-one seemed to mind. It was curious how everyone else seemed used to this sort of chaotic behaviour.

For the first six months of my using, friends had to hit me up. I would hold out my arm out and look the other way, as though I was getting the cane at school. After that I started taking control of things myself.

Becoming a junkie didn't seem like an option at first, though subconsciously I was carefree and rebellious against society. What started out as a weekend special event quickly descended into a 24/7 fact of life. You don't notice the subtle signs at first, but slowly your mind and body veer in one direction. Before you know it, heroin is central to your existence.

It was James Freud of the Models who gave me my first heroin, and he had a heavy addiction himself. Ironically enough, that week he gave up and stayed clean the whole time I was into it.

Losemore

I first met Sadie and Monique while playing stick at the Clock Hotel in Surry Hills. They had known each other since fourth grade and were both well-bred, middle-class, north-shore girls. Sadie, the blonde, worked as a nurse and frequently consulted, diagnosed and prescribed various concoctions when the other staff weren't paying attention. Monique, the non-blonde one, was studying drama and art at uni. I had a thing for Monique, though, we all soon ended up using together and having long threesomes.

When Monique moved up to the north coast to go to university in Lismore—which I was soon to dub Usemore or Losemore—I followed her.

I found smack a great sex aid; I could stay hard and fuck hard all night. After a while I felt I needed it all the time so my performance stayed the same—though eventually I didn't feel like bonking at all.

To make a little money I started doing drug runs back and forth from Lismore to Sydney. Nothing big—a gram or two. I'd catch the mail train to Lismore and be greeted at six in the morning by loyal customers, and wouldn't even make it down the road to where I was staying before I'd sold out, making $500 in profit. I never managed to save any money though. The more I'd make, the more I'd use, the more I'd spend, the more I'd make, the more I'd use.

After touring the US, Michael and the band went to England and recorded their new album *The Swing*. They had already recorded 'Original Sin' in the US with funk legend Nile Rodgers. The song is almost synonymous with INXS now. Michael was going out with his longtime soul mate Michele Bennett, and mentions her in a letter to me from then.

Dear Rhett,

Hope your doing fine up in the greener pastures of Lismore. Sorry it's taken so long for this letter but I had no idea where to send it until a few weeks ago—anyway this is express delivery via Michele.

Well the album's coming along very well—it's going to be different. Not as dark as Shaboo Shabah. *This studio (the Manor) is great but the Go Karts aren't working, some of the riffraff one has to put up with. Should be back via Japan in about 3 weeks. Worked with Nile Rodgers in NY on a single as well! I miss you a lot and love you— please take care, I'll see you around Xmas.*

Michael X

The Manor, England

I had a mate down in Sydney called Cindy who wanted three pounds of weed and had given me $4200 to organise it. I was introduced to a guy called Greg who showed me some nice heads and said he could get larger amounts. We agreed on the price of $1200 a pound, and he asked me to come over to his place later that evening.

I knocked on the door, and Greg called out to come in. I found myself facing a .22-calibre rifle with a silencer. He said, 'Put the money down and get out.' Simple and to the point. It's hard to argue with someone when they have a gun in your face, so without any fuss I put the money on the bench. I turned to leave, hoping he wouldn't shoot me in the back, and told him that he would be sorry.

Monique said she had a friend who knew people who could get things back in order. I had Greg's name and address, so he wouldn't get away that easily. That night I organised two guys to come up from Sydney. The next day I got a call from the 'rectifiers', Tony and John, who were already in town. They were big men with a no bull-shit attitude. On the way to Greg's place we went over what had happened a few times.

I had never seen the guy who answered the door. When I asked for Greg, the guy said he'd never heard of him, and that I must have the wrong address, and closed the door. I was momentarily con-fused, but I knew it was the right place, so we knocked again. This time when he answered Tony and John pushed him aside and we went in. He was a bit shocked and stood his ground until Tony winded him with a blow which somewhat restored his memory.

The guy sat down and we started turning the house over. I found the silencer under the couch cushions, and John found the rifle in a kitchen cupboard. The guy was still being a bit unhelpful, so John and Tony assisted him with memory recall a bit more, until he told us that Greg didn't live there, he'd just been staying there and he didn't know where he was. We took the rifle and left, and the guys dropped me in town. I gave them a good description of Greg, and they returned to stake the place out.

Greg came back later that night and Tony and John burst in right behind him, taking him by surprise. Greg was a desperate junkie. He had been out scoring and in the short time since he'd ripped me off he'd managed to spend nearly all the money. Tony and John beat him up, took anything of value they could find, his dope, what was left of the cash, and hit the road back to Sydney.

I was distraught. I contemplated suicide, wanting to jump in the swollen creek behind Monique's house. Instead I went back to Sydney to face the music and work something out with Cindy, who of course wanted her money back. I had a bit saved but nowhere near what she needed back. I considered asking Michael for help, but I figured he'd be so fucking angry with me, and I needed support, not another lecture. I started to entertain extreme solutions. The only way I'd ever get that sort of money was if I robbed someone myself, and given my hyper state of mind, thought a bank might be the go.

I borrowed a .357 Magnum off a friend who got it from his father, and for the next few days I walked around Sydney's CBD with a shoulder bag containing the gun, a black balaclava, and some gloves. It was a fucking hard call and stressed me out no end. I cased a few joints, but when it came down to it I couldn't bring myself even to enter a bank.

Eventually I went over to the house Michael had just bought in Paddington, and broke down. I showed him the gun and told him my plans. I really felt a failure, not even having the guts to carry through my plan. Michael kind of freaked, was angry, lectured. Then a few days later he called me up and agreed to lend me the money if I agreed to pay him back. It came out of one of his first big royalty cheques with INXS. I paid back my friend, and, years later, Michael too.

deepest, darkest darlinghurst

When I returned to live in Sydney, I moved into the city so that my habit could be closer to my habitat. So close in fact that I cohabited with two dealers. Carl, who sold speed, and Jason, who was a home delivery smack dealer.

I rode home one day, parked my motorcycle, and opened the front door. A detective calmly walked down the stairs, asking who I was. Funny, it should have been the other way around. He ushered me into my living room where there was another undercover bloke making himself at home. I could hear someone else upstairs.

The first detective asked me where I had been.

'Yoga.'

He must have thought I was being smart, because he asked me again.

'Yoga,' I repeated.

I may not have looked like a yogi, but it was true. I'd been going to classes run by an ex SAS paratrooper who made you get into grotesque poses, 'Or else!'.

The cop decided to pursue another line of questioning and asked about Carl and his dealing activities. Of course I knew nothing, but Carl's room told another story. It was cluttered with used fits, bloody swabs, magazines mutilated for packet squares and blackened spoons aplenty. Carl wasn't dealing speed big time, but had a healthy habit and made spare change.

I hated speed. I'd tried it a few times. The rush was okay but I didn't enjoy staring at the ceiling too wired for sleep. Plus it prematurely ages you. As Frank Zappa said, 'Speed turns you into your parents, man'.

The cop found a small amount of grass in my room, but luckily I'd just unloaded a lot more. I couldn't believe it when he opened up my wardrobe and grabbed the top of an enormous nitrous oxide canister with Royal North Shore Hospital brightly stencilled on the side to search behind it for contraband. If the cops hadn't broken in they may have had a legal leg to stand on. Instead he just wrote down my name and said, 'Tell Carl to watch it, cos we'll be back', and left. I watched them empty my pot on the road outside and swept it back up after they drove off.

Postcards came back from various dots on the globe from Michael. His tone was as ever up-beat, happy.

> *Hi Rhett,*
> *Hope your fine. This hotel is not so bad! Europe is good to us.*
> *Andrew says Hi. I miss you. Take care. Be good. Danke!! Michael*
> *Bad Hotel, Scheveningan, Holland*

> *Hi ya!*
> *It's very cold here −4 degrees. Had reindeer for breakfast and watched mini icebergs go down the river. Tim Dowling is here and said Hi to you. We all went to a club full of Viking descendants and got…well you know the story. Love to you. Michael (Nice hotel, it's where we played as well.)*
> *Oslo, Norway*

The band's singles and albums were now charting everywhere. Though it seemed like it took ages, it really did happen quickly for INXS. One day Dee Why, the next Detroit, so it felt. I think the speed of things was ironically one of the reasons fame didn't go to Michael's head. He literally grew up with it.

It was this stability that stopped him from throwing a tanty outside the legendary late night watering hole, the Bourbon and Beefsteak bar in the Cross one night. They wouldn't let us in because they thought he was too drunk, even though Michael was still clutching the Countdown Most Popular Male Vocalist Award he'd just received earlier that night.

Michael stayed cool. We just went somewhere else to celebrate. Imagine being that rich and popular in your heyday. The mere association got me a lot of free drinks and chicks. Though there was nothing to make my dick go limp quicker than a girl asking midbonk, 'So where's Michael?'.

My friend Larry had his fingers in many pies and was into matters botanical. I knew he was up to something, and bugged him into showing me what he was doing. One morning we headed down past Mittagong on a pair of motorbikes. From there we went bush on foot, to several isolated plots of pot Larry had been growing by a river, and which were now mature. When he had decided to grow there, Larry had bought a topographical map from the Forestry Commission to choose his sites. He was growing heads on Crown land.

We spent much of the day harvesting about twenty pounds of fresh wet buds, shoving them into two garbage bags and then climbing back out of the gorge. Larry had asked me to take it all back to Sydney as he was feeling a bit paranoid—plus he had no headlight on his bike and it would be dark soon. I strapped the smaller bag to the rack of my bike, and squeezed the bigger one into my backpack.

My sister Tina had just arrived from California to help Mum with the make-up school she had just opened in Milsons Point, and Michael and I were meeting her at Mum's for dinner. It was going to be a big family occasion. I had to get home, dry out the pot, shower and change. It had been a long day and the ride back was monotonous. When I got to the outer suburbs I thought, 'Not long now, I'll be home soon'. Then I blacked out. Either that, or I've blocked out what happened—there was a car in a right-hand lane waiting to turn right, and I ran straight up the back of it.

I must have been doing sixty to eighty kilometres per hour because I pushed a perfect tyre print into the boot, while the force of the impact popped the radiator out the front of the car. I bounced backwards, my body ending up between the car and my bike. My only memory is of trying to gather up my bags and telling the ambulance driver to please not let the police look inside them. I was taken to hospital—accompanied by my bags, which, amazingly, followed me into emergency, surgery and the plaster room before they were finally delivered to my ward.

I wasn't in good shape. Both wrists were broken. My nose was bruised and swollen and my left eye had turned every colour of the rainbow from smashing against the inside of my full-face helmet. If I'd been wearing my own helmet and not one of Larry's, I'd have shaved my chin off. I had also fractured my pelvis and bruised my ribs. I woke up the next morning sporting two plaster casts up to the elbows.

The next day Michael, Tina and Mum drove out to see me, and when Mum left the room I told Michael about the pot, and he took it home to dry it out. It made a thick carpet on his kitchen floor, and three days later he had to get Larry to come over and pick it up, as *Rolling Stone* magazine was due to come over for an interview, and his kitchen really reeked. The pot was ruined, having gone mouldy from sweating in garbage bags overnight in the hospital.

Michael didn't tell me until years later that driving home from the hospital, the smell from my bags became so pungent that Mum pulled over and demanded to know what it was. Michael had a bit of explaining to do for me there, which he did.

The only other time Mum came to see me was with a class full of make-up students so that they could study black eyes, bruising and stitches. Until now she had used her maiden name Kennedy for any film credits, even though her current name was Moolenburgh, after her fourth marriage, to a Dutch insurance broker, Kees. Mum was cashing in on the Hutchence name to attract students, thus the 'Patricia Hutchence Make-Up Academy'. She even used the promise of an appearance by Michael at the annual Christmas party. This of course placed Michael under unnecessary pressure.

Tina had recently jumped on the bandwagon too and changed her last name to Hutchence. Hell, anyone can do it if they want the association.

After a week in hospital I went to stay at Mum's and she and Tina looked after me. I was fairly incapacitated, with my arms in plaster creating a daily challenge. The accident was a blessing in disguise as I couldn't shoot up through the plaster, though, I did consider drilling holes. Due to powers beyond me, I managed to stay pseudo straight. I could still smoke pot and roll joints, except that my tongue couldn't reach the paper.

A month later I was in the bath and soaked one of my plaster casts off, only to find my arm hadn't been properly set. It looked deformed. I went to my doctor and he cut the other plaster off, and that arm looked just as bad. I had surgery in which they re-broke my arms and put four screws and a plate in each wrist, then I had my arms re-plastered for another four weeks. This time it was done properly, and I had my arms back.

Later I realised what must have happened. After a day picking plants, my hands were black with resin. As I used to bite my nails, I must have ingested some, become stoned, blacked out and crashed. The moral of the story being don't bite your nails.

Dear Rhett!
At long last your travelling brother has sat down to write!

I hope everything is A-OK with your arms. I didn't realise that you needed so much done to make them work like they used to 'so to speak'. Why don't you send me some polaroids of you + your working arms or something.

Right now I'm in our coach 'Doin 90 down Highway 24'!! as they say—I'm on my way to Memphis, things have been getting better here although the LP is only starting now, properly. I'm starting to get a little tired of touring, I miss you and Mom and Tina + Erin and Michele and, I'll be back around the 25th of Sept. I guess I'll move into the same place—hows your place going—I hope your doing OK with your health, physical + mental, mines not so good as my wisdom teeth are giving me hell—I'll have them out when I get back.

How's Sydney? I miss it very much, one day you'll have to come on tour with me somewhere, that would be great.

I might as well say that I think that if you decided to go to Hong Kong with Dad I think you would do very well, it would be a fantastic start into a new life, I could see you to and from tours and M and I could stay there, it would certainly be a great experience.

The Go Go's [the all girl LA band INXS were supporting] are a lot of fun and are playing very strongly. Their audiences are pretty good for us though we've got to start our own tour in a week. We had a hit in Canada, and in France, we had a No 1. Tres bon, non? Last week I hung around New York for a few days and met some people at last, one guy called Hunt Sales, who is, or was Iggy Pops drummer, also Soupy Sales son. He's very funny also I met Andy Warhol—He looked like a GI Joe doll!!—But otherwise nothing but gigs, coaches, hotels, gigs, coaches, hotels AAAAGH!!!

Say hello to everyone especially Tina + Mum + Erin + Kees and me mates.

Love and groovyness
Michael—Your Brother
Highway 24, Tennessee

When he was back in Australia, Michael flew me down to Melbourne for the 'Rocking the Royals' charity gig for Prince Charles and Princess Diana when they were touring Australia. It was a great line-up including the Models and the Divinyls. Michael got me a room at his hotel and I was given a protocol list. It stated that we commoners had to be inside and seated before the Royals arrived, stand when they arrived and sit again only after they had sat. But I got waylaid doing lines in my room with a friend, and we arrived late, in the middle of the Models' set. We were shown our seats and lo and behold, who should be sitting in front of us but the blue-blood couple themselves. They didn't seem overly enthralled, but when INXS came on I noticed the Princess tapping the little handbag she had royally placed on her knees.

hong kong revisited

In late 1985 I went back to live in Hong Kong and work for my dad, who by then had been living in and out of Asia for the past twenty years. I guess he had sensed things were heading askew for me, and had been asking me for some time to consider working for him. Michael had also been suggesting I take up the offer, and eventually I did.

Dad had a spacious two-bedroom apartment on a quiet, tree-shaded street in Kowloon, which came equipped with a maid, cook and driver—luxuries I've been very lucky to be spoiled with for many years of my life.

Hong Kong is the definitive sprawling concrete jungle, ever changing, constantly being knocked down and rebuilt. Its people scurry twenty-four hours a day, ant-like, amongst the old and new, adding to the hustle and bustle. There are people who live on sampans packed so tightly into Aberdeen Bay that they cannot move. Some spend their whole lives on that polluted, smelly water, and never set foot on dry land. Yet their lives are lived as fully as the most seasoned traveller's.

Dad employed me as a gofer, and soon had me busy, dropping off and collecting clothing samples, sending faxes and doing general office things. It was okay work for a while, and great to be back with Dad again.

Hong Kong must have made a pretty big impression on me when I was a kid, as I seemed to remember a lot of it, only it had seemed bigger before. When I went back to the park that backed onto our old house in Dorset Crescent, Kowloon Tong, it was just a tiny plot of land. It still had the same sandpit, swings and slippery dip, but didn't stretch off into the horizon like it did when Michael and I played there as boys.

Dear Rhett

Hi, thought I'd get a letter to you soon. I'm sorry about our call, you did everything wonderfully. The rest of the house will have to live up to it.

I don't know what your plans are, but I hope their coming true for you. Your life had been pretty hectic recently but I am sure you will cope in the outcome. If you need advice or whatever I can give you don't hesitate to call.

I had an OK time in London, though it's extremely expensive and cold. Michele and I managed to sneak a weekend in Paris together, saw a couple of friends there as well.

I haven't seen an abundance of people, I'm not interested in clubs etc. I've spent too much time indulging other people and not myself or loved one enough.

Some have asked how you are—I say unreal to them.

I hope I can see you in the very near future, we didn't have quite enough time to get down—ay what!!

Tennis is becoming my favourite sport—can you play—if so we must sometime—by the way, would you like to do a short story on anything for a magazine? You should give it a try—make it humorous as you do.

Please write back to me soon and do take good care of your body + soul. Hello to Daddio.

Love + Peace
Michael

Michael and the band were back touring in Australia, drawing huge crowds—their beer barn days well and truly behind them now.

Dear Rhett

Hi, how are you? It sounds like you are settled in a bit more, as long as you don't let the isolation get to you too much.

I talked to Croy [our auntie] tonight, she said you were great at what you were doing and speaking a bit of Chinese too.

So Dad's arm needed more attention after using it too much, well I just hope there's no complications in the future, looks like you've got something definitely in common.

I must say thanks very much for your words of wisdom in the letter, you are very honest and perceptive, and I know that you had ill feelings towards me for a while. But I'm glad you realised why—and please let me say that I respect you so much Rhett, you're a very special person, to me and especially (remember), to yourself!!

Please give my love to Dad for me.

When I take off again I'll be by to see you both—we can go out on zee town.

I miss you a lot, but at the same time I'm very happy for you doing so well. Please keep it up and learn what you can while your there.

Our tour of Adelaide/Sydney/Noosa went well. We got 21 000 people at Adelaide! And I just had some days at Noosa in the (sorry) sun, now I'm back in downtown smoggy boring Sydney. I've started writing some stuff for our 5th LP, God. It seems like INXS has been going for over 20 years, I think a few more and that'll be it, you can only be married to 5 guys for so long—I would like to go solo in about 2–3 years—Anyway blah blah…

Write back soon and I will ok motherfucker.

Take care of Kell Hutchence for everyone. Mum + Kees are doing OK, on and off, you know.

Take care of yourself

Love + peace Michael xxx

Sydney, Australia

That year INXS made yet another quantum leap forward. *Listen Like Thieves* was their big breakthrough album in the US, including the smash hit single 'What You Need'.

Michael was already moving into the life of a rock superstar, yet his letters were always personal. It was as if he had reached stardom, but it hadn't reached him.

Dear Rhett,

Ello dere boss. I hope your well and happy—you sounded in fine humour in both your last letters! They are eagerly awaited by Michele and I to brighten our humble little lives up.

Things are going to be tough when you don't have a maid anymore one day. So Honkers is lacking nite life? Although you do have a nose for whats happening, especially free entertainment.

I am sitting in Rhinocerus (not on one) at the moment were up to our 2nd song and all is very well. Chris Thomas is slightly eccentric but a 'good producer' nonetheless.

The house is good and sends its regards—it's a one bedroom but quite a good size—jolly civil neighbours too—ask us in for cocktails occasionally. I'm doing stuff to it to make it pretty. I feel like such a solid citizen it's disgusting. Anyway it's a good place and I want another in the country or overseas. Such capitalism

Speaking of money, how are you doing? Coping? Ask Dad for more responsibilty when you know you can handle it and more money when he can afford it.

Is father OK? I hope to come through to see you guys as soon as possible—maybe when I finish the LP and go to do press—Michele goes to Europe in a couple of weeks—I'll let you know of any confirmed details regarding touring soon as I can.

I hope your contented with HK and the experience is all you want it to be—I miss you lots thanx for the letters—Hope you can read this—maybe I'll start typing if you can't.
Lotzalurve
Michael xxx
Sydney, Australia

When my grandmother passed away in Sydney, Dad and I had to return for the funeral. His mother Mabel, or Mabs, and I had been close, and not knowing many people who had died, it affected me deeply. She had been slowly deteriorating since moving into the nursing home, but it was the only way of looking after her. With Mabs gone, I only had one grandparent left, Mum's mum, whom I hardly knew. Both grandfathers had already passed away before Michael and I were born.

I decided I wouldn't return to Hong Kong after the funeral because the work I'd been doing with Dad had stopped. It wasn't really what I wanted to do anyway, and my heart wasn't in it. It seemed like time for a new beginning. But I needed money to re-establish myself back in Australia.

Around that time a friend put me on to an American guy who had recently arrived from Katmandu with some hash oil to unload. I decided to buy some of the guy's stuff and take it to Sydney. I hoped Mabs wouldn't mind: I didn't think she would. The trip turned out to be really hairy though, and nearly scared the shit out of me—which at the time would have been the last thing I needed.

One Friday afternoon I went to a chemist near Star Ferry and bought antacid, constipation pills and 120 condoms, telling the giggling salesgirl I was in for a very big weekend.

The next day I started getting ready, the whole procedure being tedious and time-consuming. Unwritten rules, passed person to person, had to be followed and adhered to strictly.

The oil had first been placed in dry condoms, while the following five or six wrapped around the original were the normal lubed variety. Next I took off two layers, then added another three condoms. In all then there were six or seven condoms between the oil and me. It was a matter of life and death that there were no air pockets trapped inside.

Two days before my flight I started watching what I ate, nothing too acidic or fizzy—not too much at all really—then began a daily regime of antacids and stomach neutralisers. I bought a one-way ticket back to Sydney on Malaysia Airlines via Kuala Lumpur, and planned to leave a day before my dad, who as usual had some business ends to tie up.

The day I left, I got up at six in the morning to get ready for my midday flight. The final part of the procedure is you mix equal parts of yoghurt and milk together, then start trying to swallow the damn condoms, while drinking the mixture to help it down. The swallowing would have to be the hardest part, as your natural reaction is to vomit them back up. I was managing to swallow five, then I'd throw up two, then get a few more down, then bring a couple more up, so it was taking ages. I kept sneaking from my bedroom to the bathroom, back to my bedroom, trying not to let

Dad know what I was up to. This went on for five hours. Then, just before leaving the house for the airport, there's the last thing you take—a pill to make you constipated.

I checked in, paid my departure tax, bought a carton of duty-free cigarettes and a *Playboy* magazine (for the articles). I didn't have any money left, as it was all tied up in condoms, but Dad kindly gave me $20 pocket money. I kissed him, said goodbye, and trotted through Immigration and Customs and onto the plane. The flight to Kuala Lumpur was tough, as I was not able to eat anything and I love airline food, usually asking for seconds.

As we taxied to a stop in Kuala Lumpur, the last thing the speaker above my head blurted was, 'We hope you enjoy your stay here in Malaysia, and remember drug smuggling is a capital offence, punishable by death. Thank you'. We had a two-hour transit stop, so I checked out the duty-free shops until it was time to re-board.

When I was heading back into the departure lounge, they asked to put my carry-on bag through the X-ray machine. The operator started looking through my bag, then pulled me aside and asked me to follow him. I kept my composure, but was thinking, fuck fuck fuck.

As he led me into a little room, I still wasn't sure what the problem was, until he pulled the *Playboy* magazine from my bag. He told me that he would have to detain me as I was in a Muslim country and had committed an offence under some pornography Act. He told me that every photo brought a 1000 Ringgit fine, and as I'd happened to buy the *Playboy* Girls of Summer and every page had a photo, it was a very expensive magazine.

I apologised and explained I'd bought it at Hong Kong airport, that I'd only been in transit and hadn't left the terminal, and how I had to make my flight because I was going back to Sydney to go to my grandmother's funeral, and he could call my Dad in Hong Kong to verify that. He told me to wait a minute, then left me alone in the room, doing headmiles. It felt like I was waiting to see the school principal.

Alone in that tiny room with its wooden lattice ceiling, I figured someone might be watching me so just stood there trying not to move, trying to breathe easily through my nose. Outside I could hear 'Flight 714 for Sydney on Malaysia Airlines, this is your final boarding call'.

The guy came back in shaking his head and saying he would have to detain me. I was terrified. My heart was pumping hard and the corners of my dry mouth had turned down. I started getting desperate, pleading with him. I just had to get on that flight, as I certainly didn't want to stay and end up machine gunned or whatever they do to you there.

He asked how much money I had and I offered him the $20 Dad had given me, which was all I had on me. He just laughed. I told him he could have my leather jacket or my Walkman or the carton of cigarettes, but he shook his head smiling, saying that he couldn't walk out with that stuff.

I reached the point where I was pleading just take anything, just let me on the flight. He kept stalling, and nearly all the passengers were on board by now. He finally gave in for four packets of cigarettes, the $20, and of course the magazine, which was what he had wanted all along.

I was so relieved to grab my things and get out of that fucking room. I ran to the plane and the moment I boarded they closed the door behind me and we started to taxi away. Malaysia had never looked so good from the air. Needless to say, it was the last time I ever swallowed something that I wanted to see again.

san fran

Back in Sydney, I decided to get a place of my own and eventually found an apartment for $90 a week, which was cheap for Centennial Park but expensive because it was a cockroach infested, cold, tilted, run-down heap of shit. The tenant above me and I didn't get along from the start. He had Tourette syndrome and most nights he'd pace back and forth, ranting and raving, 'Fucking little…get fucked you…fucking cunt…fuck you…' in one long, six-hour sentence. I think my snoring and the volume of the hip-hop I was getting into didn't help his condition. Other nights he would belt out sixty words a minute on an old typewriter on the wooden floorboards above my bed or drop a bowling ball over and over. When he was evicted he left with all his worldly possessions, the bowling ball in an old Qantas carry-on.

From the far side of the world came news that Michael and the band were selling out venues that once he would have only dreamed about.

> *Dear Rhett*
> *Hope you're fine. It's snowing here but gigs are good—we sold out*
> *Hammersmith Odeon in London!! Thanks for calling that day. I wish*
> *I was on the beach right now!! Now put this on your new board in*
> *your new place on a new day.*
> *See ya, Michael*
> *Dusseldorf, Germany*

Being Michael's brother meant I got tickets to virtually any show or gig I wanted. All I had to do was ask him or someone who worked for him at MMA, INXS' management agency. I'd go to the box office mention my name and his name, and get my tickets or passes or laminates. I found that even if nothing had been organised, if I mentioned his name and insisted that tickets had been left for me, they gave me tickets anyway. After a while of going to Michael's gigs, I had to use a pseudonym myself, as someone was showing up before I arrived claiming to be me and taking my tickets. I became 'Carmen Buckets'.

As most of the international touring acts stayed at the Sebel Townhouse when they were in Sydney, more often than not the after-show party would end up in the hotel bar with Eric the barman pouring value for money, or upstairs in someone's room raiding their mini-bar. The Sebel was a legendary Sydney hang, with the walls of its comfortable bar lined with signed photographs of celebrities who had stayed there and dropped by for a drink. It was Sydney's home away from home for the stars. Now, sadly, apartments.

Early one morning a bunch of us were upstairs, partying, drinking, snorting, and toking heavily in a room, when we heard sirens outside. We looked behind the curtains, and out the window see three fire engines pull up in front of the building. While we were laughing, smoking and making wisecracks about how we were on fire, the firemen were running about, organising hoses and looking up. The next moment there was a knock on the door and it was the night manager who informed us that the smoke detector alarm signals from the rooms went directly to the fire station, and that if we were going to smoke joints, could we please blow the smoke out the window? I always loved the Sebel. I first met Ginger at a hundred parties. She gave me a job that suited me, Saturday mornings, in a groovy shop she was managing on Oxford Street in Paddington, near the markets. It sold T-shirts, books, comics, postcards, posters, bongs, papers, scales, cuts, everything Guru Adrian, hence anything funky, hip and new. The job was cash in hand and the fringe benefits exceeded the wage.

Much of the stock was from California, so when I told Ginger that I was going there, she talked to the owners and organised to give me $10,000 to do some buying for the shop. They specified a few special items to get, but the rest I could choose myself.

Whatever was affordable, markup-able, and suited the shop.

San Francisco is a beautiful city, and it being sister city to Sydney made me relate to it. I went to the Last Gasp, a distributor of underground comics and bought up stacks of RAW magazines, Zap comics, Furry Freak Brothers, Mickey Rat and Dope comics, and around three hundred T-shirts, plus various posters, postcards and stickers, spending nearly half the money there. Then I'd wrap up a dozen T-shirts and other goodies in Christmas paper, with a nice card and send them off to friends back in Sydney as gifts, saving $10 per T-shirt in import duties and taxes.

I went to the Haight–Ashbury Street Fair. It was a beautiful day, and bands played on every corner. The street was overflowing with trippers, flippers, users, losers, hustlers, bustlers, players, stayers, scammers, studs, cruds, hippies, zippies, fags, dags, wastoids, androids, babies, maybes, thickoes, sickoes, the lost, the loster, runaways, diehards, deadheads, could-bes, would-bes, should-bes, and mimes miming their own business.

I was miming mine when suddenly an attractive young blonde girl walked over, handcuffed herself to me, smiled and introduced herself as Kirsty. She told me didn't have a key to the cuffs, but that didn't really matter to me. Later that night, after tripping out together, some guy managed to pick it for us, not that we were in a hurry. I saw her again the next day and we started hanging out together.

Kirsty was a runaway who had just moved from her mother's houseboat and was staying at the various hotel rooms that Welfare could find for her. She certainly stood out amongst the other recipients seeking emergency accommodation. We spent the days panhandling to get change for wine and bread and cheese to take to the beach. We hung out on Haight and sat in the park with the old hippies and new freaks. Thomas, an acid casualty who had scratched his name backwards on his forehead, asked me for a fag one day. Each morning he had to look in a mirror to remember his name. He hadn't finished writing it yet, and only had AMOHT permanently etched. I gave him a fag.

My weekend away had turned into a six-month blur and when I finished buying and posting everything I flew home with my suitcases stuffed. I went through Nothing to Declare, but Customs pulled me over. The officer opened my bags, saw a dozen six foot blowup Godzillas I'd bought for the shop, and gave me a quizzical look. I told him they were samples and gifts. He just thought I was kinky or weird.

I'd posted some acid back to Sydney for my own use, and it became the flavour of the month at parties. One day Ginger said she wouldn't mind going to California for a holiday and buy some acid herself. As I had the contacts, we decided she'd fly me back over.

Not long after, we flew into LA and hired a car on Melrose Avenue. An hour later we were heading up Highway One in an eggshell coloured '64 Buick Skylark with the top down and wind in our proverbial hair. By nightfall we were in San Fran.

I soon found Kirsty on Haight. She had her own place now, down off Castro Street with a couple of punks. We made plans for her to send me trips in the mail on a regular basis. Sniffer dogs can't smell acid, so if there's nothing on the envelope to draw attention to what's inside, you're home and hosed.

Michael and Michele had arrived to do press for a couple of days, so Ginger, Kirsty and I hung out with them while they were in town. We had dinner a couple of times, drove them around the spots of interest, and saw the band playing in Berkeley.

After Michael left, I said goodbye to the land of the free and home of the foot-long hotdog and flew home.

Back in Sydney at our inaugural acid party I met a girl I was really attracted to, especially because of the way she wrote her name on the mirror in lipstick, over and over again, Kim Kim Kim Kim Kim. The night we met she took me back to her place and we sat in the bath full of floating fruit, island hopping, and working on the Archimedes principle till the wee hours. It had been a groovy party with sixties music, incense, oil lamps and about three hundred trippers there testing the very strong, fresh, no print, 'super blanks' as they became known. Until then, Sydney hadn't seen acid of that calibre. Acid had just made a comeback.

I met a whole new circus of friends through Kim. Nathan was one of those smarties who read popular science magazines and listened to the Cocteau Twins and Severed Heads. He also liked taking drugs, which his rich parents and the government invariably paid for.

We hit it off, then hit it up. 'You got any money?' were usually our first words on seeing each other, and if we didn't there were ways of getting some. Nathan once rented a koala suit and stood in Chinatown clutching a bucket with a 'Save The Koalas' sticker crookedly stuck on the side, sweating in the sun, hassling tourists for change. I saw him that afternoon at my dealer's house, still in costume. A tad surreal seeing a large koala trying to find a vein. Ralph was still counting the coins when I left. When Ralph got busted, we started seeing a couple called Chuck and Di. Great names for dealers: Ralph, Chuck and Di.

One day we decided to go tripping, and met up at a friend's place in the Cross. We dropped a tab each, then for some reason we each shot one up. Not something I'd recommend for anybody who doesn't want to be hurled brain first into a scary, overwhelming unreality, particularly before noon.

Before it came on even more strongly, we decided to try to make it back to my flat, not too much of a walk, but harder when your feet don't touch the ground. At first Nathan seemed like he was handling it, but somewhere along the way he entered another world. He was walking along, looking into the sky and repeating, 'Four Gods...two angels...four Gods...two angels'.

Normal conversation wasn't working with Nathan any more. I'd point to some landmark on the horizon and tell him we just had to make it there, that done, I'd point out another reference point a bit further away, and slowly we edged along. For a while it seemed like we might actually make it back to my place, but outside the Women's Hospital in Paddington he lost it again, and started running out onto busy Oxford Street screaming, 'I want to jump into the darkness!'. I went to see Ginger at the shop and told her in gibberish acid speak what I'd been practising in my head, but by the time I got there it was too late. The cops had come and taken Nathan away. He got off without any problems though. Pays to have parents in lofty places.

The latest card from Michael came from Bali. In his down time now he had the money to travel, rest up, enjoy his time with Michele.

> *Yo Home Bro!!*
> *This is not the Bali people warned us about. It's great at Sanur beach. Been dodging people etc. on the roads. They're mad!! But very hospitable. Hope all is well in Sydney. Be back wed or fri—maybe never. Hello to Heidi, Lisa and everybody else. Seeee Ya!!*
> *M + M xxx*
> *Bali, Indonesia*

I first saw Ruvé at a party in a friend's photography studio and if there is such a thing as love at first sight, this was it. Second and third too. Tall and skinny with long dark hair, with the most gorgeous face, she was absolutely beautiful. I asked her out for dinner, she accepted, and so began us.

Not long after we starting going out, we went to see Mental as Anything play at Sydney University. Ruvé disappeared for a while and returned with a white, albino laboratory rat that she had just saved from some life-threatening experiments. At first I thought I didn't want or need a pet, but if there's such a thing as love at fifth, sixth and seventh sight that was it and he was soon part of our lives. I named him Plague after Daniel Defoe's *A Journal of the Plague Year*. He was a true people pleaser—not bad going when you're born a rat. After a while it seemed like everybody knew him. Some nights, people I'd never seen before would come up acting like old friends. His good looks and charm made him a regular chick magnet with a bulging phone book and social invitations flooding in.

Plague ate gratis in the finest restaurants, never waited in lines at clubs, and could gnaw his name in any door he pleased. The social snappers favoured him, and most weeks he ended up in the social pages, or the Stay in Touch column in the *Sydney Morning Herald*. When I left the house, my mental checklist became 'money, keys, sunnies, drugs, rat'. He made the perfect housemate as I could trust him with the phone and leave the STD bar off.

It was through Plague that I met Iain: scammer extraordinaire. He invited us to join him on an all-expenses paid trip to the Adelaide Grand Prix. At the airport Plague sat in my sleeve under my arm, one of his favourite spots, as our carry-on bag went through the X-ray machine. After we boarded I put him back in my carry-on and he chewed the arms off my favourite Mambo sweatshirt.

We flew down first class, and Plague, like myself, enjoyed the food and watched the movie. Iain had somehow got passes to the upstairs of a pub that was lavishing a $1200 a ticket, all you can eat and drink smorgasbord. Champagne, caviar, smoked salmon, exotic fruits and the finest cheeses. It was the only pub actually on the race circuit, with a great view of the track, but that also meant it was smoky, loud and smelly. We spent the morning on the upstairs balcony getting stuffed and trashed. By lunchtime we decided we were over it and booked our flight home early. We never saw the actual race, though I now think the best place to watch it is on TV in the comfort of your own home.

Apart from the three of us, the entire first class section on the flight back was filled with Michael Jackson's entourage—and Michael Jackson. Plague wanted to meet him, and as I was sitting next to Michael's personal dietitian, we asked her, and she thought it would be okay. Before we landed in Sydney, the semi-gloved one went up and disappeared into the cockpit. Word had spread that he was on the flight, and I guess he didn't want to be hassled by two hundred people filing past his seat to the front exit (though why he just didn't get off first I'll never know).

After everyone had disembarked, Plague and I went up to the cockpit door and knocked (this was pre September 11, when you could still do that kind of thing!). The door opened and Michael Jackson was standing there looking at me. I pulled Plague out of my jacket and put him on the flight navigator's chair and said 'Hello, my name's Rhett, and I just wanted to say hi and introduce you to my rat'.

Michael was going through a stage when he dressed like Mickey Mouse in *Steamboat Willie*, he sounded like him too.

'Oh he's so beautiful, he's so cute,' he squeaked.

'He's a big fan of yours,' I said.

'Oh I love animals I love rats. What's his name, Ben?'

'No. His name's Plague.'

'That's so cute, I love animals, I love rats.'

'Well we'd better be going. I hope you enjoy your stay and have a good tour.'

'Oh thank you. Bye Plague. I love animals, I love rats, he's so cute.'

It was kind of eerie how he focused on Plague, and related better to him than to a human.

I picked Plague up, put him back in my jacket and we scampered off to the limo that took us home.

Plague actually got to know quite a lot of celebrities. Richard Lowenstein had him scurry up Michael's arm in his INXS 'Need You Tonight' video, and Baz Luhrmann featured him in an early Pardon Me Boys clip with Ignatius Jones. Plague of course did them for love, and a little cheese.

Then one weekend a bunch of us went up to Palm Beach. Plague seemed his normal self, scurrying here, scampering there, the life of the party. We were all laughing, when all of a sudden he was gone—disappeared. I searched high and low but never saw him again.

People still come up to me and ask, 'Where's your rat?' I tell them, like I told the press, 'I believe he went bonkabout'. It was a shock though, and for the next week I think much of Sydney mourned a great loss. I miss him still. Every now and then I'd get a postcard. Then they stopped.

It was after Ruvé went away to model in Milan that I met Lisa at the Sleaze Ball. Lisa was a sexy girl who drove a push-button Valiant. Late at night we'd head over to Taronga Zoo and park down near the wharf. There's a low point in the wall, where you could easily jump over, near the rhino enclave. You just had to be careful you didn't actually jump *on* the rhino. Once inside, the place is yours to run free. There were only two guards who drove around in a little security car, so if you heard anything or saw headlights, you just got down and hid in the bushes till they went past.

We'd take champagne and do lines on the glass display cases. The best time was full moon because of the friskiness of the animals. It was usually really peaceful there, with the quiet only broken by the wind rustling in the trees and corks popping.

I took Lisa to see the Eurythmics at the Entertainment Centre and after the show we went for drinks at the Sebel. Annie Lennox went straight up to her room, but Dave Stewart held court in the bar downstairs. He and Lisa disappeared for a while, and when I found them later she was flirting and trying on a diamond bracelet he had taken out of the hotel safe. I didn't think much of it, and we went home.

The next day when I called her she wasn't home. Then I heard she had been seen in Double Bay, hopping out of a limo and into shops with the gem-wielding guitar man himself. When we caught up later that night she didn't mention being with him until I told her she had been spotted. Lisa was nonchalant about it, and said they were just friends and there was no sex or anything. Whatever, I felt left out and didn't like being lied to. Yet who am I to disagree—everybody's looking for something.

Lisa finally got her big break acting in the movie *Dead Calm*, but ended up on the cutting room floor—and from what transpired, a few others as well. She was gone for three or four weeks, and every other night we would talk on the phone. Then one night I ring and some guy gets on and tells me that she'll tell me about it when she gets back, and hangs up. Nice one. I didn't hear any more, but when she returned a week later Lisa calmly told me she had met a Hollywood actor, had an affair and was going to join him in Los Angeles and get married. So it goes.

It was around this time I met Sallie-Anne Huckstepp. She was a complex and fascinating character, well known to the media after she alleged the police had murdered her boyfriend, Warren Lanfranchi. She was also said to be a police informer.

A friend drove me down to Botany to the house where she was living. He had known her for some time and introduced us, as I was after an ounce of coke for a friend. We knocked on the door and she answered, a beautiful woman and quite a sight in a yellow bikini with her right arm broken and in plaster. She'd nodded off driving her Mercedes home and smashed into a number of parked cars.

We went in and had a cuppa while the deal was done. Then my friend drove me back to town so I could finish the deal. It was good toot and I made a few hundred dollars and a gram for my efforts.

Sallie-Anne eventually found herself in a tight position, and had to go into hiding. Still, it was business as usual and she worried away the next paranoid month, then moved into a flat in Edgecliff with a girlfriend, Gwen.

I liked Sallie-Anne. She was generous and trusting and just caught up in the false glitz and seedy glamour of dealing big time, though probably not even a pawn in the big game. I cried when I heard she had been found floating in Busby's Pond in Centennial Park. I'd only known her a couple of months and I had seen her the previous evening, having gone around to her flat to score.

I was shocked, stunned, freaked, and cleaned out my house. A couple of days later I got a call from a reporter who had some-how obtained a copy of Sallie-Anne's address book, and got my number. I was the closest address to where she was found and would I like to comment? I told her to fuck off, not to call me again and hung up.

sorry hills

When my lease expired, I moved into a place in Surry Hills and started making scratch videos for clubs, parties, fun, splicing the most visually exciting graphics and scenes into some sort of story or flow. The three-hour tapes contained over a thousand edits, took a bit more than a week to make, and I sold copies for up to four hundred bucks each. I originally made them purely for the visual impact, quick bright sharp edits that beat with music, though they were pretty funny with their original sound too.

I was out at the Soho Bar one night when a spunk-bubble walked up to me and said matter of factly, 'I want to fuck you'. She was sexy, leggy, had a great opening line and was absolutely serious. I replied, 'Ahem…meet to please you, Rhett'. Her name was Natalie. It turned out I knew her father, John, but had no idea then that he had a daughter. He was a famous clothing designer during the sixties, making clothes for the Stones, the Who, and Hendrix amongst others. He even designed the uniforms for Sergeant Peppers, is said to have invented flares, brought paisley back into vogue, and made John Lennon's court suit for his pot charge. For some reason I didn't go home with Natalie that night. Instead, we made plans for her to come over the next day.

The next morning, I was woken early by Michael Saker, my bohemian, artist friend, carrying a large, rolled canvas. Michael was after some quick cash to score, and I was quite used to these early morning shenanigans. He unrolled his painting to start the bargaining. I liked his work and this was no exception. A two-metre by three-metre myriad of colour and multiple strokes, which Michael told me depicted a poem. He was in a hurry; I snatched it for $160 and proudly stuck it up on my living room wall. End of story.

Not end of story. Natalie came over for lunch. She was looking edible and we were chatting and getting to know each other when she suddenly said, 'What are you doing with my painting?'. So I told her about my latest acquisition. Natalie then told me that she used to be good friends with Michael. Nothing sexual; she just liked his company. She'd written a poem for him, which he had then painted and given to her. Earlier that morning, Michael had come over for a social and Natalie had told him that she had met a guy the night before whom she had the hots for. They'd had an argument and he'd ripped his painting off her wall and left. Presumably to sell, presumably to get on.

Natalie ended up moving in with me, and we were together for the next nine months. I liked her and her shoe fetish. Apart from shower, she did everything in them.

Despite the constantly building wave—INXS was now touring promoting the *Kick* album—Michael retained his cool about it all, still 'seeing what will happen'. What was happening was that INXS now stood on the brink of global stardom, and Michael of mega-stardom.

> *Gidday Rhett!!!*
> *Have just finished all my press and am on a plane to LA. New York's great. I miss you and friends + Michele though. Start playing in 5 days. The first door is open—we'll see what happens.*
> *Love MH*
> *New York, New York*

Most people agree the mid-to-late eighties and early nineties were the real heyday of INXS. The *Kick* album had become a huge success globally. Sales were being reckoned up—in record company speak—in millions of units. INXS were now one of the top bands in the world. These were their glory days and they would go on to play Madison Square Garden and Wembley and before adoring multitudes in Paris and Rio.

I was involved in a new music venture of my own—the booming dance party scene in Sydney.

One day I was in an old warehouse full of rusty machinery looking for props for a dance party, when I stepped on a nail covered in pigeon shit. The moment I pulled my foot off I knew there was something seriously wrong. That night I lay on my bed screaming in pain. Natalie got on the phone and a doctor visited but didn't know what the problem was. The next day and night I was still screaming, hardly sleeping a wink. Another doctor came, only to tell me he thought I had a low pain threshold. I didn't need a doctor to tell me that.

Late the next night, with me still screaming in pain, yet another doctor visited. This one was worried why I was still at home and not in hospital. So at five in the morning Natalie drove me over to St Vincent's Casualty, and I was screaming so loudly that a friend on the sixth floor heard me arrive. The screams certainly got me to the head of the Casualty queue, though, and I got instant attention.

That day they ran a series of tests on me, coming back with a diagnosis of septic arthritis, a horrible blood disease. They said I was lucky, because if the nail had gone in two millimetres deeper the infection would have gone into my bone, giving me a terrible bone disease, with amputation below the ankle the best cure. As it was, two months of antibiotics should do the trick. I got daily visits from Natalie and at night we'd pull the curtain round my ward bed for a medicinal fuck. I'm sure that it hastened my recovery too.

Dear Rhett
G'day mate. Hope your fit and fighting. London's good fun. So was New York. We should do it together one day (travel that is). Hope you got some income to save for it. I'll be back next Sat 22nd. I'll try + find you a present. Hello to everyone
Michael xx
London, England

Dad had a new love in his life, the wonderful Susie. That September I flew to Hong Kong for their wedding. Michael and

I then flew to Tokyo and I joined INXS on their ten-day Japanese tour.

I'd never been on tour before and Michael had invited me to show me what it was like. Daily doses of decadent debauchery is what it's like. By this time Michael's several-year relationship with Michele Bennett had come to an end, amicably, and he was joined by his new main squeeze, an American model called Jonnie, whose real name was Rosanna. I liked her. She was smart, intelligent, witty, and I could tell she genuinely liked and took an interest in me.

Dad and Susie came over from Honkers for a couple of days, before going on to their honeymoon in Borneo. We all checked into the Roppongi Prince Hotel conveniently situated in the heart of the nightclub district.

Fans had been waiting at the airport, outside the airport, following our limo on the way to the hotel, patiently outside the hotel, quietly in the lobby and sometimes suspiciously on my floor. They can wait vigilantly for thirty-six hours plus, autograph book pen poised, lens caps off, waiting for that one opportune moment. They would have to be the most patient, persistent, polite, reserved, restrained fans I'd ever seen, and the biggest merchandise spenders INXS had ever seen. When you got in earshot they would quietly ask for your autograph, or if it was alright to have a photo taken. And if you said do a tap dance juggle three balls and sing the national anthem first, they would have.

Some of them must have been financially unchallenged to do what they did. One gorgeous seventeen-year-old girl took a major fancy to Michael. In Japan, front row seats are usually scalped for exorbitant prices, yet she had not only managed to get front row, she'd got virtually the same seat in every venue for every show and she always wore a red dress, because Michael sang of his love for a girl with 'Red dress on, long black hair' in the Loved Ones cover, 'The Loved One'.

She managed to find out which hotels the band stayed at and booked herself a room on the same floors for the whole tour. When we got back to the hotel she would already be there, draped over a lounge in the lobby, with gifts. Michael and Jonnie finally snared her, invited her into their private domain and deflowered her in Osaka. I saw her at Wembley years later and she gave me a present, a nice black top.

The fans at the gigs were very restrained, sitting, watching, singing, clapping along. Security men stood with their backs to the stage looking at the audience, and didn't look around once. And you couldn't help laughing during 'Need You Tonight' when Michael sang the chorus 'How do you feel?' and stuck the mike out for the audience to reply, and fifteen thousand girls sang 'I'm ronery!'.

After the gigs the band and crew spent many hours with many models at many clubs. Japan imports a lot of models, girls from all over the globe. Some of them work a lot and return home with a suitcase full of cash, while others party hard, doing the odd shoot, slowly becoming alcoholics. Shoots or shots. There's enough work there to occupy both sorts. They've got it made. They don't have to wait or pay to get in to the clubs, they get vouchers for food and drinks for free, all because they look good and that attracts the rich. The Tokyo clubs tend to be concentrated together, so you just hop. We did, from Bingo Bango Bongo to Java Jive, to Lexington Queen, to Pineapple's, to Cleo's—a circuit that kept us going all night…morning…night.

When you're a star, or in the entourage, you have pretty well free rein with girls. I was in my element and ran riot. The hotel usually left two kimonos when they turned down your bed, though the first night I brought two girls home and from then on they left me three kimonos. Late at night we'd be drunk or bored and do silly things like fill out the breakfast menus, ordering everything, and place them on neighbours' doors, or swap their real menus for Do Not Disturb signs. Japan must be one of the only places where you can trash your hotel room in a food fight and they'll smile and bow and ask you to please come again.

Here and there we had a couple of days off, where I looked around for tin toys, cool threads and someone cute to go to the show with. I bought thirty or more battery-operated and wind-up tin toys, was given a beautiful Mr Shinju stripy suit by Michael, and took about twenty something kimonos from hotels back for Christmas presents.

The band and I got invited to constant record company lunches, lavish and expensive. Every day was full, and when it wasn't we shopped.

Flying home I was the only unmarried and non-Japanese passenger on the jam-packed jumbo. For some reason this time Customs really had me in their sights. The Customs officer went through all my kimonos, through my everything, then told me he would like me to do a strip. I have no idea what he thought I might have been smuggling from Japan, maybe some sushi strapped to my chest or a karaoke machine up my butt (or was it the other way round). I was taken to a private room, spread 'em, got dressed and left. They kept my Vegemite sachets and the little jam pots I'd kept from the breakfast tray.

I'd only been back a week when Natalie flew out to Tokyo for a month of modelling and shoe shopping. A week before she came home, Ruvé returned and I couldn't resist temptation—even though she'd been working in Europe for the last year and we'd broken up. Natalie came home and wasn't happy about it, even after I found out she'd struck up a 'friendship' with a guy in Osaka. Then Ruvé flew back to her apartment in Paris.

Michael had a new love interest too. After a couple of years with Jonnie, he met Kylie Minogue. I first met her in Michael's hotel room after an INXS gig. She was still seeing Jason Donovan at the time and he was with her that night.

I remember trying to get Kylie to smoke a joint, but she didn't want any. It was to be the first of many refusals. Jason happily obliged. She was a sweet girl, and very petite. The magazine photographs of her are pretty much actual size. It wasn't too long before I heard that Michael had left Jonnie and flown off to be with Kylie.

This was the start of the nineties, and Michael was now travelling constantly. The press, of course, was both intrigued and scandalised that the sunny queen of *Neighbours* had gotten together with

Michael. Until now he had been spared the worst excesses of the yellow press and paparazzi. Most of his contacts with the media had been interviews with rock journos for music magazines, but now he was being chased down streets by baying packs of camera-laden Pommie oafs who didn't give a fuck what they put you through provided they got some intimate pic of the happy couple for tomorrow's front page, better still, an unhappy pic.

I think Michael almost kind of enjoyed the buzz of it at first, the chase and how to beat the pack at their own game. Later on he just took swings at the bastards.

Kylie and I became friends while she was with Michael. She and I worked together to organise his thirtieth birthday party in Sydney. Michael had helped me out numerous times, and I wanted to let him know how much that had meant to me. For his present, I gave him a painting I'd bought from Michael Saker.

The party was in a photography studio in Surry Hills. It was packed with friends. Michael was in high spirits, as were all of us. At the party, social snapper Robert Rosen took a photo of Michael carrying his birthday cake, which later appeared in the English tabloids, forever stretching the ethics of friendship.

One day I got a call from Nick Egan, a graphic designer friend of Michael's who had designed the album cover for *Kick*. He'd heard about my scratch videos and thought I should come to Hollywood and he would help get me started. Michael thought it was a good idea too and agreed to help set me up, so the plan was in motion. I got my visa, tickets and departure date, and placed my everything in storage.

I decided to have an 'I'm outta here' party. It started early, and by ten-ish I was trolleyed. A junkie friend from across the road asked me if I'd like a little shot. I couldn't really leave my own party, so I asked if he could make me one up and bring it back. He did, and I went up to my room. I hit up then lay down on my bed. My house-mate, Dreadlocked Sue, came in and started talking, something she did quite a bit of. I wasn't moving, she was talking, my eyes were rolling back in my head, Sue was still talking, I was turning blue, Sue was chatting, I was outta there.

Then another friend Gerrard walked in, took a look at me and screamed, 'What the fuck are you doing?' to Dreadlocked Sue. He picked me up, rushing me downstairs. Sue talked on. The phone had been disconnected so someone had to run up the road to call the ambulance. I remember it all being very much like the cult movie *Dogs in Space* that Michael had starred in.

I came to in the back of the ambulance across the road from the house, surrounded by Natalie and a bunch of very worried friends. When I went back inside, I couldn't understand where everyone had gone. I didn't quite get it just then, but it *is* etiquette to leave when the host dies. It was all a terrible shock and for the next three days until leaving I lay in bed crying.

Lost again

When I first arrived in the sprawling mass that is LA, I moved in with Lovey, a friend of Michael's, who had a house next door to the Hollywood Bowl. Lovey was a New York actor, waiting in Hollywood for that big break that sadly never came.

Michael was paying my rent and giving me $250 a week to live on until I could get work. I didn't have a car yet, which is an essential accessory in LA. You can't do anything without a car. You might as well not even leave the house. You even need a car to go buy a car. It might be against the law to walk the streets of LA. I'm sure the cops would stop you if they saw you and want to know what the problem was. 'Where's your car...you haven't got a car? We got a walker here. I repeat, we have a walker. We're gonna need backup. Okay, now turn around and put your hands behind your back, nice and easy.'

One day Lovey saw a cable technician connecting the neighbour's TV, put on a bikini and befriended him, and, 'Stupid questions for $1000 please', we had free cable. I was fascinated having fifty-two channels and would put on my leg rope and surf remote channels for hours.

Some of the big whitegoods warehouses had a thirty-day no questions asked, money-back guarantee on appliances. So I'd 'buy' a VCR, use it constantly, but keep it in good nick, then return it before the month was up and get my money back. Then I'd go to another branch and do it again. The hustler is always right. I spent most of my time with a joint in one hand and a remote in the other. Still do.

I finally organised the money from Michael to get a car. I don't know much about cars, but I know about looks and the baby blue '59 Ford Fairlane I found in the Valley for $1999 looked good, even if it didn't have reverse. I was surprised not to see more people driving old cars. Most of them were newer, smaller and more fuel efficient. It used to cost me $5 just to get to the gas station, but it was beautiful. After being a passenger for nearly three decades, I learnt to drive in LA. I found I liked driving, the speed, the control, the flow, freeways. My new-found wheels meant more mobility, and I began scouting around for work.

About six months after I arrived I went to see Nick Egan on the set of the video that he was directing for a Canadian band—a remix of Nancy Sinatra's 'Boots'. A friend from Sydney, Lian, was doing Craft Service, which is basically buying $200 worth of biscuits, chocolate, chips, fruit, tea, coffee, gum, finger snacks, and setting up a table on set so the crew can grab whatever they want, whenever they want. Lian had sprained her wrist, and Nick asked me if I'd take over. I must have made an impression on the producer, because after that he hired me for every job he did. So after six months of trying to break in, I had my foot in the door. It's a funny industry. Once you're in, if they like you, you work forever. Fuck up and you may as well start looking for another occupation. You learn to do your job and your job only.

I did craft service for a while, which paid $120 a day cash in hand, plus I'd get to take home whatever food was left over. Then I started to move up the ladder, becoming a production assistant (if that is up). I wasn't sure what department I wanted to be in yet, and PA is a good job to check out every aspect of the industry. Before I went back to Sydney for Christmas that year, I'd worked as PA on a dozen videos including Elton John, After 7, Edie Brickell and the New Bohemians, Tom Petty, Womack & Womack, Taylor Dayne, Shawn Colvin, Jenny Morris, and Madonna. I'd also worked on a series of public service announcements with Geoffrey Osborne, Melissa Manchester, Germaine Jackson, Ray Parker Jr, as well as a German beer commercial.

Just before going home for the festive season, I went to a Christmas party put on by Virgin. Sir Richard certainly knows how to throw a party, and it seemed like everyone was having a good time. John Lydon, or Johnny Rotten, as he doesn't like to be known, was there with his long-time girlfriend. They were sitting on a couch drinking wine, and I thought I'd introduce myself as he'd supported INXS on a tour a few years before, and Michael was matey with Glen Matlock, the Sex Pistols guitarist.

I walked up, extending my hand, 'Hi, my name is Rhett Hutchence, I just wanted to say hello, you know my brother Michael'.

Though they hadn't been talking, it felt like I'd cut him off mid-sentence and he sneered at me, 'You're not Michael's brother, fuck off' and turned back to his girl. I said, 'I am', he told me to fuck off again and I told him I thought he should fuck off, and fucked off.

Michael told me later that that's the way John is, and that he was actually being really nice to me. I can picture him buying milk at the local store, sneering, tossing the money, grabbing his change, spitting on the floor, telling the shopkeeper to shove it and kicking his cat.

Back visiting Sydney, I stayed with Michael at the Connaught, in an apartment he was renting for a couple of weeks. I had a bit of cash and spent the time catching up with friends.

One night the actor Kym Wilson came over and she and Michael went out to a theatre production, leaving me to my own devices, being, watching TV. Michael had left his wallet on the table, and I peeked inside to see sixty crisp $100 greenbacks. The temptation being just too great, I grabbed one of them and went to the Cross to score some coke. I changed the money at the Gazebo Hotel, scored, and went back to the apartment to enjoy it (if I still did). It wasn't long before I wanted more, so I swiped two more of those crispy bills, left the keys inside so I couldn't get back in for more, and beelined it for the Cross. This time, to change the money I went down to the Bourbon and Beefsteak, ordered a Jack and Coke, downed it, got my change and went off to score again.

An hour later I was back in the Bourbon and Beefsteak, gulping down another drink and getting more change, when three detectives approached with the banknote I'd changed, wanting to know if it was mine. I said it was. They said they thought it might be counterfeit and asked me to come with them to Kings Cross station.

When we got there, they showed me the problem. They had all three notes, and they looked fine to me, right paper, right colour, right texture, consecutive serial numbers, except that on the front it looked like somebody had pressed their thumb down hard while the ink was still wet, smudging Ben Franklin's face.

I told them I had got them for a job I did in the States, and that I'd had them for a long time, only just deciding to cash them in. They were intrigued why I needed to cash them all that night, and I said I was having a fun night. They told me I would have to hold off on the fun until they could get them authenticated. They would have to wake up a Federal Police officer to come and check them out. By this time I was beginning to wonder about the notes myself.

The Federal Police officer arrived around five in the morning. He gave the notes the once-over, returned my last one, and told us it was a printing error. I was allowed to leave, and one of the detectives came back to the Bourbon and Beefsteak with me to authenticate it, and I got my money, quickly giving it to my dealer. I don't know if Michael ever missed the three notes. If he did he never mentioned it.

When I got back to LA, Lovey had moved back east, still waiting for the big break, so I moved in with Daman and Deni, a couple of Aussies. Daman was a production manager at a large music video production company, and Deni a freelance writer and editor. Daman was good-looking, stylish, with a penchant for the fifties, while Deni was more a country jillaroo type. They had a beautiful deco flat in a block called the Trianon, which was built by Douglas Fairbanks junior as a present for Mary Pickford. Lian and Vincent Spano shared an apartment upstairs. It was a bit of an Aussie enclave.

Daman chuffed pot and told me he knew where we could get better deals, off the hispanics up on Pico Boulevard. So one day we hopped in his '72 El Dorado Cadillac and headed down Western, the longest industrial road in the world. He told me the procedure on the way, but it didn't quite prepare me. 'Don't get out of the car, whatever you do', he added.

It was just getting dark as we pulled off Pico and cruised slowly up a shadowy street of run-down houses. Suddenly, no fewer than eight shady characters surround the car, running along with us, thrusting bags in our faces, vying for competition, yelling 'Whatchu want, whatchu need?' I'm looking at the bags that they grip tightly and push in our faces. It's really overwhelming and confusing.

Then, without warning, the dealer near Daman bolts ahead of us and everyone scatters. I'm watching as a plain-clothes cop runs past us, badge on his belt, gun in his hand, chasing this guy with a female cop close behind him as back-up. It was split second. Everything was fine, then they appeared from nowhere, very *COPS*, and we sat back and watched the whole episode. Without speeding up, Daman casually took the next right. US street dealing at its finest. I scored my first dime bag in America on the next street, barely two minutes later. And Daman was right, the deals on Pico were bigger.

Daman was working on a Janet Jackson video and gave me a job in the art department. At the time the company he worked for was making many of the videos being screened on MTV. I loved the work, and a lot of what we shot was in high rotation, so I got plenty of satisfaction viewing the finished product on TV, knowing what went on just out of frame to get that shot. There was a lot of work on, and I found myself busy working with Seduction, Andrew Ridgley, Fleetwood Mac, Richard Simmons, Boo Yaa Tribe, Taylor Dayne, Blue Nile and the Georgia Satellites. The six-week shoot for some Coca Cola Magic Summer commercials we shot with the New Kids On The Block was tiring. A couple of times I'd be driving home after an average sixteen-hour day, and fall asleep at the wheel, thankfully to be woken by the 'duh duh duh' sound of tyres on lane dividers, or an irate horn for encroaching.

One of my jobs was picking the Kids up at the hotel in the morning, dodging screaming fans out front and driving them to the set, and dropping them off after we'd wrapped, trying again to avoid the fans. The Kids thought everything was 'dope'. This was dope, that was dope, anything they said was dope. One of them commented on my dreads one day, and in an English schoolboy accent I replied, 'Yes, it's rather dope, isn't it'. They didn't say dope around me again.

I soon found out that Daman dabbled a bit in smack, and in between jobs, we started frequenting Downtown, despite its average ten homicides a day. When it wasn't too hot cop-wise, a dozen dealers lined the corner of Olive and Eighth, home of the homeless. It was better to buy off the Mexicans. They wanted the return business and were less likely to rip you off than the black dealers who were likely to sell you bunk so they could score themselves. Trying to get the money back from them was like tempting death.

The smack came tied up in tiny water balloons which the dealer held in his mouth. They were only about the size of a pea but I was still amazed at how many they could keep in their mouth. 'Brown (heroin) or white (cocaine)?' he would ask as he spat them into the palm of his hand. The reason they did it this way was that if the cops came they could swallow them. The buyer was meant to put them straight into their mouth, though I used to wipe them on my shirt first. It wasn't long before I was going downtown on a daily basis, and I never saw the same guy twice.

It was pretty easy to make drugs part of the budget. Take the money out of petty cash and put it down as courier, or gaffer tape, whatever. Petty cash is easy to cover. I used to get $10 worth of gas and a receipt for $20. On big budgets you would be dealing with lots of petty cash, and as long as you had receipts you were covered. Though sometimes I wished there was a receipt man that I could go to and buy $100 worth of assorted receipts for $10 and a receipt.

Next, Daman introduced me to crack. Crack is dirt cheap, but costs a life. For $5 you can get a little rock, a nice rush. It's as strong as injecting coke, and of course you want more. As a matter of fact, if you really want it, you do anything.

I was constantly putting myself in danger, being a desperate white guy with money. I'd spend $20, dash home, have it, stare out the window, and then go back for more, doing this for hours. I guess that was when and how my cocaine psychosis started. When I finished my rocks or when I ran out of money, I'd be on the floor, picking up anything that was white and make a pile on the table. A chicken pecking for that ever-elusive speck for hours on end. Then I'd lie in bed, staring past what I saw, doing headmiles, and sweat myself to sleep.

Sometimes I'd get ripped off. Dealers sold all sorts of bunk—soap and wax being favourites. I've also seen glass, plastic, even gum. Sometimes I'd walk three steps away, realise I'd been ripped off and turn around, and the guy would raise his arm in a 'don't even' gesture, and I wouldn't. Somehow I managed to keep my job down, but slowly I was turning from an extrovert to an introvert. I knew I was in trouble. Every now and then I'd get up enough nerve to smash my glass pipe. The next thing I'd be out buying another one.

My friend Stan came over from Sydney looking for a job. He'd been out all day and come home, parking his rented car in the crack-head car park across the road. When he told me where it was parked, I thought 'fuck!' and ran outside.

Too late. There was just a little broken glass where the car had been minutes before. I had told him not to park there. Some crack-head would have seen him, waited till he left, walked over, smashed the window and driven away with a wide-eyed grin. Stan had left everything in the car too—passport, tickets, traveller's cheques, camera, leather jacket, sunnies. A crackhead treasure trove.

Michael was in town, staying in Beverly Hills at the Four Seasons. He'd been shopping around for an Aston Martin DB5, and had finally found a fully-optioned, left-hand drive Superleggera through a friend for $150,000. I said for that he could have seventy of my cars, a fleet of Fairlanes. But it was his dream to own an Aston Martin.

We took the car out for a test drive and he bought it. For someone who didn't even hold a licence, Michael took a lot of fancy cars for test drives.

I was poolside at his hotel one afternoon when I noticed a dark-haired beauty alone in the jacuzzi. It wasn't long before I was in there too. Her name was Christina, she was from Copenhagen, and had come over for a week to interview Michael Douglas for a fashion magazine. We spent the rest of the week together, at my place, or ordering room service from hers.

The night before she left, we had a little dinner party at my place. After we'd eaten, Stan and I borrowed her hire car, a new Thunderbird, to drive down to Pico to get a little pot. On the way, we decided that a little rock wouldn't go astray either. We pulled into the dark street, and a guy came up with a few rocks in his hand. I was looking, more people were crowding around the window—busy as usual. Perhaps a bit too busy for comfort.

I thought we'd try another street, and told Stan to drive off, but didn't notice the guy had accidentally dropped a little rock at my feet. As Stan sped off, we realised the guy was still in the window. He'd wedged himself in, and was holding on for dear life. Stan was doing fifty miles an hour by now and we were both looking at each other, and at this determined guy. He was screaming furiously in Spanish. I could easily have hit him, but that would have just made things worse.

I yelled at Stan to stop. The guy's feet touched the ground, and he reached down and grabbed the rock. He was still screaming at us, so I tried to calm him and buy the rock for twenty bucks. Within a few seconds of us stopping, his extended family started introducing themselves to us.

The street was very dark and you could barely see outside. Someone opened Stan's door and whacked him in the jaw. They tried to get the keys out but luckily we were still in drive and the keys wouldn't come out of the lock. Instead they tried to pull Stan out of the car, but couldn't because of his seatbelt. They were screaming, Stan was screaming, I was screaming. There was a loud crash as a block of concrete bigger than a basketball smashed through the rear window, showering us in glass. It would have killed or crippled anybody in the back seat.

Then, as fast as they appeared, they vanished. We took a millisecond to get our senses together, and sped off. Except for Stan's jaw and the rear window, we'd been lucky. We pulled over still buzzing, shook the glass off and smoked the rock. We decided to park the car out the front of the hotel, say nothing, and let Christina think later that someone had tried to break in, but not taken anything. I threw a handful of glass on the ground and around the boot before we went inside, acting like nothing had happened. Her insurance covered it. Stan certainly didn't have much luck with hire cars in LA.

One of the good aspects of LA is that you can always get on a freeway and leave. With that in mind, one weekend Daman and I hopped in his '72 Cadillac and headed for Las Vegas. Very fear and loathing, except we didn't bring adequate drugs.

Vegas is crazy, a twenty-four hour slot machine, pa ching, pa ching, pa change. Apart from the hookers, everything is dirt cheap—hotels, food, drinks are free, so you can spend all your money on gambling, every last nickel of it. It's not surprising the numbers on a roulette wheel add up to 666.

Gambling isn't one of my addictions, which is just as well as the bug bites hard in Vegas. It's a make or break city with lousy odds. 'Place your debts.' I saw one woman in a fevered search for a lucky machine at three in the morning, clutching her buckets of quarters with more respect than she obviously had for the sleepwalking six-year-old she was dragging behind her. At least with heroin, after a couple hundred dollars worth you fall asleep and stop. Gamblers don't reach a pass-out point. They have nothing to stop them.

Work had picked up again and I'd graduated to video assist, which meant running a split from the camera and recording each take so the director could check them after. If you can do that, you're doing your job, and it pays better. I kept myself as busy as possible, working with Wendy and Lisa, Pebbles, Go West, Maria McKee, and was first assistant director for a shoot for the ever-hip Devo that we shot at Palm Springs.

Jon Farriss's girlfriend Lisa had a 'cute as' sister, Laura, who lived in Dallas. When she came to LA to see the band we met and hung out. Nothing sexual, damn it, she just liked to party.

Laura flew back home to Dallas, but a month later she invited me over and sent me a ticket. Like most things in Texas, Dallas is big. Like LA, it looks like it's been dropped from the air, flattened and spread out on landing. Opulence abounds. Oil derricks sit on front lawns pumping fortunes into their pockets and egos. And you need a car, even more so than in LA. They've adapted everything to the car, with drive-in chemists, banks, alcohol, drugs, assassinations, you name it.

Days we did the sights. The Grassy Knoll, the Book Depository. Nights we ate tex-mex and immersed ourselves in margaritas. One night we were driving with Laura's friends Putt (real name), who had a brother Chip (ditto). Who knows, maybe their dad is called Par. We were drunk and Laura and I started having an argument. I got out and was pissing in a bush when a cop car flashed its lights. Being drunk and angry, I gave them the finger and walked the other way. Moments later they came screeching around the corner, straight for me, lights flashing and siren blaring, skidding to a halt in front of me. Again, very *COPS*.

I must have been very drunk, because when they got me in the car I was virtually daring one of them to hit me, thinking for some reason that being Michael's brother gave me special privileges and police immunity.

I woke up next morning in a cell, which surprised me, as I'd forgotten everything. I felt disorientated, and banged on the door for some answers. A female officer told me if I had no outstanding warrants or such and could make bail, chances were I'd be out in a couple of hours. She was nice, and even got me some McBreakfast.

Before too long I was led out before the judge and he arranged a date for a hearing in a few weeks, and released me on $100 bail that Laura paid. The next day she drove me to the airport and I kissed Dallas goodbye.

Production companies started finding it harder to pay me cash. Short shoots were fine, but for bigger ones or commercials they needed forms filled out, information about you, social security numbers and such. When Michael told me INXS would be touring Europe early the following year, I asked him if there were any jobs. He thought I'd be wasting my brain being a roadie, that I was smarter than that. But I bugged and begged him and finally scored a job as a carpenter. I had wanted to be in charge of luggage, as that way you get to travel with the band and stay in their nice hotels, but in the end I was happy just to be included.

I decided to leave LA and go to New York before the tour, as I had an onward ticket. But until my departure I moved into Lynne and Dan's garage off La Cienega to save cash. Lynne was a fashion stylist who'd worked for INXS, and she and Dan were groovy people with the who's who of LA always dropping in. Their friends included Leif Garrett and the gorgeous Christina Applegate. Harry Dean Stanton came by and played guitar there a couple of times.

Lynne and Dan were always getting invitations to parties and we went to a fourth of July barbecue at Julian Lennon's house in the Hills. Julian had a nice place, with a sculpture garden that dropped away to reveal LA in all its smoggy finest. He put on a spread that unleashed my inner freeloader, and I spent the afternoon on the lawn snacking and helping myself to the open bar, as did we all. Michael was back in town and turned up, and because he and Julian were friends we got a tour around the house. I got to tinkle on the famous white grand piano that John had written 'Imagine' on. Imagine.

Another night a bunch of us were invited to a record launch for Vixen, an all girl, very metal band, being held at the old Joan Crawford place. The current owner rented the grounds out for weddings, parties, anything. Joan's spread was Golden Years Of Hollywood grand. The house backed onto an Olympic-sized pool and a cabana that doubled as the star's private screening room.

The gardens were set up with bars and food marquees, and the Hollywood glam set was there, aging LA rockers stuffed into their spandex and lycra ensembles. We grabbed a drink and did the rounds, then headed back to the house and set up in the TV room, where we weren't supposed to be. I was leaning against a wall when there was a click, and a hidden door opened to reveal a secret bar. I saw three bottles of vintage Bollinger inside so I grabbed one and opened it. It didn't last long and I soon grabbed another and went outside. The owner of the place came over and introduced himself, and I offered him a glass and we sat around for a while shooting the breeze and consuming his stash, unbeknownst to him. I even managed to nip back in and nab the last bottle before we left. When we got our coats, we kept the hangers as souvenirs. My coathanger dearest is a wire one.

Michael was still with Kylie, and they were even getting time out from dodging the press to take a holiday together. Word came from Thailand, where they were holed up in the mountains.

> *Yo Bro!!*
> *Hope all is well with everyone there. The hills are alive with the sound*
> *of gunfire! Poppys not roses. Rebels not Germans. Chickens that fly—*
> *and smiles all day.*
> *Mikey*
> *Kylie xxx*
> *Chiang Mai, Thailand*

The week before I left, the swing arm on the Fairlane's front left wheel snapped and I had to get it towed to the garage. It meant I had to get the bus downtown, which added an hour and a half to my journey. I searched for the right part to no avail, and not having the $200 it would cost to get the car back in running order, I left my beautiful heap with Dan to sell for me. He got it running again, but never sold it. Last I heard a tree had fallen over on it, damaging the tree. As far as I know it's still on the corner of Fourth and La Cienega. The first person to send me twenty bucks is welcome to it.

new new york

I heart NY. I must have been there less than a day and I already liked it more than all the time I'd spent west in sunny California. New York reminded me of Hong Kong, busy and bright, pulsing, people on the street, walking, jaywalking, hustle, bustle, pizza by the slice. Even the panhandlers were nicer than in LA.

I was staying with a friend Vicky, whom I'd met in LA. I had a few friends living there and rang Gerrard, the guy who saved my life when I OD'd in Sydney. We had a drink that night, caught up. I was tired so he walked me home, dropping me at the corner of my street.

He'd only just walked off, and I was trying to find the door key when three guys came up behind me, telling me they didn't want to hurt me, they just want my money. I was a bit drunk and slow to respond, and they were saying, 'Give us da money dude', shoving their hands in my pockets. Then one of them said, 'Where's the knife?' and they started looking in their own pockets. It was then that I realised they only came up to my chest, kids basically. I wasn't willing to wait while these incompetent bubs found their switchblade, so I pushed past them, ran off and hid behind some parked cars while they scarpered, laughing, with the twenty bucks they'd swiped from my pocket. Welcome to New York.

I met Disturbed Jennifer the next day. I was on my way to a restaurant in the meat packing district when a black guy ran past me screaming, 'Man! A snake…man…jus' come out of the sky…man, a snake!'. Sure, in New York City. Crack-head. But then, sure enough, further up the sidewalk I see a fat, six-foot snake. When we were kids Michael and I used to keep a pet snake in our cubby house, which we successfully managed to hide from our folks, but it was nothing like this one. This was big.

Maybe because we'd kept a snake and I figured this one was non-venomous, I hunched down and slowly crawled up to it, my arm reaching out, but when it hissed scarily, I ran off. Two minutes later I walked into the restaurant, headed for the bar, ordered a beer and mentioned the snake to the girl next to me. She took my beer out of my hand and put it down on the bar, grabbed my hand and dragged me outside. She was pulling me along shouting, 'Where's the snake, show me where's the snake!'.

By now there were two chubby NYPD cops standing with two members of the Tactical Animal Response Group, who had the snake draped across their hands. These are the guys trained to catch all those rats, escaped zoo animals, giant flushed sewer gators and the occasional, misguided, wayward snake of the metropolis.

We ran up to the cops and she said, 'My snake, you got my snake. He must have got out a window. My snake you got my snake'. Then she grabbed the snake and wrapped it around her neck, saying 'Sorry, it won't ever happen again, thank you, sorry'.

'You better be more careful in future ma'am', they told her. 'You nearly gave some poor guy a heart attack.' It turned out the black guy had been sitting on the sidewalk when out of the blue the six-foot Burmese python fell out of an apartment window, smack-bang into his lap. He freaked and started running like a headless chicken.

Of course it wasn't her snake at all. But after that it was. She'd just got herself a $300 python for free. We wore it all the way back to her place on the Lower East Side.

Jennifer was a singer–songwriter who played many instruments, and was a natural talent. She was attractive, with light brown hair, energetic and ballsy. She performed under the name A Disturbed Jennifer because her psychiatrist had called her disturbed on her first visit, and she had kind of liked it. Her parents were Army brass, so she had grown up on various US bases around the world, and when she was old enough her musical interests led her to New York.

Just after she arrived, she started having an affair with her gynaecologist, who rather than a diamond ring had given her herpes. Dr Feelgood, as Jennifer called him. She sued, and ended up settling out of court for $100,000, various fringe benefits, and his apartment in Trump Tower rent free for a year and a half.

As well as being a talented singer, she was a budding artist. Back at her place she showed me some of her creations. She would shit in a nice pile on a piece of cardboard, push diamantés and semi-precious stones into the shit, then shellac the lot to keep it all together (and the smell in). On the other side of the cardboard she would write a list of the foods she'd eaten the day before that had gone into each masterpiece, and paste on the labels of all the foods jars and cans. By this time though she had moved on to other genres. She wasn't so much a frustrated artist, more a constipated one perhaps.

Disturbed Jennifer introduced me to her girlfriend Judy, who worked in a mid-town editing suite cutting commercials. She had some coke, and of course I was just a boy who couldn't say no. Fifteen minutes later she was on the phone to her dealer for more.

Judy said I was welcome to stay at her place on Tenth, and I took her up on it. When Jennifer told me about the local smack dealer, I was fully back in business. The first time I went there with her, the dealer didn't know me, of course, and was suspicious. I had to plead that I was a user, and show him my arms. It was embarrassing.

I'd never seen such an open drug market. Every day after dark I joined a line of other desperates and waited my turn. We went in three at a time. You'd go up to the door and a guy would open a little hatch in it and check you out individually. Once satisfied, he opened the door and you hurried in. The doorman yelled to keep to the left, get your money ready and keep moving. The waiting was pretty tense because all you wanted to do was score and get out. When it was your turn, you'd move up to the guy at the bottom of the stairs, tell him how many packets you wanted and give him the money. Cash only, and no $1 or $5 notes. He took your money, counted it, added it to his wad of wads and pulled your packets out of his bumbag, then you'd hurry away.

I hate to think I corrupted her, but in the two months I was there, Judy went from dabbling to needing, losing her job in the process. I myself was in ever deeper trouble, and needed to do a geographical to stay alive, so I booked a flight back to Sydney. There is something about sitting on a plane, cruising the clouds, that relaxes me enough to assess my situation. I can stare out the window, doing headmiles, watching the world whiz by, reflecting on this or that, in an 'it will be okay soon' daze for ages. Something of a gift, I'd say.

paris

I'd only been back from the US a week before I boarded a flight for England to join the INXS road crew for the job Michael had organised for me. The band are loyal and the road crew are close-knit, and I'd known some of them for years. Of course I'm not a carpenter, as the two real carpenters found out when they asked me to build a small box on the first day.

It didn't really matter, as nearly all the construction had been done anyway. I found other ways to help out, and so after a few days getting to know everyone and learning the nuts and bolts of carpentry, we were ready to start the European X Factor tour.

The X album had been yet another smash hit with sales in the millions, and the European leg of the tour lasted nearly two months, playing twenty-four cities in fourteen countries.

Funnily enough, lots of tours seem to start in Holland. Ours began in Rotterdam, and we had a day off there. Half the crew took advantage of it and went out to stock up on various blends of hash and bags of heads, which, carefully hidden amongst several semi-trailers of equipment, could last a whole tour.

This was to be my first taste of the famous Dutch cannabis cafes, and I was like a kid in a candy store. Drugs are one of the few ways to break up the tedium of the road and boredom of the bus. The days were very much alike, the same routine. Arrive at the venue, load in, set up, watch the show again, load out, shower, then back on the bus and off to the next gig. On this tour, the band was playing stadiums so big that the buses and semis could drive all the way in. Sometimes I'd get on the bus after lugging out, crack a beer and smoke a spliff, and fall fast asleep, only to wake up in another country, at another venue. A couple of times all I saw of a country was the gig. What's Sweden like? The bricks are bigger and slightly more orange.

The work was constant and tiring, and I soon realised being a roadie doesn't live up to the myth. It wasn't all the sex, drugs and rock & roll it was cracked up to be, though, if the sex had been there it would have been another story. The crew buses were alright, though, state-of-the-art Mercedes that slept nineteen comfortably, had seating up the front and a rumpus room down the back, and came equipped with TV, video, and a fully stacked kitchen and bar. The band flew from gig to gig and stayed in expensive hotels while the crew drove and slept on the bus, unless we were playing a couple of nights somewhere, when we got a hotel bed.

It wasn't until about halfway through the tour that the other members of the crew realised I was Michael's brother. They were amazed, not understanding why I would be working, rather than just hanging out with him.

The tour was a good chance for Michael and me to do some catching up. We went out to dinner, drank, talked. It was the best time for INXS—they were getting their just desserts. Every seat was first class, every bed five star. Michael was revelling in it. The world was his oyster.

After Rotterdam we played Brussels, then drove to Zurich and checked into a Novotel, as we had a day off. That night a few of us crew hooked up and headed into town where there was a wine-tasting festival being held on some barges moored on Lake Geneva. With over 2200 wines to taste from all around the globe, it was billed as the world's largest public wine tasting. For only eight Swiss francs it was a bargain—all the wine you could taste. I thought it would have attracted every wino in the vicinity, but it didn't, and I was surprised at how stylish and civilised everyone's behaviour was. It wouldn't have been like that in too many other places.

I decided early not to mix, and stuck to pinot noir with the occasional champagne chaser, but by the time we left we were all pretty rotten.

Not long after midnight we sauntered back along the cobble-stone streets. There was a park next to the railway station, and as we got closer we saw a big pagoda, with a bigger crowd milling about it. I thought it may have been a party at first, but the closer we got the grimmer and more bizarre the scene became.

Around the pagoda were a dozen tables stacked with neat piles of needles, spoons, water, swabs and cotton wool. Dealers waltzed around brazenly hawking their wares, calling out 'Brown sugar!' and 'Coke!' for all to hear, while buyers shopped for bargains. All dealing was done by sight, no scales needed, except for large amounts. The dealers would tap out stuff with a switchblade from big sandwich bags. You tend to trust the judgment of a guy with a switchblade.

Inside the pagoda the freebasers huddled in splinter groups sucking on glass pipes and bongs. We mingled amid the chaos, with people mixing up and blasting all around us like some surreal yet familiar nightmare. The park was known as Needle Park, and it fascinated me that such an open drug market existed in Zurich, in prim little Switzerland. There must have been at least a couple of hundred people there, all with one purpose. I suppose I was one of them too, because I scored some smack. After a while we regrouped and headed back to the station and our hotel. I ended up sick as a dog because I hadn't had anything since leaving Sydney.

After Zurich was Frankfurt, Copenhagen, Stockholm, then a night off in Hamburg. Hamburg is renowned for its sprawling red light district that caters for every desire imaginable. In one area the streets are walled off from prying eyes and women don't enter. Inside, men window-shop, checking out the women displaying their wares in the large glass windows. The further down the street you go, the kinkier it gets, with whips, Alsatians and bondage gear dominating the scene.

After Hamburg we played Cologne, Strasbourg, Montpellier, Bordeaux, Toulouse, Madrid, Barcelona, Lyon, Milan, then on to London. Each show was a sellout, packed. Back in London, INXS played to full houses at Docklands, and four shows at Wembley Arena.

Each night was an electrifying experience. The band would come on and the crowd would roar. When Michael came on, the pitch heightened even more, and I could feel the adoration of everyone there for him, in my own heart.

Most of the fans were girls, surprisingly young, and would have been in nappies when the band first started touring.

Michael was very short-sighted. He wasn't born that way, it just came on later in life. He told me he couldn't see past the first few rows of people in the crowd. One night he wore contact lenses, and said later that the sight of so many people freaked him out so much that he didn't wear them any more.

I first met George in Glasgow, at the tail end of the tour. The snow was so heavy that the roads were blocked and half of the equipment was stuck in Birmingham. INXS had to cancel their gig. Not bad really—Glasgow was only the second show in sixteen years that they'd cancelled.

We got an extra day off, and hotel rooms for the night. That evening I went down to the bar for a warming nip and saw a guy in an expensive suit with a woman on each arm, drinking champagne. I had my tour jacket on, he mentioned something about the band, and we started talking. He bought more bubbly, and I joined them for a glass. That turned into another glass, then another bottle. George was a Londoner, shortish, stocky, with a cockney accent. He was living in Amsterdam, gave me his number and said if I ever went there to give him a call beforehand and he'd look after me.

Amsterdam had always fascinated me, and I'd decided to go over for a few days before heading down for Christmas at Michael's villa in the south of France.

The rest of the tour ran to plan—Manchester, Paris, Brighton, Bournemouth, and we ended up going back to Glasgow and doing an extra show to make up for the cancellation. We finished with a bang in Dublin a week later, when the stories I'd heard about roadies and groupies finally came true, and I got laid on tour.

We all said our goodbyes and, cashed up, I flew back to London to stay with friends. The night before I was leaving for Amsterdam, I called George to tell him I was on my way with a couple of friends. He said he'd make a hotel reservation for us, and would see us tomorrow.

Next evening we were standing in a plush hotel foyer in Amsterdam. George was there to greet us, all smiles, like we'd known each other for years. He had set us up in two large suites with views. There were bottles of champagne in buckets and fruit platters in our rooms. George said to help ourselves to room service, as we had £600 credit. I nodded, smiled. I didn't quite get it, but was happy enough to receive his generosity. How often does someone pay for a five-star hotel room for you and friends, and lay on room service too?

We drank the bubbly and George asked if I'd like any coke, or 'eck-ta-tee', as he pronounced it. He said I shouldn't buy from anyone on the street, as it could be risky and the quality questionable, and that he could organise anything I needed.

That afternoon we hopped in his brand new Mercedes 450 SL and sped south. After an hour and a half we pulled over at a roadside restaurant near the Belgian border and went in. There George introduced me to a German couple, Hans and his wife, who had driven up from Belgium to meet us.

We grabbed a table, ordered Heinekens all round and made small talk for ten minutes. Nodding and smiling. We finished our beers and walked outside, and Hans said 'Vellcome to Holland, I hope you enjoy your stay here'. We shook hands and he placed a packet of Marlboros and a sandwich bag, quite unexpectedly, in my palm. I said 'Thank you very much', and 'Goodbye', and smiled and nodded. When we got back to George's car and I looked at what I was holding, I discovered the sandwich bag had an ounce of uncut coke, and the ciggie packet roughly seventy ecstasy tabs, together worth a small fortune. I broke off a small rock and made a couple of lines and we snorted, chatted and sped back north to Amsterdam.

That night George drove us over to the Paradiso nightclub and introduced me to an old girlfriend of his, Petra, and her girlfriend, Paris, whom he had kind of lined up for me.

Paris was extremely cute. She was tall and blonde, with light olive skin. She told me she was twenty-three and born and raised in Amsterdam. Paris was a good talker; witty, with a snappy repartee. She had a university degree, and told me she was working as an art dealer, mainly modern, buying and selling around Europe.

We were having a great time, and I thought it was soon going to get greater, when Petra came looking for us to say goodbye. Paris wanted a lift, and all of a sudden she was saying goodnight. After she went, I trawled the bar for my friends, who had gone, and was just about to leave when Paris came back in. She had missed her ride on purpose, and come back. It was freezing, so we jumped a cab back to the hotel and went straight to my room. We woke next morning to a beautiful day and a totally trashed room, clothes strewn, empty bottles everywhere. It looked like I'd lived there all my life.

But doing excessive amounts of paranoia-enhancing drugs, in a strange hotel, lavished on gratis by a strange man in a strange country, apart from not being that strange at all, can still cause a deal of concern and sense of worry unparalleled, and I spent most of the next three days at the door peep-hole looking, staring, watching and peeping. Meanwhile my friends were telling me to relax, it was all okay, while singing me 'Welcome To The Hotel Paranoia'.

Paris took me over to her place. She had a generous-sized flat for Amsterdam, with a big lounge and kitchen, and a spiral staircase that led upstairs to the bedroom which looked up and down a canal, and out across the city.

The next day was Christmas Eve, and I was due to take a train down to Cannes for Christmas with Michael, but George insisted on hiring a car for me to drive. He continued to be ever obliging. I was intrigued, but soon stopped trying to work it out and just enjoyed it.

I asked Paris to come with me, but she had other arrangements. Then at the last minute she changed her mind. We had a long drive south to make it in time for the Christmas festivities. Whenever we felt fatigued we'd pull over and have a line. Finally, early on

Christmas evening, we pulled up in Michael's driveway. North Sea to the Med in twenty-two hours and three grams.

Michael's new property, which he had bought from Duran Duran's manager, was in Roquefort Les Pins. It was in a beautiful rural area minutes from the quaint cobblestone village of Valbonne. The 250-year-old farmhouse property was walled and gated, with spacious, manicured grounds of olives, figs, lavender and herbs. Sheep used to sleep downstairs at night in winter, and during the olive picking season, lunch for the pickers was cooked in its massive wood-fired oven. Over time the house had been modernised, and now had central heating and a pool and cabana. All in all your perfect five-bedroom country retreat. It was going to be a small gathering, with Michael, Kylie, Nick Egan from LA, and a couple of other friends. Paris and I unpacked the car and went inside to a chorus of 'Merry Christmas!', presents and drinks. It was wonderful to see Michael at ease in his new home playing host. He gave me a Swiss Army officer's watch for my present, and I gave him a couple of grams of coke and a handful of pills. The others had already had Christmas dinner, so we nibbled leftovers, and being exhausted, crashed early.

For the next few days we lapped up the good life, and lounged around drinking champagne and enjoying stimulating conversation. I can adapt very well to Michael's habitat, though of course nothing lasts forever, plus we had to return the car, so after a few days we loaded up and drove back to Amsterdam.

During these few days together, Paris and I had already fallen in love. It was heady, pure intoxication. I loved her, and she loved me. I hadn't even been looking for her, and there she was in my lap.

On the way back north I mentioned how I wished I could stay with her for a while, but that after my money ran out I'd probably have trouble finding work and have to leave. I had saved about £2000 from the tour, but that wouldn't last long in Europe. Paris told me not to worry, and that she would look after me.

'Are you rich?' I asked.

She told me her grandfather used to be the chairman of Shell, and that when he died he'd left her 4,000,000 guilders. This was something of a sore point with her father, as he himself hadn't been left anything. She told me her mother was dead. The money had been put into rollover accounts in Switzerland, and now she had 10,000,000 guilders, and was sitting very pretty indeed.

When we got back to Amsterdam I moved into her flat. On New Year's Eve, George and Petra came over with lump of coke and a sixpack of Bollinger. We partied hard, took some 'eck-ta-tee' and watched the fireworks. When the champagne was gone George invited us over to his house to continue.

George asked me if I'd ever shot a pistol, and pulled out a size-able Smith and Wesson 9 mm automatic. I said I hadn't, so he took me into his garage and gave me a run-down on how to gun down. Then he fired a few rounds at close range into a large cardboard box in a corner. When my turn came I fired several shots into the box. It was so loud I thought the neighbours must have heard. That, and the sudden, odd feeling that there may have been some-one in that box, made me stop shooting. I'd had enough anyway.

Paris and I decided to fly down to the beautiful city they named after her. She had some things to do there, and we could stay with her father. But Paris and her dad really didn't get on. On our first afternoon there they had a huge fight, screaming at each other in Dutch. I had no idea what it was about. We ended up going to stay at a friend's place before our train back to Amsterdam.

The first Gulf War was starting, and around the world millions of people were gathering for anti-war protests. We took the Metro to Bastille and I bought two bottles of champagne before we assem-bled with the half a million other demonstrators. We made our way through the throngs to Place de la Bastille and the Colonne Juillet. We got as high up the column as we could go, and there were about forty of us up there with everyone milling around us. I popped a champagne cork, sending it sailing over everyone's heads to a roar of approval, and we sat up there drinking and smoking, staring out over the sea of protestors stretching to the horizon.

Not long after our return to Amsterdam, George came over and gave me the gun that we'd shot before. Loaded. As a gift. I was shocked. I kind of liked it, but was kind of scared too. I asked him if it was clean, meaning had it been illegally procured or used, and he got suddenly angry that I'd asked. Then he explained that he'd picked it up at the open-air gun black market in Belgium, and that after we'd shot it that time, he thought I might like it. But still I wondered.

That night I carved a perfect hiding hole in one of the thicker books in Paris's shelves, just like in the movies. Apart from taking it out and looking at it every now and then, the gun lived there in the bookcase; an unasked and unanswered loaded question.

The South-American leg of the INXS tour kicked off in mid-January in Mexico, and even though I hadn't been hired for the crew I decided to fly to South America and surprise Michael for his birthday, and see them play Rock in Rio. Paris didn't need a visa, but I did. I phoned the consulate and was told I could get thirty-day tourist visa when we arrived in Brazil, and so I could just buy my ticket at the airport. We booked a flight and packed a small bag with skimpy, beachy Rio essentials.

When we got to the airport, Paris told me she'd forgotten to bring her purse, which had about $6000 in it. She thought it was on the dresser back at the flat. Her friend Lars, who had come to see us off, did a mercy dash back to look for it. We went in to buy the tickets, but the airline told me that even though I had a reservation, and no matter what the consulate had told me, I couldn't buy a ticket without a visa, and I couldn't get a visa without a ticket. Catch-22.

Lars returned, having looked everywhere, unable to find her purse. As we were packed and ready to go, I walked over to the

south of france

I arrived in Cannes to find Michael had gone to the wrong station to pick me up. I phoned his place and told his housekeeper Jean where I was, and eventually he found me and drove me home. We didn't talk too much on the way.

Michael was now happily with Helena. She was an extraordinary beauty—from the moment she woke until the minute she closed her eyes to sleep at night.

They had guests staying and friends over and there was a party in full swing. I didn't feel like socialising, and hung in my room, sorting my stuff out. The next day Michael showed me the ropes, how to mind the house and the car while he was gone. Strict instructions not to drive his Aston Martin.

Michael and Helena both lived extraordinarily structured lives—planned a year in advance. The night before Helena left to rejoin their busy schedules they took their remaining guests and me to Le Moulin de Mougins, Roger Verge's famous restaurant in the hills above Cannes. I ate pigeon, a small pigeon, which was *très étrange* as I couldn't recall ever seeing a baby pigeon. Michael let someone choose the wine, and they accidentally ordered a couple of bottles of a $1200 sauternes, which I might add was rather nice—until *le check s'il vous plaît*.

Later that night I tried to call Paris, but she was out. Every time I called over the next few weeks, she was out.

Michael and Helena soon left, and I was in the *maison* alone. Jean and her husband Pierre lived in the guesthouse down the driveway, so the main house was all mine.

I didn't bring a lot of dope with me as I wanted to get clean, so after I'd run out, it didn't take long for the withdrawals to start. The restlessness, sore muscles, tossing, turning, sleepless nights, were eased slightly by lots of hot baths, cheap wine, and catching any sleep I could, any time of the day. Smoking hash only seemed to accentuate my hanging out, so I even gave that a miss for a while. I've always preferred to cold turkey it. Feeling the agony my body suffered reminded me of what I'd put my body through. No pain killers, no pain, no gain. After five or six days I felt much better and it showed when I looked in the mirror.

After a month of 'She's not here', one night I finally got Paris on the phone. She'd been busy, she still loved me and she told me she was coming down and arriving in Cannes on the next morning's train. I was looking forward to seeing her and being with her again, as I was lonely already, having never quite learned just to be with myself, or how to experience boredom fully.

I slept well that night, and the next morning hopped in 'Pepé', Michael's new Mercedes four-wheel drive and raced down to get her. I got there early and sat down on the platform and smoked a cigarette, waiting. I wondered how many years, all up, I'd spent waiting. Anxiously fucking waiting waiting waiting.

Finally, the train was coming up the tracks and pulled to a stop. Carriage doors opened and people got off, then more people. I looked up and down the platform and couldn't see her. The guard blew his whistle, the doors closed and the train left. No Paris.

I felt bitterly disappointed with her again, and hollow inside. I'd believed her again, and I should have known. I drove home slowly, thinking about her, and tried to ring her again. The number was engaged. Then I got through and was told she was expected home later that night. I didn't hear from her.

The next day I decided to go for a drive, get out of the house. Chateau Hutchence was situated halfway between Grasse and St Paul de Vence, at the base of the Alps Maritime, and surrounded by some of the most picturesque countryside in France. Narrow tree-lined streets zigzag from the mountains down to the Med, through little cobblestone villages, past farmhouses and chateaux and shepherds tending flocks.

I was starting to feel better. Everything looks so new and fresh in early recovery. Nature's beauty returned and I was smelling the roses, not vomiting on their roots. I was enjoying my clarity, my senses, my surroundings and myself.

Over the next three months I stayed mostly at home, not straying far from the pool during the day and the TV at night. Once a week I'd go down to the supermarket and stock up on supplies with the 900 francs allowance Michael had given me, being just enough to get by. I wasn't over Paris though. I had tried calling her nearly every day, even though she never called me back.

I was starting to get bored, and apart from the friendship I'd developed with Jean, I had no intimate contact at all. Jean and I got on fine, then finer. She was driving us home one evening after we'd had a Pernod or two in Grasse, when I put my drunken arm around her. I thought she was leading me on, saying, 'Ahhh Rhett…ahhh Rhett'. I kissed her neck, 'Ahhh Rhett…' Then she screamed 'Ahhh Rhett!' and told me *'Arrêt!'* is French for 'Stop!'. And I'd thought she liked it. But that kind of broke the ice, and it wasn't long before we were somewhat closer than before.

Techno had arrived in a big way to the Med, and the techno crowd liked their drugs. I had a connection, a guy up in Paris who could supply good acid. I did the clubs in the towns nearby, and made good money moving a lot of tabs each night. Suddenly I was making money, but I wasn't spending it all on drugs myself.

But my quiet days at Michael's were coming to an end. Everyone was coming for Christmas. Michael, Helena and her parents, Mum and her latest husband Ross, Dad and Susie, Tina, Erin, Brent and Tina's boyfriend and his daughter, would all soon be converging for the first family Christmas we'd had since I could remember.

Michael was first to arrive, as he had a lot of things to organise. It was good to see him, as it had been five months since we'd seen each other, and he'd only called me a handful of times. We went out shopping and bought lots of cheese, pâté, fruits, ham, chicken, breads, smallgoods and alcohol. Plenty of beer and two dozen bottles of champagne.

Helena arrived soon after with the assortment of cheeses she carries with her wherever she goes around the world. Next Mum arrived with Ross, in the middle of an annual round-the-world trip. Tina and her crew followed, then Helena's parents Elsa and Fleming, who came bearing schnapps and herring. Dad and Susie flew in from Sydney. By the time my old girlfriend Kim came, the house was as full as the fridge.

We all got dressed up on Christmas Day. The pile of presents was almost as tall as the tree. Michael was very proud to be able to host such a big family gathering at his lovely home. He was beaming with love for Helena, and this was their first Christmas together.

It was a nice feeling, and a strange one too. For years I'd tried to escape the memories, and for years all I'd wanted was my family to be together again. Now they were, and everyone got on well, and more than ever I was willing to be open-minded—yet still I wanted some questions answered. I wanted to ask Mum why, and find out what had been happening to her, for her to be able to do what she did when she left me behind in Australia, and fled to LA with Michael all those years ago. I hadn't really talked to anyone about that fateful day in 1974, except for Michael, and to him only rarely, and never about his own feelings about what happened. I always figured I was the only one really hurt by it all.

I told Michael I was going to talk to her about it, and he asked me not to. He said he didn't want any fights. Mum was happy for the first time in ages, having recently remarried, and it wasn't the right time. So for the next two weeks we all sat down for breakfast, lunch and dinner, and I acted the part, played the game, and every-one must have thought things were resolved, because I was clean, and Mum and I seemed to get along. Charades is a French game after all and everyone played their roles.

But overall it was relaxed time, with a sense of family. We went on family outings down to Antibes, did a perfume factory tour in Grasse, and a lot of drink-driving *après* long lunches.

At nights Michael, Tina's son Brent and I would go down to Cannes and Nice, and hit the hottest nightspots. One night Michael and I drove into Monte Carlo in his Mercedes but were pulled over by the gendarmes and politely told to go back to France. Why, we didn't know. Perhaps they just didn't like the look of us.

Lenny Kravitz was playing in Nice so we went down for his show, which was amazing, then went backstage to meet him and the band afterwards. Michael invited him back to his place for a couple of days. He was friendly and outgoing, and invited me to see him in New York. When he left, I drove him down to Nice station and we literally had to run for his departing train, Lenny calling back thankyous and goodbyes.

Then, as fast as they had come, everyone left again, and I had the house back to myself.

One day I got a call from Disturbed Jennifer in New York. I'd mentioned to her a couple of times that she was welcome to come over and stay. When she took me up on it I asked her to please bring something over because I'd been so good lately. Two days later I drove down to Nice to pick her up. The international airport then was unique and quite bizarre, in that you could have contact with the incoming passengers before they went through Customs and Immigration. And if you only had carry-on luggage, you could disembark and walk straight out of the airport.

It wasn't long after touchdown before I saw her coming towards me, wearing a large brimmed hat with skull and crossbones scarf tied around it which half-hid her tired, relieved-to-see-me face. We hugged and greeted and she told me the stuff was in her hat. I took it and her carry-on bag, and showed her where to collect her other bags and go through Customs and Immigration, while I waited in the arrivals lounge. I'd been waiting twenty minutes when I saw her up ahead, walking towards me with a Customs officer right behind her. As she got nearer I could see she was wide-eyed and dramatically mouthing 'THE HAT'. I quickly placed it on a nearby phone box, picked up her bag and walked towards her. Hello again, was there a problem? The agent asked me if she had any other baggage or luggage. I showed him the carry-on and he asked us to follow him.

We walked over to the Customs area and went into a little room where another Customs agent was going through Jennifer's guitar case, looking in the strings packets. I asked him again if there was a problem, and explained that Jennifer was a friend who had come over for a one-week stay. They told me it was just routine.

The room had big windows, and strangely enough I was able to keep an eye on the hat through the blinds. I saw a guy walk up to the phone, pick the hat up, look around and place it under his arm while he made his call. I'd been clean for six months, give or take a few trips, ectattys, and joints, and wasn't about to let someone just come along and take all my wants and desires away, so I asked them if they needed me anymore, and could I go and bring the car around? No, they said, that would be fine. I excused myself and hotfooted it to the phone, shoved the surprised guy aside, grabbed our hat and hurried away to hide it in the car. Wrong hat, mate.

The Customs people found nothing, so we loaded up the car, got in and drove over to the automatic toll gate, laughing like kids who'd just pulled a swiftie over their parents. I tried to sneak out and not pay by following the car in front of me very closely, but the swing arm came down too quickly onto the roof, and snapped off, flying through the air behind us. I floored the accelerator and we were out of there.

Jennifer had four packets of smack, and kindly gave me two of them. She had actually started the journey with ten packets and had only consumed six by the time I saw her. I gathered she was having trouble with her boyfriend Steve and had come over to talk to me about stuff, and dry out in the process. We sat in the kitchen, got high and caught up. Apart from the nausea that follows, it felt nice being high again, with that reassuring warmth.

I told her about Paris. How I'd not heard a word in six months, which felt odd for someone I'd spent nine months with, twenty-four hours a day. It didn't surprise her.

Jennifer played me some new songs that she'd written on her four-track, which were brilliant. Then we went out to lunch in Ezé at a wonderful restaurant perched high on top of a mountain crag, with magnificent views up and down the Med.

On the way home, Jennifer put it to me, asking me to consider coming to live in New York, at her place, rent free, manage her and get her a contract with some label, any label. She had been trying unsuccessfully to get a record deal for nearly four years and was about ready to chuck it all in. She told me she thought I was her last chance to leave her bite marks in the apple.

I'd always thought she was extremely talented, and had met some A&R (Artist & Repertoire) people from a few different record companies through Michael, so I had half a Reebok in the door. I mulled it over. I believed in her talent, thought she just needed a break. I had some money left over from my acid dealing, and decided I'd give it a go.

By the time I left I had been at Michael's house for seven months, more time than he had spent there, and apart from the extra 16 000 kilometres (Barcelona, Venice, Milan) on his car and a biggish phone bill, I hadn't caused any real damage.

The day before I left, a letter turned up from Paris. She apologised for not coming down and said that she'd chickened out at the last minute. She had been on methadone and was now off it and clean after completing a rehabilitation course, and wanted to see me.

I decided to fly to the United States via London, where I needed to get a new passport, and use my return ticket from Amsterdam to stopover and see Paris. I wrote to her telling her my plans and gave her my phone numbers. When I arrived in London she had called and left her number so I rang her back. It was nice to hear her voice again and she sounded clean and serene. We caught up on the phone several times while I was in London and I was excited at the prospect of seeing her again. She would meet me at the airport in Amsterdam with a large welcome joint.

Touching down, I rushed through Immigration to the Arrivals area. The corners of my mouth turned down soon enough when I realised she wasn't there. Again I'd believed her, and again I'd been let down.

I had bumped into Kylie in London, and as she was going to be in Amsterdam too, doing some press, so we decided to hook up. That night I rang her and went over to the American Hotel to see her. She came down to the bar and we had a drink and chatted. It was nice to see her, and it helped relieve my loneliness. I tried to get her to come across the road to the Bulldog, the famous touristy cafe/pub hash hang, but Kylie was not into that. What is it about her that just makes you want to corrupt her? So after a couple of drinks, as it was late already, we called it a night. She went up to her suite and I traipsed back to my horrible little room in a cruddy hotel.

I had booked a week's stopover, anticipating a wonderful time with Paris, and it turned into a cold, sad, lonely week. I felt like using a number of times. I knew where to get it easily enough— right outside the front door—but somehow refrained. Then one day, it was too much. My usual triggers clicked, and before I knew what I was doing I had scored and was back in my room, smoking smack. Relief only a junkie would know about. A cure-all for end-alls. A couple of stoned, cold days later, I flew out, and arrived in even colder New York.

new york, you nork

Jennifer was living with Steve on the Lower East Side in an apartment above a Chinese noodle factory. According to our arrangement, I moved in with them and we got busy on a demo tape. My plan was to use my connections to get in the door, and the product should sell itself, or else we could invite the right people to a showcase at, say, CBGBs.

The problem was that she was using again. The other problem was, so was I. Only a little at first, after dinner sort of using. But I didn't want to fuck at all with that shit.

We finally got a demo together, and I went to go see Shauna, a relocated LA friend who was now high up at a new record company. Shauna liked what she heard, thought Jennifer had potential and wanted to meet her, so we made an appointment for a week later.

A week to buff her image up enough to get her a deal. Not that her image was bad, just that record companies like a whole package. Apart from Jennifer being stoned, the meeting with Shauna went well, I thought, but when I called a few days later, Shauna told me she thought Jennifer could be trouble. In a nutshell, Disturbed Jennifer was what record companies called a 'temperamental artist', meaning not worth the hassle or babysitting fees. Besides, what do you find in nutshells?

By now Jennifer and I were hoeing in. Drugs had got a hold of us again. Whenever I got some money or Jennifer got a cheque we'd be straight off to a dealer.

I'd been there about two months when one day Steve told me he wanted $300 back-rent—rent Jennifer had said I wouldn't have to pay. New York habits are expensive and I didn't have anywhere near that amount. I told him Michael was arriving in a few days, and that I thought he would help me out. Steve said I couldn't leave the apartment until I paid up, and proceeded to take the doorknob off the front door, and double-locked the entrance to the street downstairs. I was effectively a prisoner. Steve was an ex-Hell's Angel, big and very scary. And Jennifer, possibly because her last chance of success had come and gone, possibly because of the drugs she was on, was solidly on Steve's side. I was up against the two of them.

That night when they were lying in bed in their room near the front door, stoned asleep, I found a big screwdriver and tiptoed over the creaking floorboards to the apartment door, put the screwdriver in the hole, turned it, and it opened. I was opening it up enough to squeeze out, when it creaked loudly and woke up Steve, who was still groggy and unsure what was happening.

I ran down the stairs, and started kicking at the door that led to the street, but Steve was onto me, punching and pulling me backwards. I gave in, scrunched up in a ball on the floor at his feet, which then decided to kick me. He dragged me upstairs and beat me more until I ran terrified into my room. Steve then lovingly kicked my door off its hinges and started a barrage of verbal abuse that lasted most of the night.

The next morning he continued his intimidation. I thought of jumping out the window, but being on the first floor, I probably would have broken my legs. Later that day I went out to the kitchen to get some water, hid a carving knife under my shirt, and put it under my pillow for protection.

After three days of imprisonment I was over being held against my will and devised an escape plan. The street outside had recently been changed from two-way to a one-way. Cars were to detour around the long way, or go illegally about twenty metres down the one-way street to save time. The police were onto it, and had stationed a cop in a car on the corner opposite ours to nab offenders. He was booking around ten drivers a day.

I wrote a note saying, 'Please help me. I owe the people here $300 and they are keeping me against my will. I am a tourist and don't know my rights and the laws here, and I fear for my safety. I need help. Please come up', and signed it.

I went to the kitchen and got a glass of iced water and went back to my room. Steve and Jennifer were in their room watching cable. I opened my window, and pelted the cop's car with ice blocks until I finally got his attention. He got out and crossed the road slowly in typical 'Don't bother me, I'm eating a doughnut', NYPD fashion. I scrunched the note into a ball and dropped it, praying the wind wouldn't blow it away. He read it, and I pointed to the building's front entrance.

A few seconds later the doorbell rang. Jennifer had ordered some Chinese, and I hoped she would just go down and open the door. But Steve looked out their bedroom window, saw it was a cop, and called out to Jennifer not to answer it. I knew they wouldn't let him up, so I grabbed the knife, ran out into the living room and started yelling out the window to the cop below to come up. He's looking up at me, all blasé-like, and I'm waving the knife around screaming 'Get the fuck up here, he's fucking crazy, he's trying to kill me…GET THE FUCK UP HERE!'.

Steve came towards me wrapping a belt made from three welded motorcycle chains around his fist chanting 'Get away from the fucking window man…I'll fucking put you in hospital scumbag…get away from the fucking window!'. I was still screaming to the cop to get up there.

The cop had his baton out now, and was trying to break in a small window by the front door. I don't think he'd ever worked so hard in his life. I was holding the knife in my left hand so I could defend myself with my right. Steve took a swing at me. I put my hand up, and the chain cut me on the forehead, knuckles and into the back of my hand. Then he swung at me again and I managed to grab hold of the buckle, and at the same time I stabbed him in his right side and twisted the belt out of his hand. The blade snapped from the handle and fell bloodied to the floor. I dropped the handle and started wrestling with him. Steve was trying to get the blade, and there was no way I was going to let him.

We rolled around on the floor, with Jennifer—and all the people inside her—now hitting me with a broom. I managed to get on top of Steve, holding him down by his ponytail, and somehow got to the blade first and promptly threw it out the window. I still had the belt in my hand and ran over to the window and smashed it, to emphasise to the cop that I needed help and now. I stood in the corner, catching my breath, wondering what was going to happen next. I could hear the cop still pounding away downstairs.

Steve discovered he was bleeding, and started screaming, 'He stabbed me...he fucking stabbed me!' in a surprised pitch. 'He stabbed me, Jennifer...get the cop up here!', and Jennifer ran downstairs with the front door keys.

I was still in the corner, breathing heavily, adrenaline pumping, about five metres from Steve, when he picked up the large screwdriver that I'd tried to escape with the first night and threw it at me. I put my hands up to try and stop it. It swooshed through the air and lodged itself deep in my thigh. I couldn't believe he'd made the shot and I don't think he could either. I pulled it out of my leg, and threw it out the window too.

Then I noticed that the door was now open for the first time in days, dropped the belt and bolted. I ran down the stairs and encountered the cop on the middle landing as he was trying to get his gun out. I ran behind him, with Steve chasing after me, wielding his belt. The cop called for him to stop and he did, still screaming, 'He stabbed me, he stabbed me!'. But I felt safe for the first time in days. It was like the end of a movie, when the back-up finally arrives, except there was no music or credits rolling.

The cop kept Steve at bay until another cop arrived, who handcuffed and escorted me to an ambulance. The paramedics checked me over, and whisked me off to hospital where my wounds were treated. Then I was taken to the local precinct for a statement.

I was charged with assault, before being taken to the Tombs, the infamous holding cells below the courthouse—so named because some people never get out. On the way in the squad car a cop told me it would be better for me if I didn't talk to anyone down in the Tombs, and that I shouldn't cry down there.

Once you've been handcuffed, you can forget about your rights; you're in another world. At the Tombs I was uncuffed, strip-searched, fingerprinted, photographed, had my shoelaces removed, and then put into a holding cell with forty or fifty men, young and old, black and Hispanic. I was the only white guy. I found a seat in the corner, sat down on the cold cement and buried my head in my knees. My hand wasn't too bad, but my leg had a steady throb from the screwdriver wound, and I was withdrawing and exhausted, though hardly relaxed enough to fall asleep.

Later that day we were led out in pairs and given our daily sustenance. Processed cheese and a Spam sort of meat thing, on white bread, a cup of orange soft drink and three packets of white sugar. The sugar apparently calmed you down if you were hanging out.

Every hour or so, a Corrections Officer would read out half a dozen names, and those called would file outside, get handcuffed to a long chain and disappear. A quick glance around revealed that at that rate it would take another six or seven hours until I was called.

Those who tried to strike up a conversation always started with, 'What you in for?' and I always answered, 'Assaulting a police officer'. I figured it raised my cred enough for me not to get hassled. Everyone I talked to was in there for drugs. One guy came in and, when he thought it was safe, started selling stuff the cops somehow hadn't found on him. The asking price was $20 a packet, and I wished I had more money because they were being snaffled quickly and I was feeling like shit. I offered him $8 in change and eight cigarettes, which he accepted, thank you very much. Then he sold the smokes for $2 each, making even more.

In the graffiti-scrawled corner, exposed to all, was a stainless steel toilet, completely stained, on grimy tiles, with no paper. I had to wait my turn, then went to the toilet, sat down, leaned forward and snorted my stuff while flushing the toilet to cover my loud inhale through my semi-blocked nose. I flicked the empty packet out the bars at the back of the cell, where it joined piles of cigarette packets, empty crack vials, and other rubbish.

I'd seen enough cop shows to know I was entitled to make one phone call. I racked my brains for the very best person to call, and decided on Martha Troup, Michael's personal manager and INXS' New York-based international manager. The Corrections Officer told me I would have to wait for a while, then finally called me over and escorted me out to a phone, telling me to make it quick.

It was late now and I hoped Martha would be home. It rang and rang, until finally she answered in a friendly tone. As I started explaining where I was and what had happened, she leapt into action, telling me what to do and reassuring me that it would be alright, I was not to worry, she would call Michael and work things out.

I listened to her, trying to hold back my tears, and for the first time since I'd been in custody I felt a sense of relief and hope. It was so good just talking with someone I knew, and now with Martha on the case, I felt better. I said goodbye, dried my eyes and pulled myself together before the officer took me back.

Around midnight my name was finally called, and with seven others in tow, our right hands were handcuffed to a chain and we slowly shuffled out. I was taken to another cell to wait until hearings started at eight in the morning.

Robert, the lawyer Martha had organised, visited me. He assured me not to worry, asked me for a brief summary of what had happened, and wanted to know how I would be pleading. I told him not guilty—it was pure self-defence.

Nearly a full day after my arrest I was led up into the courtroom where normal-looking people were going about their day, like normal people do. I was sitting up front, and every now and then Robert would turn around and nod to me with a reassuring smile.

We all had to rise when the judge entered. On the wall behind the bench was a large plaster relief of Justice, blindfolded with scales. Written next to it in big gold letters was: I GOD WE TRUST, the N having fallen off.

The judge read my police brief, and asked Robert how I intended to plead. Robert said not guilty, and asked for an adjournment. The judge looked in his diary and said, 'The 11th of October'. And this was only April. Robert agreed, and I was uncuffed, made to sign and receive a piece of paper for bail, and we both walked out. Free at last.

Robert lent me $20, which I quickly scored with, then limped up

Canal Street to my friend Skate's place to crash. I phoned Martha and thanked her, and she told me Michael would be in town in the morning, taking the first available flight over from London.

I had a bath and inspected the damage. My head and hands were scratched, though not too scabby, but it was my leg that worried me. My knee was stiffening up and the back of my thigh was black, blue and quite swollen, though the puncture hole looked fairly clean. The pain had subsided to a dull ache. I lay in the bath with my bad leg sticking out, so as not to wet the wound, closed my eyes, and felt relaxed for the first time in ages. Relaxed enough to cry again.

Next morning Michael was on the phone, and we had the first of many words on the subject. At first he was understandably very worried about me. Then he got on to 'I knew this would happen', and how it was my fault, and when was this sort of thing going to stop because he wasn't going to bail me out forever. He was staying at the Royalton Hotel uptown, and told me to get up there pronto. I didn't have any money, so he organised someone to be there to pay for my cab when I arrived, and hung up.

Not long afterwards I was knocking on his door, and entered his suite. Michael was in the hotel's white fluffy robe, picking at his expensive breakfast. As soon as I sat down I started crying again. I wanted to be close, needed some support and love, but he was angry now and being the big brother he tended to be when I was in trouble. As only Michael could, in only Michael's way, he lectured me again, and I couldn't stop crying.

'Do you know how much this is going to cost me?' he asked and told me, at the same time.

I wished I could have met him on more neutral turf, and not in his $500 a night suite. Helena came back with bags of shopping and plonked them down and went out shopping again, so that we could continue our chat. She just said hello. I was surprised she didn't even ask if I was alright.

I was hungry and asked if he had finished his breakfast, and devoured what he hadn't picked at, surprised he didn't even ask if I wanted anything to eat. He reckoned it would cost about $15,000 to get me out of the whole mess. It wasn't the money;

he just wished I'd grow up, clean up my act and do the things normal people do—work, pay rent, buy food—normal things. I agreed with him and promised I would get some help. Michael told me I'd better not be lying, and that I should start looking for somewhere to live, which he'd inevitably have to pay for. I emotionally blackmailed fifty bucks out of him before I left.

This was the first time that I had seen Michael after he had been injured in an incident in Copenhagen. One night about three months before, he had an altercation with a taxi driver there. He had just left a club with Helena and some friends, and they were on bicycles. They'd stopped to get something to eat from a stand in a narrow cobblestone street. A taxi started honking at him to get out of the way. Michael gave the driver the finger, at which the guy got out and punched him in the face, and he fell down cracking his head on the pavement. Michael's friends beat up the taxi driver.

Over the next two months he was nursed back to health by Helena in her apartment in Copenhagen. It was a very serious matter, and Michael was lucky not to have suffered serious brain damage. He told me that he went to one of the best neurosurgeons in France. The guy drew a picture of a brain, with ten stems going down from it. 'This is the human brain'. He then proceeded to rub out eight of the stems. 'This is your brain now'.

He had lost 80 per cent of his smell and taste, and was often quoted as breaking down to friends that he couldn't even taste his own girlfriend any more. That must have hurt him very much as he'd even written a song about her taste called 'Viking Juice'.

In a way, from that day on I saw a different Michael, one I hadn't met before. He could become very angry at the drop of a hat. And though he had reason, I'd never seen him get so angry, and so quickly, as he did in New York that day. Michael seemed to get better over time, and was still the same guy, but now his moods could fluctuate quickly at times.

A few days later I went uptown to talk to Robert. He thought he could talk to the District Attorney and get the whole thing sorted out a lot quicker than October. Robert thought that if Steve would drop his assault charge against me and I dropped my assault charge against him, the police wouldn't have a case—end of story.

He said Steve had been in hospital for three days with a punctured kidney and spleen, handcuffed to the bed with a police guard watching over him. When fit enough to be charged, he was bailed until October too. Then he promptly vanished. Robert said we had to track him down to put the proposal to him that we both drop our charges, and he had a friend called Dan, an ex-cop and bounty hunter, who would do that.

Michael was still angry with me, and I don't remember that we saw much of each other after our first meeting. The stab wound in my leg had reduced my mobility, and it was hard to get out anyway. I lay low at Skate's place. A week after Michael jetted in, he and Helena returned to Europe, and even though I had friends in town, I felt alone and alienated because of my addiction.

After some shopping around, I moved into the Chelsea Hotel on Twenty-third Street. It was actually the cleanest, cheapest place I saw. It's a beautiful old building and Stan the manager is helpful and friendly and has been there many, many, years. Among other famous people he knew Brett Whiteley quite well, with the foyer and the area behind the desk proudly displaying two of the New York-style works Brett did during his two-year stay there with wife Wendy and daughter Arkie.

In New York you need two things, a lot of money and a lot of money. Michael was generously paying my rent and gave me an allowance of $250 a week for food, so I could get by. As soon as all this was over I was planning to be on the first flight to Sydney, and as I'd promised, get some help, some form of rehab. Stan put me on the first floor in room 109, near the room where Sid Vicious had stayed, and his lover, Nancy Spungen, died. I wanted Sid's room, but a couple had been living in there for a year.

My room was scant and quite grotty really, but for $325 a week plus tax, I couldn't complain. Now I can. The carpet was pock marked with cigarette burns, the little porcelain sink mottled brown from steady drips, the curtains frayed and tatty, the sheets and bedspread stained, and the small dirty kitchen had rats, acting like they were the rightful residents and ratepayers.

One morning I went out for a walk only to see a headline with the terrible news about the death of Brett Whiteley, and went back and told Stan. Another untimely, tragic end, to yet another sensitive genius.

Every week I'd call Robert for the latest. Dan had tracked Steve and Jennifer to an apartment in New Jersey. Steve was thinking about the proposition, though for the next two months he still wanted go ahead with the charges. Robert believed that was on his own lawyer's advice. Steve's lawyer was one of those types who advertised on cable channels watched only by the stoned or dysfunctional.

Robert agreed that Steve wouldn't have a chance if the case did proceed, as it was pure self-defence. Plus, Robert would get them both charged with kidnapping, which carried a minimum seven years in jail. Steve was hard to keep track of, however, and from time to time he would disappear. I think he knew it was costing me a small fortune to stay in the country, and was just being a pain in the arse.

After I'd been at the Chelsea for three months, Robert called to say he'd finally struck a deal with Steve to drop the charges for $1000. It would be the quickest, cheapest, easiest way to deal with the whole shemozzle. A week later Steve and I were in court again, the charges were withdrawn, the case was closed and Robert gave Steve an envelope with ten Ben Franklins in it.

Michael and Helena flew in again and invited me to dine at Indochine with a catwalk of supermodels. Michael told me to wear the Mr Shinju suit he'd bought me in Tokyo. The one you need a licence to wear, and I felt really uncomfortable in it as I was the only one dressed up.

I was seated across from Christy and Elle, next to Yasmin and Helena, with Gail Elliot, her husband John, Michael and some other fashion guy making up the table. Yasmin was nice. We'd met before in London so we chatted, and she made me feel welcome. It was

Christy who mesmerised me, even though Helena had told me, 'You wouldn't like her, she's got no tits'.

Elle had met Paris through me, and we talked about her pathological traits. She said she'd expected and suspected as much. Elle had quizzed Paris about her family fortune one night after a show in London, and Paris had been evasive. I asked Elle why she had never told me about that, and she said it was because I had been so much in love: I would never have believed her anyway. Elle was right about that. As Goebbels said, 'The bigger the lie, the more believable it is'.

One day, way out of the wild, blue yonder, my phone rang. I picked it up and it was Paris. The last time I had heard from her was at Jennifer's, when she called me to apologise about the airport. She told me she had picked up again and couldn't bring herself to face me. I wondered how she got my new phone number. Paris's latest story was that her cousin in Colorado was getting married and Paris was a bridesmaid. She was flying over in a week and wanted to visit me on the way. She gave me the date and flight number and actually sounded like she believed her story, as pathological liars do. There was no way I was going to the airport so I told her that if she called me from the lobby downstairs, I may go down. She called the next few days until the morning she left, promising to see me. I've never heard from her again.

Early in August I booked a flight back to Sydney. A couple of days before leaving, I went out early, walking along Canal Street, past Little Italy and through Chinatown, to score. I finally did so, but I'd only got two or three blocks away when a car screeched to a halt in front of me and I saw two cops in bulletproof vests inside.

I was put into a van with other unfortunates. Back to the precinct, back down in the Tombs. When I got my single call, I rang Robert to tell him about my stupidity. He was nice, reassuring me again that things were okay, that these things happen. The next morning he spoke to the District Attorney and I plea bargained and pleaded guilty to a charge of 'disorderly conduct' instead of possession. My sentence was to pick up rubbish with a stick with a nail in the end along the Queens expressway for two days while wearing a bright orange boilersuit. The day after completing my debt to America, I was at the airport ready to fly home.

bearing the cross

I returned to Sydney on a Friday morning, and in keeping with my promise to Michael and to Dad, by Monday morning I was on the methadone program. The reason I chose methadone was that I was coming off a pretty strong habit and thought free drugs were a good option.

Dad and Susie had been back from Asia for a year now, and I moved into their apartment in Darlinghurst. Dad wanted me to get back into making videos, but I needed a car and licence for that. On my birthday he surprised me with a second-hand Suzuki Sierra four-wheel drive. I art directed whenever work came up, but it was very different to working in Los Angeles. In LA I worked in the art department. In Sydney I *was* the art department. The work was harder, but the satisfaction greater.

One day Dad showed me a letter addressed to Michael, care of him, that a fan had sent. Nothing new or strange there; that kind of thing was always happening. It was from a girl called Adrian who had flown over from the United States just to be close to Michael. I'd never heard of her, though I guess that if she thought that Michael might dump Helena for her, she must be something special, to fly to Sydney on the off-chance.

She had given a local phone number, so I rang her the next day. She sounded nice enough, and we made an arrangement to meet at the Tropicana cafe. When she turned up, I was more than a little surprised. She was a typical chatty American fan, with the weight problem of four people, who just wanted to hear all about Michael. She said she was psychic, and had virtually dropped everything— her job, her husband, sold her car—all because she'd had a dream that she should be near Michael. I thought she must have weird dreams, politely finished my coffee and bade her adieu.

When I next talked to Michael he said, 'What...Adrian...the fan?'. He told me she was a nut who wrote crazy letters, that yes, they had met once on tour in America, and he couldn't believe she was now living in Kings Cross, within a stone's throw of Dad's place.

Dad hated me using. One day he caught me having a hit, and threw me out. I went off to the Tropicana cafe, had a cigarette and a coffee, and then Adrian walked up. She detected that something was up, and when I told her what had happened she offered me her couch. As I didn't have too many options, I took her up on it.

Adrian lived in a bedsit, two single beds in one little room with an ensuite and a depressing kitchen, on the third floor of a run-down block on Darlinghurst Road. The next day I grabbed every-thing from Dad's and moved in. It wasn't long before I had bor-rowed $50 off Adrian until cheque day.

She had never tried smack, but curiosity was getting the better of her. As an addict you're always eager to find new people to exploit, especially ones with money who, unlike you, like you. We went to the ATM, she gave me some cash and I went into the Cross to score. When I returned, I injected her with about $2 worth, then had my share. It was new, it was exciting and she didn't mind it.

One morning outside Adrian's flat I noticed a folder full of letters in a garbage bin. Fifty or more letters, some of them twenty-five pages long and written on both sides. Hundreds of pages of letters, and all written to Michael, by Adrian. The cover sheet was a list of every letter she'd written to him, how many pages were in each, when she sent it, how much each cost to send, and whether it got through or was returned to sender.

They made for spooky reading, showing a whole other side to her. For the most part she wrote about how much she loved and adored him, but then she started writing about finding hidden meanings in his videos, and thinking that Michael was singing about her. She wrote that they were destined to be together, that they were soul mates, and there wasn't much anyone could do. Some letters were erotic, describing acts that showed me yet another intriguing angle. Others just rambled on and on. Half of one page would have been enough for Michael to read and know not to read any more.

straight back where you left off, and fast. While you may think that you've got the monkey off your back, it's actually been in the closet doing chin-ups, push-ups and sit-ups, and returns stronger than ever.

With the help and support of Mandy, family and friends, I decided to give rehab another go, and contacted the Buttery again. Being a pseudo-local now gave me preference, and I was able to be admitted within a month.

I arrived in good spirits and relieved to be there, and knowing the ropes, swung straight into a healthy daily program. But recovery and remaining that way above all rely on honesty. And it was my telling a lie regarding detoxing just before admission that soon caused me to be asked to leave. The community all voiced their opinions, concerns and disbelief, but rules were rules. After only two weeks, I had to go.

The following morning I was given a cheque for the money I had left, and taken into Bangalow. I was angry at myself and at them, so I cashed my cheque and hitched into Byron. I called Mandy and told her my predicament. She was surprised to say the least, and organised to get off work early to come and get me before it was too late.

Unfortunately it already was. I left my bag at the Railway Friendly Bar and hurried off. I got to the dealer's place and sat in line with the other repeat offenders. I hated that house. Nobody had given the place any loving attention since smack moved in years ago. And being the only dealers in town, they just did not have it together. It took them forever to weigh some dope, do some origami and count a note or two. Eventually I grabbed a packet and some fits and headed back to the bar, stopping at the toilets in Railway Park for a quick shot. Due to past experience, I've always been very careful about how much I use after being clean for any length of time. But this time I fell for the one where you have the second half before the first has fully come on. Around three hours later my eyes opened to see concrete. Very close concrete. So close I could smell it, concrete. My bum was still on the toilet and I was still very stoned. It took me a minute to work out who and where I was, and what had happened. I'd OD'd in the toilet. Not a great way to go. I looked everywhere for the fit and as I couldn't see it anywhere, figured it must have fallen out of my hand and rolled under the door, where hopefully it had been disposed of more thoughtfully. I pulled myself together, got up and went to the pub where Mandy was seated with my bag, looking concerned at my appearance. I told her what had happened and she drove what was left of me home.

Mandy and I moved into a nice house in town in Byron. It was there that Zoe Angel decided to choose us as her parents, and we in turn discovered Mandy was pregnant. We talked seriously, joked lots and agreed it was meant to be. I told Mum, who was happy, and immediately started buying presents. Dad asked if we were going to get married, and I mentioned that with previous family marriage attempts as a reference point—Mum (five), Dad (two), Tina (two, soon to be three), I had been put off the idea for some time now.

zoe angel

We started nesting and preparing for the unknown. At first things were good. We both started attending weekly birth classes. I took up yoga again, doing a number of one-month intensives. But as much as I wanted to be clean for my new child's sake, I found it too difficult. It seemed easier to get some money together and drive the fifty minutes to Nimbin to score on a daily basis, which I was soon doing. Of course Mandy didn't like it, though in the end there was little she could do.

The night we moved into our new house we were eating pizza and watching *Dead Ringers* on video when Mandy's stomach started to hurt, so she had a bath. It was when we saw a little blood floating in the water that we knew. *Here we go, here we go.* As we didn't have a car, we called a friend and grabbed the pre-packed bag and headed into the Mullumbimby birthing clinic, arriving around three in the morning.

After they took Mandy's vitals, the nurses called Mark, our obstetrician, and we made Mandy as comfortable as possible. Mark arrived a short while later, and as Mandy's waters hadn't actually broken yet, he suggested she get as much sleep as she could, and he'd return in the morning. We made ourselves comfortable and tried to catch some winks. It was quite surreal, as the woman in the next room was screaming, and continued to do so for the next seventeen hours.

The next day Mark told us that if her cervix hadn't dilated enough by that evening, he would have to induce, as he was worried that when the time actually came Mandy would be too tired to push. There was nothing much we could do except wait, and inform those who needed to be.

That night Mark returned, and as there had been little progress, the decision was made, and at around six, he broke her waters with what looked like a barbed knitting needle. If Mandy thought it had been uncomfortable and painful up until then, she was in for a bigger surprise.

As soon as her waters broke, she went into instant agony. It was terrible to see someone you loved in such pain, and there is nothing you can do but hold their hand and wipe their forehead. Luckily the labour didn't last long, and within a couple of hours, after much huffing and puffing and straining, a beautiful being emerged and I told Mandy that she'd had a beautiful little girl. It was incredible. We literally watched her turn from an arctic blue to a living pink, which radiated out from her chest after her first breath. I cut the cord, bundled her up and put her on Mandy's breast, and they left us alone. It's funny, you think you've been in love, then when you meet your child you realise there are far deeper levels to love than you ever dreamed possible.

Mandy and I had guessed we were having a girl, so we had whittled down a short list of half a dozen names. It's not easy choosing one, especially with everyone trying to help with their sometimes silly suggestions. Old girlfriends were out of the question, and you mentally cross off people you consider dysfunctional. Tina had faxed a list, Mum and Dad had their ideas. Michael had recently parted from Helena for his new love, Paula Yates, and he phoned in her suggestion—Saucy Cupcake.

When our baby started crying I began reading out the list, and when I got to Zoe she stopped, choosing her own name. After that Zoe fell fast asleep, and was an angel for the rest of the night, hence her middle name. The next morning I phoned everyone with the wonderful news, and after I had rubbed Zoe's feet in the earth to ground her, we headed home sweet home, not even twenty-four hours after labour had begun. The next few days, weeks and months were spent doting, taking many photos, and showing off our pride and joy to family and friends.

We were up on the Gold Coast seeing Mum one day when I bumped into my friend Vincent Stone, who was up there with his band doing a corporate gig. After the show we went to a few clubs and ended up with TV rock guru Molly Meldrum, quite sauced at a bar on Cavill Avenue. I had met Molly on a few previous occasions, and we got on, though I have to admit, personally, I prefer him in small doses.

The conversation naturally steered to INXS, and he started telling me that they wouldn't be anything if it weren't for him. He said Tim and Andrew were the only two with any talent. I listened to him blabbering on for a few minutes, then for some unknown reason I grabbed his hat, jumped the railing and bolted off towards the nearest taxi rank. I hopped in a cab and looked out the back window to see him racing up the street after me. But I got away with the hat. There were a few black hairs inside it, and if I get any bad reviews for this book I swear I will clone millions of him. Be warned, critics.

Before Christmas we decided to have a naming ceremony for Zoe and started organising. Mum and Ross, and Dad and Susie were coming. As Michael was going to be in town with Paula, we asked him if he would be Zoe's godfather, and he readily agreed. Mandy's best friend Jo was asked to be godmother. Mandy and I made invitations and planned the ceremony. Everyone was asked to meet at sunset at The Pass, a favoured spot up the beach in Byron, and to bring a wish for Zoe on a piece of paper. I thought it was to be a private affair, but spotted two photographers with long lenses trained on us, who must have been following Michael and Paula. I went over and asked for a bit of respect and privacy, but all they did was walk ten metres away and set up again.

Mandy's friend Stella Kinsela was the mistress of ceremonies, and after we had all gathered in a circle, she began the proceedings. It was a wonderful event. Mandy and I stood together holding Zoe as friends came forward and offered her earth, water, fire and air. Then it was time for me to walk around and gather all the wishes in an urn. The wishes were then burnt without being read, and Michael rubbed the ash into Zoe's forehead and feet. Meanwhile, as if on cue, two dolphins slowly cruised along just off shore. After the ceremony we all went back to our house for champagne and dinner. Fleet Street had a field day of course, with 'Paula's Pagan Christmas', and 'Paula's Hippie Holiday' headlines.

Michael and Paula were staying at the Beach Hotel, though they decided to leave his new Bentley at our house. With its style and a new-car smell, we enjoyed the luxury of it just sitting there on our front lawn.

It was the first time I had met Paula. She seemed quiet and demure, giving all her attention to Michael, but that was no doubt because she was meeting all our family and friends for the first time.

The next day I went over with Zoe to see them at their hotel. Michael and Paula were out by the pool, and I joined them. Half an hour later a cute girl walked over and sat down on the deck chair nearest mine. It turned out that she was English, on holidays she said.

Not long after, I noticed a guy taking photographs of us from an upstairs room. When I mentioned it, the girl got up and promptly left. I spoke to Michael about it, and we went into the hotel to see which room the guy was shooting from, then went back down and asked for the manager, who said the room had been taken the day before by some English press. Great, mate. Management respected our need for privacy, and asked them to leave. Within an hour the room, which happened to be the hotel's most luxurious suite available, had been vacated.

The girl came back down to the pool to apologise. She said she was not part of the team, trying to get any dirt they could. She didn't mean any harm; her boyfriend was a photographer and he'd sent her down to chat to us and see if she could get any nibbles.

Michael had some security with him, Tony Woodhall, who looked after his Harley when he was out of the country, and worked for free because he enjoyed the association. Tony told us he headed them off in the car park, and made the guy wet his pants before ripping the film out of his camera. Nonetheless, ten poolside 'hot shots' appeared the following week in *Woman's Day*, under the heading 'Michael and Paula's Lust Down Under'.

Over the time Michael and Paula were in Byron, Mandy and I got to know her better. She was witty, smart, extremely quick. Michael was obviously very taken with her—but no, personally I wouldn't have swapped Helena for her.

Christmas Day that year was in Sydney. Michael and Paula were staying at the Park Hyatt, overlooking Sydney Harbour, and we commandeered the hotel library for Christmas lunch. The hotel had set up the big reading table for our lunch, and decorated it. The courses were brought in one by one by four hotel staff. It was all very civilised with everyone putting any issues aside in order to have a pleasant family gathering. Apart from Dad accidentally sitting on and breaking the Donna Karan sunglasses Michael had given me, it was all good.

After lunch Michael stood up and clinked his champagne glass for everyone's attention. He had an announcement to make. He wanted us to be the first to know that Paula was pregnant and they were expecting a baby in July. We were all very excited and happy for them both. Dad, Michael and I were the last male Hutchences in Australia, and so were the only ones who could keep the family name going. The name is English, comes from Wiltshire, and goes back until at least the eighteenth century. (Any other willing candidates to help keep the lineage going can contact me at willingcandidates@hotmail.com. Photos and bio please.)

Mandy was delighted with the news too, as it meant Zoe would have a cousin of around the same age. Dad told me later that Michael had actually told him about it the day after Zoe's naming ceremony. It had been Zoe's day though, and they didn't want to take any of it away from her.

We didn't know it then, but that Christmas was to be the last time the whole three generations of our family would be together. INXS has just released a song of Michael's called 'Flesh and Blood', with each of our family members getting a verse, the essence of it, hope, being that there's nothing said that can't be undone.

On Boxing Day Michael and Paula moved up to Palm Beach, to a beautiful house they had rented over New Year, and asked

Mandy and me to join them. It was a vast, *Vogue Living* type of place that stretched down to the water with a private jetty.

Then, just before New Year's Eve, Paula had to fly back to London as one of her girls was unwell. Michael had only just got back from dropping her at the airport when he got on the phone, talking sweet nothings to somebody, finishing off with 'See you soon'.

An hour later the doorbell rang and I opened it to see an old girlfriend of mine, Lisa. She dropped her bag, said hello and headed off to Michael's bedroom. Michael asked me to bring her bag inside and I told him to do his own dirty work. They went into his bedroom and he did. That New Year's Eve I stayed in watching the fireworks on TV while she and Michael went out in a limo from Partay to Partbee to Partcee.

A couple of nights later Michael and I went out for a cruise around town in his Jag. We were driving from the city out along New South Head Road when Michael pulled over to pick up a hitchhiker near Rushcutters Bay Park.

Jane looked like an old hooker because she was. She was surprised when she saw who it was who had stopped to pick her up. As we drove she said she wanted us to take her to The Gap on South Head (Sydney's most famous suicide leap down onto the rocks in the Pacific). She said she was planning on jumping.

In the fifteen or so minutes it took to drive there, Michael and I talked her out of doing it. I can't remember what we said, beyond the obvious, 'Life's worth more than that...' but she didn't do it. After cruising around for a couple more hours we dropped her back in Rushcutters Bay. She thanked us for helping her get a little reality back into her head.

tiger

On 22 July 1996, the day after Dad's birthday, Paula gave birth to Heavenly Hiraani Tiger Lily. Michael was ecstatic, as he wrote to Mandy and me.

> *Dear Rhett, Mandy, Zoe.*
> *Hi there people of Byron Bay. Guess what? I'm a daddy!! She's a beautiful baby girl as you know she seems to be turning into a tigerlily—tiger being the operative word. She has a glint in her eye, a wonderful little grin and we're both very happy. Exactly what we ordered, sleeps all night with us—never wakes up or cries. It's great having her here in Sth France, gurgling in the garden and sunlight all over her. I'll send you some photos soon as their developed. Lots of love from Pauls, the girls, tiger and me.*
> *xxx Michael*
> *PS happy birthday Zoe, yaaaahoooo!!!*

Of course they were being hounded for photographs by the press, and thought that by releasing one it would quench their thirst. Well it didn't and they were followed and harassed just as much.

Later that year they flew in to Sydney to show us all their new bundle of love, and for INXS to perform at the annual ARIA record industry awards. Mandy and I went down to see them and got a room near theirs at the Sir Stamford. It was great to catch up again. Michael was in good spirits, obviously due to Tiger. He had always wanted to be a dad, and naturally made a great father. And Tiger was gorgeous. It was also a good time for me as I was in one of my 'Try a bit harder though I'll still have a little dabble when I wish while I can get away with it' times. But on the whole I was straight, tish.

The night before the awards Michael and Paula received some news that would quickly put a damper on things. Drugs had been found at their house in London. By the next morning it was on TV and the front pages of most papers. I went over to see them and find out the story. It appeared that Tiger's nanny, Anita Debney, had found opium under their bed. She says that she was at home when for some reason the car alarm started going off outside. Not knowing how to turn it off, she starts looking for the car instruction manual. And of course, she looks under the bed. I mean where else does one hide their manuals? Nup, no manual there, but what's this? Two packets of Smarties? But maybe the manual is inside one of them? No, just some brown stuff. My God, I think it's drugs, I'd better call the police and they can inform Michael and Paula about what's been found in their house.

Why did she do it? She'd been working with Paula and Bob for a number of years. Perhaps now she felt genuinely concerned about drug use.

A set of polaroids showing Michael and Paula in compromising positions with leather and sex aids were also found and later became saucy breakfast table newspaper fodder for sexually frustrated Poms.

All of it made Michael furious and upset, totally freaked out. Paula was staunch, like a rock, coolly taking it in. Michael told me it was untrue. Somebody was trying to set them up, he said. Who, he wasn't exactly sure, though he said he had a sneaking suspicion.

A little while later Colin Diamond came over. He was Michael's tax specialist. I had only met him once, with Michael at a coke-fuelled Bolivian boardroom party in Kirribilli. I had pulled him aside and said how smart it was he had managed to get Michael's Hong Kong residency, as he was now only paying 17 per cent tax. Colin replied, 'You don't understand mate. If you don't generate the money in Hong Kong, you don't pay any tax'. I thought this was just another way of saying that Michael really wasn't paying much tax at all.

Colin was concerned about the opium discovery, and started advising Michael and Paula on what should and should not be done. He suggested Paula fly back to London to find out the story, and Tiger stay with Michael. No charges had been laid yet, but if there were to be any, Tiger might be taken away by Social Services in Britain if they deemed Paula an unfit mother. He suggested Michael and Tiger leave Sydney the day after the awards and fly to the Gold Coast where they could hide out at Michael's place on the Isle of Capri.

Colin was adamant about one thing—that I was not to go with them. As a matter of fact, I could not even be seen with Michael. He said if someone were to get a photo of us together, with me being a known drug addict, it wouldn't help the situation one bit. I didn't accept that, but Michael was swayed, and Mandy was asked to accompany them up to the Gold Coast and help out with Tiger while Paula was away.

Colin had been working for Michael for a number of years by this time, and exercised considerable influence over him in various matters, both legal and otherwise, which had nothing to do with his brief as tax adviser. Over the years Michael had come to trust him, and Colin's influence had deepened.

Paula left before the ARIAS, and Michael insisted I come with him while Mandy kindly looked after Tiger and Zoe back at the hotel. The band played brilliantly as per usual, and Michael sang a truly heartfelt rendition of 'Searching' from their latest (and last) album, *Elegantly Wasted*. Teardrop heartfelt. And, unbeknownst to anyone, it was to be the last public gig INXS ever played in Australia with Michael.

Michael wasn't feeling social, even with many friends there, and wanted to leave soon after playing. He waited for me in the limo, as I had promised I'd get some autographs for a friend, for his ever-growing collection. I saw Molly Meldrum, who apologised profusely about rabbiting on that morning in the bar on the Gold Coast, and even said I could keep his hat. English pop star Neneh Cherry had earlier co-presented a couple of awards with Michael, and asked me to pass on her best wishes and love to him in regards to the bad press about the opium, as she hadn't had the time during the event.

The next morning Michael, Tiger, Mandy, Zoe, Colin and Tony Woodhall flew in a private plane up to the Gold Coast, and I moved into Michael's hotel suite. Two days of getting stoned later,

I flew up the join them, but was only able to see Michael in the privacy of Mum's apartment in Broadbeach. I thought it was ridiculous covert crap. Mandy told me Michael spent a lot of the time in the dining room having meetings with Colin, apart from the time he showed her a video of an island Michael and Colin had invested in off Lombok in Indonesia. When the hullabaloo over the opium was dismissed as not worth a taxpayer's fart of prosecution, Michael returned to sunny London and we went back down to cloudy Byron.

A friend of mine had thought for years that all I needed to do to achieve and maintain normality was Vipassna, the pseudo-extreme meditation course. Apart from rehab, the ten-day, no talking, no eye contact, fourteen hours a day of meditating in the same position, periodically supplemented by hippie tucker, turned out to be the hardest thing I've ever done, but it was well worth the renewed clarity I gained, and the feeling of achievement upon completion. I returned to Byron, to the cute little house that I shared with Mandy and Zoe, clean and serene.

I guess if Mandy hadn't gone to visit Mum while I was away, I might never have known the truth about that day at the airport when Mum took Michael away. I doubt if I would have ever remembered it. Those sorts of things one tends to forget, erase or delete. To kill the pain or hide the hurt. A coping mechanism you put into action to get on with life.

I cried when Mandy told me what had really happened that day. I cried because I didn't know the truth and I also cried because I knew it. I cried while listening to Mum's side of the story.

Over coffee with Mandy one morning, unprompted, Mum had told Mandy she regretted taking Michael and leaving me with Dad, but she thought she was doing the best she could in the circumstances. Michael was older, and easier to manage for a single woman. I still seemed to need the guidance of a father. The marital situation had left her stressed and really unable to understand how much all of us would be affected. Mandy said Mum told her the toughest memory to deal with was me at the departure gate begging to go with them, crying and screaming, 'Please take me with you. I promise I'll be good'. Michael of course was disturbed by how upset I was and just wanted to go through the barriers and onto the plane. With all the emotional turmoil going on, Mum felt she couldn't turn back, thinking that with the bags having gone through it was too late. And so she and Michael went.

I still don't remember going to the airport. I don't remember crying or screaming, pleading to be taken too, promising that things would be different, I'd be different, that I would be a good boy from now on. 'I promise, I promise, I promise.' I don't remember Michael yelling, 'C'mon Mum let's go, let's just go', and dragging Mum away to the plane because he couldn't handle the scene, the noise or the tears. Nor do I remember going home with Mum's sister Maureen, alone. I'd been to Sydney Airport dozens of times with my family before, but usually we had left together. I honestly didn't remember being at the airport that life-changing day. I always thought I'd stayed at home.

That Christmas and New Year, Mandy and I had to be out of the house due to one of those stupid clauses they put in your lease stating that we had to clear out while the owners came back to sit on our couch and fuck in our bed for six weeks. As much as everyone else wants to be there, at Christmas time Byron is the place where most locals would prefer not to be, as the town, that doesn't cater for itself, strains to breaking point.

We decided to go on a vacation while Zoe was still under two and travelled for free, and flew to Bali. It was wonderfully relaxing as the Balinese adore children, believing them to be the closest to God. It was in Bali that I started writing this book. The airport story had inspired me, and every day I took time out to write about my life.

After the Bali trip, we took the bus down to Sydney to visit Michael. We met up with him in his hotel room, wearing a gold suit for a magazine photo shoot. We had hardly said hello when he was called downstairs for the shoot. About an hour later I happened to look out the window and saw Michael stepping into a limo to leave town. He'd forgotten even to say goodbye. As it turned out, that was the last time I saw him alive.

Back home, I got into doing some stage work and set design for a couple of local theatre productions, even though there was little or no money involved. Mandy started getting more involved with her art, which was now being noticed. Her exhibitions were always popular and she sold well from the beginning. After all, who wouldn't want a Nolan original?

Zoe was an angel of course, as the light reflecting the halo in her hair acknowledged. And best of all, I managed to maintain a semblance of sobriety. When I relapsed, I was straight back in, but if I could refrain from using, I really felt that I wanted to stay clean. I hadn't thought like that before, always being mind-tricked and sucked back into doing what I didn't want to be doing.

Mandy and I rented a car one day and drove to Wondai, in south-west Queensland to see Mandy's mum, Carol, and introduce Zoe to her great-grandparents.

Carol had lived in the same house all her life, as had most of her neighbours. Every evening they would all arrive back at their respective homes, pull up in their respective driveways, and sit on their respective porches watching the family across the road, who in turn watched them. Nothing much else tended to happen. Comical really—maybe that's what got Mandy started as a standup.

Mandy's father had died when she was six years old. He and Carol had been having an argument which ended with Carol shouting, 'If there is a God, how can he let someone like you live?' He had stormed out, slammed the door and driven off, only to die in a car accident later that night. The wreck was towed to the police station, which was right behind their house. Mandy could see it from the kitchen window, or when she bounced high on the trampoline. Her father's dog, ever faithful, sat and howled by the wreck until it lost interest in food and life, and died too.

Carol became religious, even speaking in tongues for a year. And Mandy aspired to get out of Wondai, leaving for good when she was nineteen.

There was quite a story with Zoe's great-grandparents too. After his son's death, Mandy's grandfather had a fight with his wife, and locked himself in the bedroom—for six weeks. They even got the local priest to try to coax him out. Apart from sneaking out to raid the fridge when his wife was asleep, the old man stayed in that room.

Then one day, out of the blue, he unlocked the door and stepped out—and didn't speak to his wife for the next thirty-odd years. Yet they still shared the same house, she still cooked him three meals a day, and he still ate them in the same chair, at the same spot in the kitchen.

His days were spent with his new interest. He started making two-foot-high concrete mushrooms, and his backyard still has about fifty of them spread around. When he did speak to anyone, it was without any pleasantries whatever. Not a single 'please' or 'thank you', ever again. Mandy actually thought he was the gardener.

Mandy told me that she was visiting one morning and her grandpa was in the kitchen having breakfast. Without warning Mandy's grandma poured two litres of orange juice over his head, and he didn't even blink, just finished eating and went out to his shed and started making more concrete mushrooms.

As we pulled into their driveway I saw her grandfather out the front near a lovely rose bush. He grabbed a rose in his hand, looked over at us, then snipped the flower off, letting it fall to the ground.

I got out of the car to introduce myself.

'Don't you work?' he said, before I spoke a word.

It was seven o'clock on a Saturday night.

'Hi, my name is Rhett'.

'Rat?'

'Rhett.'

'Rot?'

'Rhett.'

'Rut?'

'Rhett?'

'Root?'

'Rhett.'

'Wreck?'

'Rhett.'

'Wretch?'

'Rhett.'

'Brett?'

'Rhett.'

'Got yourself a new paper boy?' he asked Mandy.

In comparison, the mushroom-surrounded house with its bright green Astroturf flooring, faded brick wallpaper and faux log fireplace, seemed quite normal.

His name was Norm.

michael

Mandy, Zoe and I were in Sydney for her first solo exhibition there. She'd been nervous, as it was a big step and test for her. Byron had always been good to her; now it was Sydney's turn. She had just sold thirty-five drawings and paintings at her Byron show, and deservedly so, as she'd worked really hard. Yet Mandy has a way of doing ten things at once, making them all seem easy at the same time. Many nights she would simply and quickly churn out another masterpiece on the kitchen table. Not going to art school had taught Mandy lots: she had nothing to unlearn. I've always believed totally in her talent and work, so I knew she would do well, and selling another thirty-five down in the big smoke proved my point. The other thirty sold later too, because Mandy has the knack of making art that sells itself. Sometimes it takes a little while, though eventually everything goes.

We had been there around a week, staying with an old friend Angela and her English boyfriend Tom in Bellevue Hill. It was about as long as I could handle Sydney. Too many memories. Scored here, dropped there, tempted and ripped off everywhere. However, as Michael was flying in from LA to finish the last leg of the INXS 'Don't Lose Your Head' tour, we decided to stay a few nights longer to catch up and say g'day before we saw him play up in Brisbane. I was looking forward to it as we hadn't seen each other all year, only talked on the phone.

Mr Nice had checked out of the Chateau Marmont in Los Angeles and Mr Murray River had checked into room 524 at the Ritz Carlton in Double Bay. I rang him and we chatted. I always loved how he answered the phone in a happy surprised way when I rang. 'Rhett, hey, how are you? How's Mandy and Zoe? Let's get together'. He sounded good, yet there was a tiredness in his voice. He said he was happy to be having a break soon, as the tour had been long. I don't know how he did it, being on the road so long, when not even the nicest hotels and restaurants alleviated the boredom or homesickness: instead, it all added to the alienation.

Troy Planet, a mutual friend of ours was opening his one-man show, 'Breakfast in Rio', at the Kirk Gallery the following night and Michael was keen to go. I was to call him the next night around six, after he got back from rehearsals at the ABC studios in Gore Hill.

I rang Michael as planned, but he had decided to give it a miss as he was feeling tired. He asked me to apologise to Troy, and invited me over after the show so that we would get together downstairs for a drink in the bar instead. Angela and Tom, Mandy and I, set off for the show, and were joined there by Dad and Susie. Another friend was there too, who had been kind enough to save me some smack he had bought earlier. Not an easy task for an addict. I never could understand how people could buy stuff and still have some left a week later. It just wasn't logical to me.

Troy is a comic genius and he easily pulled the show off, getting a number of standing ovations. Dad and Susie were keen to get back to the Ritz Carlton to see Michael again, but we decided to hang backstage afterwards with Troy, making plans to see them later at the hotel. Then after some bubbly and salubrious salutations, Angela, Tom, Mandy and I hopped in the car and headed over to the Ritz Carlton, getting there around 11 pm.

The others went to wait in the bar while I found the house phones and asked to be put through to Mr Murray River in room 524. Michael answered after a couple of rings, still sounding tired. 'Come on up', he said. I told him that I was with Mandy, and Angela and Tom, whom he knew as well, and we were in the bar downstairs, and that I thought he was coming down to join us. That had been the arrangement. We ended up in a Mexican standoff. I thought it was rude to leave my friends there, and he didn't want to come down. I stood my ground, and for some reason he said, 'I'll see you next year then', and I said 'What do you mean? I'll see you in Brisbane next week'. Then I hung up, angrily. Angry with myself, and angry with him.

I went back into the bar, ordered a round of drinks for us and signed for them, courtesy of Murray River in 524. Mid-Jack Daniels I thought, no, fuck it, I want to see him, and went back out to the house phones asking the operator to be connected again. The phone rang and rang and after a while I figured he had fallen asleep. He had sounded really tired. Dad and Susie had already been and gone, having sensed this themselves. After our drinks we decided to go home, as we had to get up early to catch the day train and bus up to Mum's on the Gold Coast, where we would stay for a night before heading back down to Byron.

We got to Mum's to find that Michael had phoned her that morning. He had asked her to convey his apologies for not seeing us at the hotel, and said that he had merely fallen asleep, exhausted.

I've never really liked staying at Mum's, especially as we stay in Ross's office, which is covered in Michael's awards and gold records. I don't know if I dislike it because it makes me feel insignificant, or because I feel bad as it was stuff that I had hocked and Ross had kindly redeemed.

No-one could have guessed it, no-one could have known, the next day seemed like any normal day. Get up, have something to eat, shower, decide what to do. As Christmas was looming, Mum had given us $500 to go out and buy some new clothes, and drove Mandy, Zoe and me down to Pacific Fair shopping centre. It's weird how when I have money I don't see anything I want, and when I'm broke I see everything I need. After a couple of hours of searching, we managed to find a few things, then regrouped and headed home. Normal day. Normal as far as the eye could see.

Or was it?

We got back, and I was in the office unpacking the things we'd bought, when I heard Mum start screaming my name. I ran into the kitchen and she was sitting by the answering machine, freaked out. I instinctively tried to calm her down to find out what was wrong.

'There's a message on the machine from a journalist friend of mine and she said she's heard some terrible rumours about Michael.'

Mum played back the message and it basically said she'd heard something had happened to Michael.

I told Mum to calm down, I was sure it was nothing, and I'd ring the Ritz Carlton.

'Can you put me through to 524, Mr Rivers's room please.'

'Certainly, please hold the line.' Ring ring ring ring ring ring ring ring ring. 'I'm sorry, there seems to be no answer, can I take a message?'

'Yes, tell him his brother phoned and to please ring me back at Mum's as soon as possible, thanks.' Click.

Next thing the phone rang. I picked it up and it was that journalist 'friend' of Mum's again.

'Hi, so what's happening?' I asked.

'I'm not sure, I've heard some rumours, have you spoken to Michael yet?'

'No, look, I can't talk now, okay.' Slam.

Michael's manager would know. Ring ring ring ring, 'Gary, it's Rhett, mate. Listen, I've been hearing stuff that something's happened to Michael. What's the story, have you heard anything?' Gary sounded agitated and slightly worried as he told me he knew nothing, but the phones had been running off the hook. I asked him to call me as soon as he heard anything.

I tried calling Dad, but his phone was engaged, so I rang the hotel again. The duty manager asked me for my phone number and told me he'd call me back.

The problem of distance was starting to get to me. We were hundreds of kilometres away. A twelve-hour drive or an hour's flight away. We simply couldn't get down there. After waiting barely two minutes, I rang the Ritz Carlton again.

'Hello, my name is Rhett Hutchence, I'm Michael Hutchence's brother, I've been hearing rumours about my brother, can you tell me anything?' I said rather sternly. I wanted answers. Still do.

'I'm sorry sir. Can you please hold the line.' Hold hold, hold hold.

'Yes hello, my name is Rhett Hutchence, can I please speak to the manager?'

'Hold for a moment sir.' Hold hold, hold hold.

'Hello, I am starting to get a little angry, so don't put me on hold again, are you in charge there?'

'Yes sir, I'm the day manager.'

'Okay, finally. My name is Rhett Hutchence, I am the brother of Michael Hutchence, he's staying at your hotel, room 524 under the name of Murray River. I've been hearing things and I'd like some answers. Is there anything you can tell me?'

'I'm sorry sir, at this stage I cannot help you.'

'You're in charge and you can't help me?'

'I'm sorry sir.'

'Well, is there anyone there I can speak to who can help me please?'

'Sir, I think it's better that you speak to the Rose Bay police.' He gave me the number. 'Thanks.' Click.

I was starting to feel that things really weren't quite right, but I was still trying to keep it together for Mum and Mandy's sake. They were crowding around me, waiting on my every word. Mum was still crying, and I told her again not to worry, that everything was fine, I was sure it was all okay, and would work out. It wasn't like we'd never heard bogus reports from the press before.

'Hello, is that Rose Bay police? I'd like to talk to someone in charge there. I'm the brother of Michael Hutchence, and I've been asked to call you.'

Mum's screaming was getting more frantic. Mandy was hovering close by me, ashen-faced, with Zoe in her arms.

'Can I have your number? It's procedure to verify who you are.'

'You can get me at my mother's.' I gave him the number. 'Please call me back as soon as possible, goodbye,' and I hung up.

I tried to call Gary again and his phone was engaged. Things were looking bad and sounding worse. I waited a few harrowing minutes and, not receiving a call back, phoned Rose Bay police again.

'Hello, I'm Michael Hutchence's brother. Is there someone there I can talk to?'

'Rhett, I think you should talk to the detectives downstairs,' the cop at the other end said. 'I'll try and patch you through.' Patch patch, wait wait. The fact that the cop knew my first name confirmed my fears that something bad had indeed happened.

I knew then, from the way I was being bandied about. I knew.

Someone had to keep it together though. Mandy and Mum were suspecting the worst by then too. The tension in the room had become unbearable. Only poor little Zoe was saved from it, by the innocence of the very young.

When the detective answered, he told me he thought I should call my Dad. I didn't tell Mum and Mandy what I was doing, I just dialled.

'Dad, it's Rhett mate, what the fuck's happening?'

'Oh son…' He was crying. Dad. Poor Dad, I knew immediately from his tone that the unthinkable had happened.

'Michael's dead.'

'What do you mean?' Shaky voice. 'What happened?' Tears streaming down.

'I don't know son, I don't know.'

'How?'

'He hung himself.'

'What do you mean, what happened?'

'Oh son…my God…I don't know. He hung himself with his belt off the back of the door at the hotel. The detectives have just arrived.'

Mum was bawling, 'No, no, no, no, no, no.' Mandy was screaming and crying and Zoe was looking at us sensing that we were very upset. 'Mummy cry, daddy cry, Zoe cry too.'

'Dad I love you, I'll call you back.'

'I love you too son, please come down here quickly. I want to be near you.'

'Bye, I love you mate.'

'Bye.'

So that's what 'friends' are for—and that's how I found out my brother was dead. Through the media first, like always, through the fucking media.

I told Mandy and Mum, and they just shrieked louder.

Mandy was hugging me, 'I'm so sorry'.

The phone rang. It was that fucking bitch 'friend' journalist again.

'Hi Rhett. Any comment?'

I had numerous, none nice and none for her. I gave the phone to Mum, who was still crying, 'No, no, no, no, no, no'. She was actually quoted saying 'no' the next day in the *Sunday Telegraph*. The reporter didn't have the guts to use their name as the writer of that front page story. As far as I could see, no-one wrote that article. I imagine someone would have been paid for it though.

I looked out the window. We were on the thirteenth floor, looking out over the Gold Coast. It was two in the afternoon with a gorgeous blue-sky day outside, and a surreal fucking nightmare inside.

The phone rang again and Mum answered it and started talking to someone, still crying. After a minute she passed the phone to me.

'It's Linda.'

Who the fuck is Linda I thought.

'Hello.'

'Hello Rhett, it's Linda.'

Ka-plunk. Linda is the Filipino housekeeper for Michael's house in the south of France. I've never met her and she's bawling down the phone.

'Rhett, I am sorry, so sorry.'

'That's okay Linda, thanks for calling, it's so sudden, I can't talk now. Look after yourself, we'll talk another time. Bye.'

It puzzled me how Linda knew, at five in the morning her time, on the far side of the world, and it was only ten minutes since we'd found out ourselves.

I needed a drink and mixed Mandy and me one of Ross's fine stiff scotches, which I chucked down in one swig and poured another. Mum wanted me to ring Ross, so I had him paged at the golf club, and asked them to find him and tell him to call home or come home urgently, as there had been a terrible accident.

The intercom buzzed.

'Channel Nine news team down here. Would you like to make any comment on Michael's death?' said some insensitive bitch.

'Yes. Fuck off and have some respect for a grieving family would ya.'

Unbelievably, she did. I hung up. Jesus Christ, we'd only known for ten minutes. 'Ahem, oh yes, we are deeply saddened.' Fucking hell, I went back into the kitchen. I wished I had some smack. Where are your friends when you need them?

A few minutes later Ross walked in to the screaming turmoil. He was wide-eyed and shaking, like Mum. Ross had a slight shake at the best of times anyway, though it was clearly notice-able now. I poured him some of his scotch and told him what had happened, what I knew, and in seconds he was comforting Mum, who still didn't believe it, naturally in the denial stage. But fuck, 'Mum it's true,' I told her repeatedly. It seemed like I was the only one handling it at all.

Then it was my turn to be in shock. This could not be true. My thoughts up until then were only natural. I was not supposed to outlive Michael, and go to his funeral, he was supposed to go to mine. That and my belief that he would not have, and could not have, killed himself.

The buzzer went again. This time it was Channel Seven. 'Any comments?' Comment, yes, comment. I picked up the receiver. 'If it was not for arseholes like you turning my brother's life into a media circus anyway, he may be alive today. So, if you don't fuck off right now, I'm gonna come downstairs and smash your fucking heads in and you can quote me on that.' Sadly, they didn't.

It was all a bit too much, though I still thought I was fairly sane. Michael was everywhere in that apartment, in photos, awards, and the various platinum albums scattered about. The room that Mandy, Zoe and I were staying in was a shrine to him even before he died.

The balcony was the only place I could go to get away from it all, and I went outside and wept again until I could recompose myself. Normally, I never would have tried to hide my crying in front of people, but this was not normal, this was ridiculous. I would cry oceans that week.

Okay, snap out of it, back inside. 'Mum, we have to call Tina.' Mum still couldn't really speak, so I tried Tina's mobile and got her message bank, speaking in my calmest voice, asking her to call me at Mum's ASAP.

A belt, a belt. I thought of how, not even two hours ago, I was in Hound Dog at Pacific Fair. They had these baggy corduroy pants that I liked, though when I tried them on they were too big. When I had asked the sales assistant if they had any smaller, he told me it was quite fashionable these days to wear them baggy with a belt. I said, 'A belt, I never use a belt', and didn't buy them. I realised later that the time I made that comment would have been somewhere between Michael's last phone call, and when the hotel maid found him.

Mum also told me later that she had noticed something odd from the salesgirls as we walked past the make-up stands at Myers as we were leaving Pacific Fair. Being in that business, she was friendly with quite a few of them, and they knew who she was. Apparently they had already heard news of Michael's death on the radio while we were going about our carefree shopping. We weren't to hear for at least half an hour after they did.

The phone rang again and it was Tina. I asked her if her husband Ken was there and told her she had better sit down, as I had some bad news for her. Tina didn't believe it at first either, until she heard Mum in the background crying, 'It's true, Tina…it's true'. I told Tina that she had better make arrangements to get a flight over. After I hung up I remembered that we were supposed to call Tina later that night anyway—it was her forty-ninth birthday.

Either time passed quickly from then on, or I don't remember the events of that night. The TV news was full of stories. No answers, just facts. I flicked through and watched every report. Wanting to see stuff, then bursting into tears each time. I don't think we had any dinner. I drank until the Coke was gone and the scotch too. Ross had organised flights for us down to Sydney the next day. Mum wanted to stay at the Ritz Carlton and I talked her out of it, saying that the Sir Stamford was nearby, and God, she wouldn't want to stay at the Ritz Carlton anyway, would she? It would do her head in. Later, after a few drinks and a joint on the balcony, I cried myself to sleep.

I woke up crying around four the next morning to see Michael staring down at me from pictures on all the walls. I rolled out of bed, rolled a joint and sat on the balcony watching the sun come up. I was thinking of my last conversation with Michael, and how I wished I hadn't been so stubborn and had just fucking gone up there and seen him. The words and the way he said, 'See you next year then' would stay to haunt me, and made my superstitious mind work overtime—like he knew something I didn't and maybe I'd be joining him sooner than I thought. (I was actually relieved just to make it through the following year.) I also thought of how I had asked both Mum and Dad to go out and buy *The Tibetan Book of Living and Dying*, which they had, as though I had foreseen something and was somehow helping them prepare.

Mum got up early too. She couldn't sleep either, though, she did seem a bit better for someone who was still in deep shock. I made her a cup of tea, we didn't say much. Soon the others got up and we shuffled around solemnly getting ready to go. Ross had booked a car to take us to the airport.

We got upgraded to first class, which at least made the flight down more bearable. We arrived in Sydney about midday and I ran into a friend, Gavan, who was coordinating the visit of the Indian guru Amma, otherwise known as the Mother. She goes round the world hugging people and spreading peace. Gavan gave her a front-page photograph of Michael and she gave him a blessing to help him on his way.

We were picked up by John Martin and Dave Edwards who worked for INXS on the tour. They told us there had been a change of plan. Instead of going straight to Dad's, we would go to the hotel, check in, drop off our bags, and meet Dad and Susie at the morgue in Glebe. There were too many press outside Dad's place, they said. A shitload of press. It's become my own collective noun for them.

It started hitting home again on the way to the hotel, as we passed numerous newsagents with front-page headlines out the front proclaiming 'Michael Hutchence Dead At 37', and 'INXS Singer Found Dead In Hotel'. It was the start of a bizarre week of hiding, ducking and weaving. What transpired could not be deemed normal, and I would not wish it upon anyone. With so much public interest, speculation abounded aplenty, and I wasn't given time to grieve.

It's odd how we all mark some deaths, knowing exactly where we were at the time, like the death of Elvis. I think Michael's death was like that for a lot of people. I certainly know where I was, and share that with the whole country. In fact, with people all around the world.

After a quick check-in using the name Edwards, we went over to the morgue. It's a characterless government building. The main entrance is on Parramatta Road but we went in via the small rear entrance. Dad and Susie were already in the Coroner's office when we arrived. I'd never seen them so sad. We hugged a long time; nothing new, I could always hug Dad, though this was a strong one. We just stood there, speechless, lost. A woman came in and told us that they were just getting Michael ready for viewing. He had a little cut above his left eye that they were cleaning up.

Finally they allowed us to go in. I waited, as I wanted time alone. As did we all. It was all so sombre. Dad and Susie, Mum and Ross, then Mandy and me. I stayed in the small room alone for a while, looking, thinking, crying. Michael, naked, wrapped in a big white blanket, actually looked as beautiful in death as he did in life. He could have been sleeping. The corners of his mouth were turned up into a secret smile, and the lights above made his eyes sparkle.

The odd thing was he was so cold, stone cold. And the slight cut above his left eye. The cut had been bleeding which showed that it must have happened before he died. That, and the bruising caused by the belt buckle on his Adam's apple, seemed the only things out of place. Except for ten other things I soon noticed. He had green metallic nail polish on his toes. Knowing Michael, it made me wonder who had applied it. It wasn't something he would have done himself. Yet another unusual thing was a healing burn to the webbing between the second and third fingers of his left hand. Past experience led me to surmise he'd nodded off with a cigarette in his hand, which made me wonder.

Before I left him I kissed his forehead and whispered, 'I love you mate, rest in peace bro'.

I went outside to let singer Jimmy Barnes and his wife Jane, the next viewers, come in. Outside was still quiet and sad. Not that I asked, but no-one offered any answers. I had lost my brother, who had showed me the world. Who was going to help me now, who was going to rouse on me, or give me precious advice? And why had I not listened more intently? After a little while, the cars took us back to the hotel.

I wanted to go and get some flowers and place them at the Ritz Carlton, so Mandy, Zoe and I headed off to a florist on New South Head Road. I wrote a card, which I placed in the dozen roses that the assistant had wrapped.

'Oh, did you hear about Michael Hutchence? Apparently they found him with the belt around his arm not his neck,' said the mis-informed idiot. What the? 'Sorry buddy,' I told him, 'you've picked the wrong guy to talk to, I'm actually Michael's brother, and I would get your facts straight before you start regurgitating shit you picked up from small-shop Double Bay gossip.' His jaw hit the floor. Not sure why, but I paid for the flowers.

At the Ritz Carlton, fans had been gathering outside and made a shrine with flowers, cards and photos, even an INXS number plate. I walked up and placed my flowers among the others, and started crying again. I looked up to see a photographer snapping away at me. Hurry, capture that grief, give me sadness for the camera, once more with feeling. I grabbed Zoe and Mandy and we started running back to the hotel, up a little laneway, to find a dozen of the motherfuckers, shooting, running, flashing after us, hunting in packs. We had to backtrack, up another alley to lose them, before we got to the safety of the Sir Stamford with Zoe, who was crying all the way 'Men with cameras chase me'.

Later, on the 6 pm news, I read the private note I had written to Michael, like anybody else who happened to be watching. Meanwhile the paparazzi set up camp on the pavement across the road, with a dozen tripods and big fuck-off lenses trained on my windows. Every now and then I would finger salute them just as Michael had done in the past. I wasn't handling this at all. Neither was Mandy. No-one was. I raided the mini-bar with the efficiency of an expert.

I'd called up Kym Wilson on her mobile and asked her to come over later that evening with her boyfriend, Andrew, to please explain to the best of their knowledge what the fuck had happened two nights before. I needed some answers for all the questions accumulating in my head. When Kym arrived she was dressed conservatively, like a pilgrim almost, with her hair slicked back.

After a glass of wine she relaxed a bit and started telling me about what had happened. Kym said they had met him downstairs in the hotel bar, and after a few drinks went up to his room. She said that he was in a jovial mood, though he was waiting for a phone call from Paula who was going to confirm that she was coming out to Sydney for Christmas with her girls. He had wanted Kym and Andrew to stay until he got the call, so they sat around chatting. That all seemed natural to me: Michael hated being alone. Kym mentioned that they talked about me that night and I asked her what she meant. A few years before, Andrew's brother had died of a heroin overdose, and the following day, his anniversary, the family all got together to celebrate his life. So as they were talking about brothers and addictions, naturally I came into the conversation. Kym told me that Michael had said that he was thankful that I had saved his life, because he had got to experience a full-on addiction without having to go through one himself.

I was shocked at what she said next.

'Oh Rhett, I saw the belt.'

'What do you mean?'

'The belt, I saw the belt.'

'What do you mean?'

'When we first went upstairs, there was nowhere to sit. There was a pile of clothes on a chair so as I moved them onto the floor I saw the belt.'

'You touched the belt.'

'Well I had to move it.'

'So your fingerprints are on the belt?'

'Yes,' she said. Though barely audible.

'Your fingerprints are on the belt?' I repeated.

'Yes.'

Kym also mentioned that she had been offered a lot of money to do an exclusive story on her last night with Michael. She then assured me she would never do a story. I told her that I didn't care, but added sarcastically, 'Though, if you really really need a new house…'

Her six-figure exclusive, 'Kym Wilson—Michael's Final Hours', appeared in *Woman's Day* two weeks after he died. Kym said some of the money was going to Tiger. I believe a small fraction did.

Another statement that proved not to be entirely correct was a claim that there had been no drugs involved, something I later found to be false, as the toxicology report and Kym and Andrew's police statements verified.

Before they left, Kym said she had something she wanted to give to me. She pulled a US one dollar bill from her wallet that Michael had given her in the room, saying he wanted her to have it, as it was his lucky dollar. Why would he have given away his lucky dollar?

I needed to see the room where Michael had spent his last night, morning, feelings, and thoughts, so I contacted the duty manager again to make the necessary arrangements. As the press were swarming everywhere, Mandy and I got a hire car with tinted windows to drive us the 100 metres between hotels.

Michael's room was not very Michael at all. If it was suicide, the wallpaper alone may have instigated it. I wondered why he wasn't

Above: Rhett (aged 4) and Michael (aged 6), Kowloon Tong, Hong Kong, 1966.

Above: Schoolboys, Michael (aged 8) and Rhett (aged 6), Hong Kong, 1968.

Left: Rhett's fifth birthday in Hong Kong.

Above: Michael and Rhett, Hong Kong, 1971.

Left: First time in Bali. Rhett, Michael and Kell (Dad), 1972.

Below: Rhett and Michael, Victoria Peak, Hong Kong, 1972.

Above: Our last Christmas in Hong Kong. Dad, Mum, Michael (with broken arm) and Rhett, 1971.

Above left: Michael on his tenth birthday, Hong Kong, 1970.

Above right: Rhett at Kowloon Tong, Hong Kong, 1971.

Above: Michael, Kell and Rhett in
Frenchs Forest, just after Michael
had returned from LA, 1976.

Right: Rhett in Manila,
Philippines, 1980.

Below: Michael, Kell and Rhett
in Manly, 1980.

Above: Rhett, Michael and
Vicky Kerridge, Neutral Bay,
Sydney, 1980.

Left: Michael performing
at the Royal Antler Hotel,
Narrabeen, Sydney, 1980.

Left: Michael
sings for his
supper. Chequers
Nightclub, Sydney.

Right: Rhett and
Sir Les Patterson,
The Domain,
Sydney, 1981.

Above: Tina, Rhett and Michael, Sydney Airport, 1983. Tina was leaving for California and Michael had just returned from a tour.

Below: Michael somewhere in nowhere USA.

Above: Michael, Hong Kong, 1984.

Left: Michael in a Mr Shinju suit in Japan, 1986.

Below: Michael and Michele Bennett in 1985.

Left: Rhett and Michael
on the way to Kell and
Susie's wedding in Hong
Kong, 1986.

Below: Rhett and Michael,
San Francisco, 1986.

Above: Michael,
Kell and Rhett,
Hong Kong, 1986.

Right: Michael
celebrating in
London.

Below: Michael and
Kym Wilson outside
the Freezer nightclub,
1991. *Photo courtesy of
Richard Simpkin.*

Above: Kylie and Michael at Michael's thirtieth birthday party, 1990. *Photo courtesy of Ronnie Stein.*

Left: Michael and Kylie. *Photo courtesy of Ronnie Stein.*

Left: Michael at the Polish Club, 1992. *Photo courtesy of Richard Simpkin.*

Below: Michael and a mystery date at a sound check.

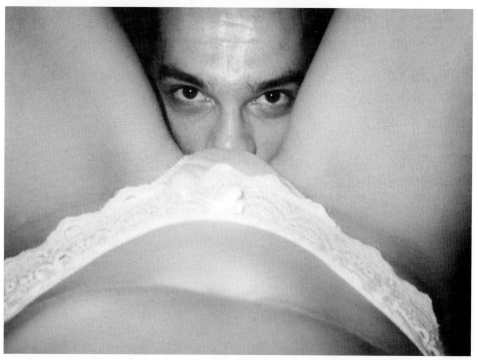

Above: Rhett, Lenny Kravitz and Michael, enjoying Christmas at Michael's house in the south of France, 1991.

Below: Michael, Kell and Rhett, Christmas, 1991.

Left: Michael, Helena and Rhett at Michael's house in the south of France, Christmas, 1991.

Below: Helena in Thailand in 1993.

Below: Michael, Rhett, Kell, Helena, Elsa and Fleming Christensen (Helena's parents), celebrating Christmas, 1991.

Above: Kell and Susie in the south of France.

Below left: Rhett and Kell, Capertee, New South Wales, 1994.

Below right: Michael, Helena and Rhett at Christmas on the Gold Coast, 1994.

Above: Fresh out of rehab, at Mum's place on the Gold Coast, Christmas Day, 1994.

Below: Paula, Mandy, Rhett and Michael, Christmas Day, Sydney, 1995.
Michael had just announced that Paula was pregnant. It was the last family
Christmas together.

Above: Rhett, Zoe, Mandy, Mum, Michael and Paula at Zoe's naming ceremony, Byron Bay, 1995. Michael was the proud godfather.

Left: Tiger and Paula in Sydney in 1996.

Above: Tiger, on the Gold Coast, 1998.

Below left: Michael, Tiger, Rhett and Zoe, 1996.

Below right: Tiger and Paula at Tiger Lily's christening in Sydney, 1998.

Above: Happier times. Tiger, Paula and Kell, Sydney, 1997.

Below: Kell, proud grandfather with Tiger, Sydney, 1997.

Above: INXS at a press
conference, 1996.
*Photo courtesy of
Richard Simpkin.*

Left: Tiger Lily, 1998.

Opposite top: Rhett with members of INXS, carrying Michael's coffin.

Opposite bottom left: Kym Wilson, who was the last person to see Michael alive.

Opposite bottom right: Rhett in the Mr Shinju suit Michael bought him, with Kirk Pengilly of INXS.

Above: Kylie arrives at Michael's funeral.

Left: Mum and Dad at Michael's funeral.

All photos on these two pages courtesy of Peter Carrette/Icon Images PMA.

Above: Michael and Paula with Tiger. *Photo courtesy of Richard Simpkin.*

Below: Rhett and Zoe Angel, 1998.

Above: Susie, Kell, Rhett, Zoe, Mandy and Tiger, one week after Michael died, 1997.

Below: Mandy and Rhett, Mandy's thirtieth birthday, 1998.

Above: The last photo taken of Michael the day before he died, with friend and photographer Richard Simpkin. Photo taken by Kell. *Photo courtesy of Richard Simpkin.*

Below: Rhett with Sophia Rose and Zoe Angel, Byron Bay, 2002.

at the Sir Stamford, which was similar, yet in a funky New York loft sort of way. The Ritz Carlton was too opulent, gilt edged, old money, proper. Boring. Mum had recommended it to him. I guess she didn't know him very well any more.

As housekeeping had already made the room up, our visit didn't reveal much, apart from the fact that the door jamb was the only thing there he could have used to hang himself on. In the half hour we stayed, before security knocked on the door to see if we were okay, I searched high and low for anything, any sign as to what may have happened, a why, a how. It was weird, a writer and no note. The only thing I noticed were two little white pockmarks in the ceiling just outside the toilet door, where it seemed someone had tried to stick something in. They looked freshly made. I thought that I would have to see the police photos if I was to have a better understanding.

We got back to our room to find the beginning of an avalanche of phone messages, flowers, cards and condolences coming from every corner of the globe. It was all getting too much again. Strange that there was nothing from any members of the band. Mind you, they were in deep shock themselves. I needed to numb myself, so I called a couple of mates and made plans for them to come and sneak me out of it. They thoughtfully cancelled everything they had pencilled in and were over before I could say 'My shout'. One of them brought a large sombrero for me, which I put on, much to the dismay of the pack of photographers who waited outside. They must have taken over two hundred photos of a very large hat as we sped away from the car park.

Things up at the Cross were just as weird, as over the years I had gotten to know most of the dealers and hookers and they knew me. Or at least thought they did. Not that I stood out any more than before, it just really felt like all eyes were on me, that people were talking about me. And they were. As soon as I had a few packets in my hand, we had a quick hit in the car and raced home.

Tina arrived with Michael's personal manager Martha Troup from the US the next morning. While Tina was at the morgue saying her goodbyes, I went to see Martha, to see if she could shed any light on things.

It was good to see her. She had been good to me in New York, and we'd always gotten on. We hugged and held each other tight.

Martha told me some strange details, stuff I didn't know. Michael had been seeing a girl named Erin, and she had joined him at most of the shows on the American leg of the tour. He was really falling for her. He'd also been getting into some kinkier sex, S&M. Hardly surprising that someone like Michael might get bored of ye olde missionary position.

Martha told me she went to see him at the Chateau Marmont in LA around a month before, and when she was in his room he had said to her, 'Martha, I'm going to get into trouble'. When Martha asked what he meant, Michael said nothing, and instead just looked up. She followed his eyeline to a ring-bolt screw, like the type used to put up a hammock, which someone had screwed into the air conditioning duct. Martha didn't ask for any elaboration, and Michael didn't offer any.

Over the next few days, the family met at the Sir Stamford to organise Michael's funeral. It was not an easy task. I thought we could get by with something private, but Dad insisted we had to think of the fans, as there would no doubt be many. We had to think big, and so St Andrew's Cathedral was chosen. I think the Anglican denomination and service had more to do with pleasing Mum and Dad than any religious views of Michael's. If anything, he was a still-searching Presbyterian atheist with Buddhist punk beliefs.

It was decided that there would be four eulogies. Andrew Farriss was asked to speak, Tina wanted to tell us something, for some reason music journalist Richard Wilkins was asked, and myself.

Richard was as surprised to be asked, as I was that Dad had asked him. Don't get me wrong, he's a nice guy and all, and Dad just wanted someone from the music industry to say a few words. But then I suppose who else do you have—Molly?

As for pallbearers, as we needed six people, I thought it might be fitting if the rest of the band and myself carried him, so I rang them all up and asked. Everyone seemed okay with the idea.

Next was to choose the music to be played. Paula had arrived in town with half of Fleet Street accompanying her on the flight across.

She was staying at the Quay West apartments, and was naturally a mess. When I phoned to check on her, she mentioned that Nick Cave had flown in, so I got his number off her to give him a call and ask if he would play something. It was appropriate enough as Michael had asked him to be Tiger's godfather. Nick was slightly reluctant at first, not knowing what to play. I thought that his classic 'Into My Arms' was the most suitable, and he agreed on the proviso that it not be televised.

That was the odd thing: Mum had gotten a deal with Channel Seven and brought media entrepreneur Harry M Miller into the picture to negotiate the whole package. Right up until the day of the funeral I kept telling her that it was not too late to stop it and pull the proverbial plug, but she insisted. By having one live feed coming out of church, we could maybe stop a media frenzy, at least on the inside.

Finding a song to start the ceremony, for the procession and the cremation, would be another problem. Of the hundreds of songs that Michael and Andrew wrote for INXS, some were plainly out of question. 'Not Enough Time', 'Elegantly Wasted', 'Devil Inside', 'Kill The Pain', 'Don't Lose Your Head', 'Suicide Blonde', 'Burn For You' and 'Disappear' were all obvious no-noes. Lucky there were still many to choose from, and 'By My Side' and 'Never Tear Us Apart' would be emotional yet appropriate send-offs. Paula had wanted to ask Tom Jones, who was also in town, to perform 'What's New Pussycat?'. Whose funeral was it again?

As I'd come to Sydney unexpectedly, I didn't have a suit to wear. Matter of fact, I didn't actually own a suit. The only suit I had ever owned was the stripy Mr Shinju. I needed something to wear, and thought the best option was to try and get my old suit back from the fancy dress shop in Paddington I had sold it to.

Mandy went in to see if she could hire it, but it was out at the time. The assistant told her that it was a popular rental. They called it the flyer, as it was never in the shop. Mandy explained my predicament, and why it was important for me to rent it back, and they rang up the renters who kindly agreed to return the suit. The next day, after paying a hefty deposit, Mandy picked it up and I was reunited with it. The last time I had seen it was on the cover of *WHO* magazine, being worn by Ben Mendelsohn.

With the white cotton shirt I bought from Wheels and Doll Baby, new black leather shoes, and some tissues, I was complete. Over the next few weeks I was to cop a flak of shit from radio shock jocks John Laws and Alan Jones for wearing that suit, but luckily, small-minded, self-opinionated dickwads don't bother me.

The day before the funeral, the family all went to the funeral parlour to pay our last respects to Michael. This time he was more presentable, in his green Vivienne Westwood suit, looking like he was sleeping, except in a casket. We took our turns going in and spending time alone with him. Mum cut off some of his hair and took some buttons off his suit, which she gave to Tina and myself, and later had hers made into a ring.

Dad told me later he'd taken three photos of Michael. I told him that they would haunt him, as he'd be left with that image in his head. I remembered how I had once seen a picture of Marilyn Monroe on the autopsy slab, and how every time I'd thought of her since, it was that image.

Dad had gone to see a friend in the Cross who owned a photo developing shop. The friend cleared the staff away early one evening so he could develop them privately. Out of all the twenty-four shots Dad took, the three he took of Michael for some reason came out black. I thought it was help from above.

As for me, I spent a few minutes talking to Michael alone, and then placed a Marlboro Light in his inside jacket pocket. It was a personal thing: he was always asking me for a ciggie. I also placed a photo of Mandy and me. Paula later told me she put a gram of smack in his pocket.

On the morning of the funeral, I got up early, had some break-fast and finished writing the eulogy. I had made a decision that I wanted to be straight for the service, so I made up a shot and put it in my jacket pocket for later. When Mandy and Zoe were ready, we went down to the lobby to group up. For a fairly small family, we had grown quickly, as there were suddenly a lot of distant cousins, and aunts and uncles I'd never met.

Sydney's Lord Mayor, Frank Sartor, had given us carte blanche, meaning that our procession would have police escorts, and any cross traffic would be blocked for the cortege. For some reason, the whole thing didn't really hit home with me until we left the Sir Stamford and walked to our limousines.

Traffic had been stopped and a crowd of around three hundred people stood outside, watching our every move. My heart froze and reality slapped me in the face, bringing tears to my eyes, again. We got in our designated limos and started the slow procession up New South Head Road, down William Street, around Hyde Park and finally up George Sreet to Saint Andrews. People lined the streets all the way and I spotted many familiar faces. It was a grey day, and everyone we passed knew who we were, and looked with sad eyes.

Inside the car we were all very quiet. Zoe was sleeping. Mandy and I just looked out the windows at the people by the roadside. I felt numb.

Outside the church, thousands of people had gathered to pay their respects or catch a glimpse of what was going on. Family, friends, fans, the bored, the idle, the curious. It felt too real to be true, and too surreal to be real. After signing the register, we went inside and took our seats. The place was packed and the heat stifling. After the family was finally seated, the service started. Not the type of service Michael may have envisioned, being formal and religious. But then who ever envisions their own funeral?

The turnout would have made him proud, however. I wondered if he knew how loved he really was. Everyone was there, old girlfriends, young girlfriends, family, friends, fans, and many associates from the music industry. It would be honest to say that if someone dropped a bomb on the church that afternoon, the who's who of the Australian music and fashion industries would have been no more. Virtually the only so-called friend not there, Colin Diamond, supposedly one of Michael's best friends, was too busy to make it. What he was doing that day, I don't know. He'd flown in the day after Michael died and found a more pressing engagement in Queensland to attend to on the day of his funeral.

I didn't get the chance to speak to anyone. Kylie was there of course, and Helena. Paula arrived with Tiger, and came over to kiss my dad sitting in his pew. My mum hissed 'Piss off, get out of here, get back to your seat!' to her. Paula didn't respond, simply returned to her seat. But then Mum and Paula didn't see eye to eye at the best of times.

Bono, who was one of Michael's best friends in the industry, couldn't make it as U2 were still on the American leg of their Pop Mart tour. Instead his lovely wife Ali came, and the band sent a huge floral tribute. The six-foot floral arrangement depicted a claddagh, an Irish symbol of love, friendship, and loyalty.

Everything went as planned and somehow I made it through my eulogy without being reduced to a puddle of tears, though my last words, 'Rest in peace bro, I love you, I will miss you', truly brought home the finality of our mortal relationship.

In the eulogy, I mentioned that I had a book of lyrics Michael had written back when he first started with the band, which included a list of things he wanted to achieve in his life, one of them being to conquer the world. I wasn't entirely accurate, and only later did I find his book again and see what he had written way back in the early eighties. Number four in his list of goals to kick was, 'Start my own strategy for world domination!!' With number five being, 'I'm serious!!!'

Strange that in the INXS 1997 Australian tour program for the their 'Don't Lose Your Head' tour, which was never distributed because it never happened, are the following lines, 'It's been a long hard trip for the six members of INXS. A long, strange, twenty-year trip that has seen the band work their way up from total obscurity to triumphant world domination'. Then in another paragraph, it says, 'Now, in 1997, in a musical climate where any-thing goes, and success is measured in internet hits, things like world domination don't seem to matter so much.' I wonder if Michael thought that too.

The rest of the service and eulogies went off without a hitch. When Nick Cave started a soul-deep rendition of 'Into My Arms', no-one could contain their feelings any longer. Including trump card. I know Michael would never have considered it had he been alive. Anyway, Tiger didn't need Colin Diamond and Andrew Young as godfathers. She already had one, Nick Cave, whom Michael had chosen. It also bugged me that I was Michael's closest blood relative, and had not been asked to be a godparent.

Security was tight around the church as the press had found out the location. There were photographers everywhere, at the gate, peeking over the fence. Before going inside I was having a cigarette and saw Paula's car arriving. As it pulled to a stop close to the door, a photographer climbed the stone wall to get a better shot. I was surprised when one of the security guards ran up and pushed him backwards off the wall, a five-foot drop. The poor guy landed hard, and lay there motionless. I didn't like what I saw, and went inside to wait for the other guests and play-actors to arrive.

Soon enough, everyone else turned up, and the charade began. All of Tiger's new godparents were up at the altar, Now, instead of just having Saint Nick for a godparent, Tiger's lineup included a lawyer, an agent, a publicist and a tax avoidance specialist. Funny that. In the end there were seven godparents, and yes, Saint Nick was one of them.

I somehow managed to take a whole roll of film, with flashes, without anyone noticing. I was still frightened though, especially after seeing the way that photographer had been treated outside.

After the ceremony they all raced off, even leaving the christening certificate behind. It was about that important. Oh, and there had not been a single reference to, or mention of, Michael. I don't know where the christening certificate ended up.

Outside I saw an ambulance with lights flashing. The paramedics had put a neck brace on the unfortunate photographer and were lifting him onto a stretcher. Security denied any pushing or shoving had taken place. He just fell, okay. And don't you forget it.

On the way to Mezzaluna restaurant for the post ceremony reception, I rang up the magazine assistant and made arrangements to meet her in the Cross to give her the film and the mobile phone back. After seeing her I quickly found someone to score off, had a shot and headed to the restaurant. It was busy there, and after a few drinks, I did some socialising then thought it would be alright to take a few photos with my own camera. No-one seemed to mind. Then, stupidly, I took a shot of Mandy, Zoe and Colin Diamond on the stairs. I put my camera down for a minute to get a drink at the bar, and when I returned, lo and behold, it was gone.

After a few inquiries I found out Colin had taken it and removed the film. I had a feeling his smile had been too cheesy. He gave me back the camera. Fortunately the only photos in it were shots from the previous day, and the ones I took at the reception. He told me that he would develop the film and return the shots to me if they were okay. He never knew I'd had another camera, and he never gave me my photos back.

The whole incident basically scared the fuck out of me, and if I could have turned back time I would have. Morally, it was a bad decision I made that day to take the photographs for the magazine. I went back to the hotel, burnt my contract in anger and self-disgust, and flushed it down the toilet.

The next morning I went into the *Woman's Day* office, and saw Jenny Brown who was the assistant editor at the time. I cried for half an hour, telling her how angry I was at myself for doing it, and begging her that they forget the deal, and please not publish my photographs. But it was too late. They had scooped *OK* magazine, and were not about to renege. The only thing they did renege on was my payment, as I had told them I had burnt my contract. I got half.

That afternoon, Dad and I had the first and only meeting with Colin regarding Michael's estate, at Dee Bee's restaurant in Double Bay. Colin is, in my opinion, an evasive character and hard to track down and lock in at the best of times. Colin explained nothing much at all and had no answers to our many questions.

Colin then went on to scare me by telling me that I had better watch myself as he knew some Federal Police and he reckoned that they were onto me. I was only using, not dealing, so I didn't think I was worthy of investigating, but Colin did put the fear into me that day. He thought I should go away to a health farm for a retreat, and suggested Camp Eden. I agreed, leaving a week later. I told Mum what he had said, and she freaked out and thought she was being followed for the next few weeks. She even made me write out a statutory declaration about what Colin had said.

Maybe I'd done too much coke, because I arrived at Camp Eden paranoid, tired and scared. Even though it was a very beautiful environment, in the Gold Coast hinterland, for the first few days I couldn't relax. I just didn't trust Colin, wondered why he had suggested Camp Eden, and wondered which of the other clients had been sent to engineer a fatal accident. It wasn't until towards the end of my stay, and I had met most of the others and discounted any fears, that I learned to relax and take in what was being offered. The good food, group therapy, pampering, and nature had sorted my head out a bit, and again I felt renewed.

All this time, Yo Yo had been doing well, and except for the 'I'm at home I'm at work' aspect, I enjoyed it. Ironically enough, the only real problem was the money it was generating, and the fact that somewhere along the line I had made an unconscious decision to spend it at the dealer's house.

As addictions tend to skyrocket, the money quickly dwindles, then disappears altogether. As soon as I got $50 in the till, I'd lock the door and race up the road to score. I decided I needed help and rang the Buttery again, asking to put my name on the list. Then with SALE signs up, I got rid of nearly everything I had left in the shop, taking what remained to store at Mandy's place.

sophia rose

I was veering out of control again, trying to maintain some semblance of normality, but it wasn't something I could eradicate or get together in time for the birth in February of our second daughter, Sophia Rose. Another beautiful girl, another seemingly easily made work of art. It was fate that I would be clean for her birth: I had no money and Mandy wouldn't give me any. This time Mandy opted for a more populated birth, with her girlfriends in attendance and photos taken. Two weeks later I got the call and went off to the Buttery again.

Third time lucky? I still had an obsession, though thank God not a compulsion, to use. I wanted and needed recovery so badly, I kept it simple, slooowwed down, trusted the process, then, over time, I'd get stronger in mind, body, and spirit. It's strange that you can be there for a week, then one day you wake up crying, realising that you are just an addict in a rehab. It had been years since I was there, and I still needed to work on my old issues of self-responsibility, self-acceptance, self-worth and self-esteem.

It wasn't easy being in there with Zoe and Sophia only twenty minutes away, even though inside I knew it was the best thing for me and for them. And though I missed them terribly, I realised whatever freedom I gave up then meant more for the future.

One day, bored in art class, I picked up a Q magazine which had an article and interview with Michael. Nothing wrong there, I'd read so many—but this one was different, and greatly upset me.

It was about Michael and Mum, and the time they spent in LA when Mum left Dad. They had asked Michael why he left LA, and Michael had answered that he had missed his brother so much that he had saved his money up and returned to Sydney. I started bawling, and had to go to my room to rest. I'd had no idea he'd done that, and it made me feel there was so much more he and I hadn't talked about, so much I hadn't said to him and now never would, and was reminded again of how much I missed him. I resolved to stop reading trashy magazines in case Michael was in them.

Sundays are a concern at rehab. Three times a month the community votes on a day out, being the beach, the movies, or a trip to a waterfall or park. The other Sunday is a stay at home, which is where the concern starts as boredom is not the best thing for an addict. They say that relapse is not really a spur of the moment thing, and one makes the decision to use three or four days before it actually happens.

That Sunday I talked with a girl I had previously been using with in Byron, and we both got to thinking, and a seed started germinating. Four days later she said she couldn't hack it any more, it was time to go, and I decided I'd leave too. We called a community meeting to let everyone know. They tried to talk us out of it, but we packed up and got a lift into Bangalow. If rehab is for quitters, I hadn't quit quitting.

We called a cab to take us into Byron and went straight to a phone box, called the dealers and asked them to hold a couple of bags, as we were coming over.

Slowly slowly I blew $50, and even more slowly I went over to my sponsor Peter's place and waited for him. I was stoned, ashamed, unsure of my next move. Peter arrived and we had a talk about things. I told him I believed that what I had done may seem wrong, but I believed with some help and common sense I could get and remain clean. I thought what I had gained most from rehab this time was the belief that my life was up to me. I knew what was good, bad, right, wrong, and I knew the consequences. It was self-responsibility. Using the program it could be done. Oh, and I was only planning on getting stoned that once.

After a troubled sleep I got up next day and re-started my morning program of affirmations, prayer, journal writing, and a walk. Then I went to the anonymous, recovering-addict-friendly coffee shop, for another reality check with my sponsor, and to explain myself once again. Something a chronic relapser is frequently doing. I really felt that what had happened the day before was a one-off, and I'd try harder from now on.

He gave me a lift to Mandy's and for the next hour I crawled around on all fours entertaining the girls. It was wonderful to see them, and in only a month they had grown in the way only kids can. I rang my parents to let them know of my early departure from rehab, and naturally they were concerned, though they still believed somewhere in their hearts that one day I would beat this addiction, as did I. Mandy drove me back into town where I managed to get emergency accommodation.

I started seeing Astra against Peter's advice. She was slender, with long dark hair, a Betty Page look. She was witty and bubbly, full of life.

Early recovery was supposed to be about me working on myself, not on others. That was understandable, though difficult, as my libido had bounced back as it does when I'm clean for any amount of time. When I'm using, forget it—I have other things on my mind.

Astra was good for me, helping me get to meetings, and giving me confidence. It wasn't long before I moved in with her.

I came home from a men's group meeting one night to find out that a friend had overdosed earlier that afternoon. My first feelings were shock and anger, then sorrow for her five-year-old son. I had only seen her the day before and we had talked about lots of things. She had told me she was planning on giving it up and getting back into meetings, the next day. Tomorrow, always tomorrow—the tomorrow that never comes.

I went to bed crying and awoke the same way, hating this disease and how, wolf-like, it plucks the weak away from the flock.

Later that day I bumped into the guy who had sold her the lethal shit, punched him in the face and told him that for his own good he'd better leave town. Her death really affected everyone who knew her, and it showed at her funeral.

The next day I awoke to a phone call from a friend in Melbourne. Apparently I was on the front page of the *Sunday Age* in a piece headlined 'The Life And Lusts Of A Rock Enigma'. It stated that while in New York I was kidnapped by a heroin gang that I owed money to, and was taken to a storeroom in the meatpacking district. When I tried to alert the police, my kidnapper noticed and I lunged at him with a screwdriver. A passing meat packer saw all this and notified the police, who charged me with attempted murder. Nice one.

The article was an excerpt from the upcoming book *Michael Hutchence—A Tragic Rock and Roll Story* written by Vincent Lovegrove, a rock journo. I knew Vince had written a book because he'd interviewed me. A couple of months later he had sent me the transcripts of our conversations, which I yayed and nayed, then faxed back. The thing was, we had not talked about the New York incident, so I wondered where he had gotten his misinformation.

The next day, after a few more calls from concerned friends, I wrote a letter to the editor in chief of the *Sunday Age*. I said I was appalled at the inaccurate and wildly exaggerated report they had published, stating that I had never been charged with attempted murder of anyone, anywhere, nor had I ever been held for ransom by a heroin gang. I asked for them to print a retraction and an apology, or I would have no choice but to refer the matter to my lawyers.

The following day they faxed me back saying their report was based on passages contained in Vincent's book, and that they thought the article summarised what he had portrayed. They would need further information before they could take my complaint to the next stage.

I phoned up Mum's lawyer who told me if that was the case, what they had written was highly defamatory. Then I called up Vincent's publishers to find out when the book was coming out. They said release was imminent, but that they would send me a copy the next day. A week later it arrived in the mail and I sat down with it. When I found the bit about my 'kidnap', it was completely wrong. Again I wondered where Vincent had got his information, because for a start there was no mention of it at all in the transcripts he'd faxed me. It must be second-hand Chinese whispers.

The next day, after being clean for nineteen days, and thinking how well I was going, I went out and scored. Same story, it made me feel like shit. One shot and my sparkle was tarnished. Again I had jeopardised the relationship with Mandy and the kids, my relationship with Astra, plus the one I've been working on with my own head and heart. Not that they are the things one thinks of when using. It's all about the now. Me me me, now now now.

I went to see some lawyers and explained about the newspaper story, and they thought I had a good case. We would have to contact Robert, the lawyer in New York, and get details of the case. Robert got back to me with the truth, and some bullshit too. The truth was that yes, I have never been charged with attempted murder, and the bullshit was that for some unknown reason, the authorities in New York only had a record of me doing one day's community service instead of the two that I honestly did. A bench warrant had been issued, but I believe that the Statute of Limitations has come into effect by now, nullifying it.

June that year saw the opening of Stadium Australia, with INXS booked to play their first gig in nearly two years, and I went down to Sydney for it. There was a problem of some sort and the band couldn't organise me a ticket, so I wore an old tour jacket and went to the box office to talk my way in. Explanations, pseudo-tears and determination got me through the gates just in time for the opening song.

I didn't expect the boys to be doing anything other than what they'd been doing for the past twenty-plus years, which was playing good music to appreciative punters, but I felt that Terence Trent D'Arby was the wrong choice for a singer. With a falsetto voice and delivery very unlike Michael's, it was, I'm sorry to say, sad. I decided not to go backstage afterwards, and left.

My new-found health didn't last long, when slowly, then quickly, my monkeys returned. I decided I needed to get out of the country for a while with a friend, Alex, and managed to get a ticket together for Bali.

We both arrived relieved to be there. The sights, smells and heat were enough for us to forget where we had come from and reinvigorate our senses. The first night we bumped into a friend from Byron. She invited us to a party in Ubud, and on the way we stopped off at an Italian friend's place and did some liquid acid. Not much, just a drop, enough to blast like crazy. By the time we made it back to the hotel the next morning we were still at it and on it, staring at the ceiling wondering when the visuals would end. That was when we decided that a little hit would not go astray.

The nearest stuff we knew of was in Thailand, so we checked out of our hotel, went to a travel agent and got the next available flight. The acid colours were only starting to calm down when we arrived in Bangkok, where a sizeable reptile with four eyes and the long tongue gave me back my passport at Immigration.

After a couple of days, Alex and I got a bus up to Chiang Mai, to find what it had to offer. Hookers and Yaba ('crazy medicine') is what we found. Yaba is no doubt Thailand's biggest drug problem, with a plague of addicts countrywide.

When Alex got an email from a girl saying she was going down to the island of Ko Pha Ngan for a party, he decided to follow, and I decided not to. Laos was so close, and had always held an interest for me, so Alex and I said our goodbyes and I.got a bus to the Thai–Laos border.

Before roads were built, the Mekong River was the main thoroughfare for the Laotians. I took the slow boat to Luang Prabang, a beautiful, 300 kilometre, two-day journey. I spent the whole time up on the roof, checking out the sights.

It was in Luang Prabang that I met Ran, an Indian guy who had just ridden in on his bicycle. He had a cardboard sign wired to his handlebars stating 'Calcutta—24th April 1982'. Ran told me that on that day he had hopped on his bike, that same bike, with a dream of seeing the world. It was a big clunky metal bike, your classic Indian basic bike. For the past seventeen years he had pedalled around the world, country to country, town to town, village to village. The newspaper clippings he carried proved his point.

Laos was country number ninety-nine for him. Ran was in the *Guinness Book of Records* as the holder of the world's biggest passport. This was because he'd kept every passport issued to him since his departure in 1982, and stapled them together into a very heavy tome. Because of his fame, he now received all his visas gratis, and usually with the biggest, nicest stamp that Immigration could find. He also got most of his food and hotels for free too. I liked him, and found his story inspirational and told him so one morning before he cycled off north, towards China.

I took the bus down to Vang Viang, a little riverside port with limestone pinnacles jutting up into the low clouds. The Guilin of Laos. The days were filled with bike rides and walks around the countryside to caves and waterfalls, or getting dropped twenty kilometres upstream in a tyre inner tube and just floating downstream back to town. The evenings were dinner and the opium den.

It wasn't long before I had to leave, even though Laos was my new favourite destination in the world, and not just because they had opium. The people are friendly, considering what they have been through, the landscape is extraordinarily beautiful, considering what has been through it—and it's very cheap to visit. Something like Thailand may have been twenty, thirty years ago. I liked it so much that when people asked me what it's like I'd tell them it was terrible and very expensive. I didn't want it to get overrun and change.

Back in Bangkok I received an email from Astra informing me she was pregnant. I phoned her saying I'd rather talk about it in person, and I'd be back soon, and we could work things out.

We still had a flight to Bali before going home and spent the next week cruising around the island. Being a spiritual and healing place for me, I found what I needed in Bali. For some time I had been open to anything that might help me achieve a life free from addiction. Previously I'd been sceptical. Living in Byron Bay, Australia's most easterly new-age capital, one tends to notice that the notice boards are filled with quacks offering their services. Over time you tend to stop believing that you can heal your car with crystals, get reiki blowjobs, or that a clairvoyant will call you. I guess it was my search for healing that led me to Rachel. She was from Tasmania but had settled in Bali. Rachel was pure love and light and a sucker for ceremony. In the short time I had in Bali, she got me a booking with Pak Circus, a local healer and shaman, who quickly dismissed me and worked on Rachel for half an hour. Rachel also arranged a crystal healing with her friend Luka who led the Circle of Light, a healing meditation group. I fell asleep and woke up covered in a hundred different crystals and stones.

As per usual I got the inquisition upon arrival at Customs in Brisbane. With so many South-East Asian visa stamps, you tend to arouse suspicion. After the usual inspections, the Customs officer asked for my wallet, placed a small square of paper in a hand-held wand, and proceeded to swipe it, as well as my Medicare and debit cards. He went away and returned asking, 'Have you been doing any cocaine?'

'No, I haven't, why?'

'Well, traces are coming up on your wallet.'

I still didn't quite understand. 'To be honest with you, I've done cocaine, I've even had a huge problem with it, but I haven't done any for over two years, so if any traces are showing up, they're pretty old.' He thanked me for my honesty and let me go.

Apart from a few nights in the opium dens, I had been pseudo-clean for over a month now, and I arrived back in Byron clear-headed with a new outlook. I went to Mandy's place, where I could stay in the spare room for a while, and spend some time with the kids.

The next day I went around to see Astra. She was well, and had already made up her mind. She wanted to have the baby. I told her I thought we needed to think about it longer and weigh everything up properly—well, I needed some more time to think, but for her the matter was closed and 'Not subject to revision', as she put it.

That night I was having a long shower, thinking about things like what to do and how was I going to explain it to Mandy, when the door opened and Mandy said 'Astra's pregnant, isn't she?'.

For various reasons Mandy, like me, was initially adamant that having the baby was not the best solution. Astra was only twenty-two, was thinking about career choices, and had just been accepted into university, in the top 98.2 per cent bracket. And knowing what Mandy and I had been through made me realise that in the long run it wasn't the easiest option. After a long conversation with Mandy, I decided to try the hard love angle and say I wanted nothing to do with the baby.

The next day I told Astra I couldn't really see us being together for any amount of time, and if she wanted to have our child it would be totally up to her to bring it up. She said her mind was made up, and if I wanted any input it would be appreciated, but otherwise she would be okay. It was up to me.

That month we had a naming ceremony for Sophia Rose, in the park near The Pass at Byron. Mandy and I stood holding Sophia in the middle of a circle of family and friends, wearing white and holding hands, and made speeches. Sophia looked gorgeous in a fairy dress that Rachel had made and everyone had been asked to bring a bead, which we later strung together to make a necklace for her. It was another lovely, thoughtful ceremony.

Dad had just received some cartons from Michael's storage container in Hong Kong, and asked me to come down and take some of his belongings. Originally the executor of the estate had stated that this comprised all his personal effects, there being nothing of value. Why the estate had been paying its expensive storage fees for the past eighteen months if it held nothing of value, I couldn't comprehend. Apart from the odd bits and pieces he had left in the storage space he and I had shared in Sydney, no-one in the family had received one piece of anything that Michael had ever owned. Except for Mum, that is, who had rung Michael's old friends after he died, trying to track down and secure his anything.

Knowing that Michael had purchased paintings at various auctions, and just plain curious, Mum and Tina flew to Hong Kong to check it out. Mum rang me up crying one night as they were being treated awfully while there, with Andrew Paul making it difficult to do an already difficult task. In the end they were allowed to leave with two bags with some old clothing, books and CDs. Mum also somehow managed to swipe a stack of documents which would later help with her legal inquiries into 'Where's Michael's everything?'.

I went down to Sydney and Dad and I went through what had been sent over of Michael's stuff, and it wasn't much at all. I guess anything is better than nothing, even if is dirty, dusty, mouldy and musty. It was divided fairly fairly, and I loaded up my keepsakes for the trip back up to Byron.

For some time now I'd wanted to see the police photos of Michael to get a better understanding of what may have happened. They say the state of your room is the state of your mind. I made the necessary arrangements, and went down to the Glebe Morgue.

I was introduced to a grief counsellor who would help if need be, and taken into a small room. The counsellor handed me a large file containing all the police statements, the Coroner's report, toxicology report, and about thirty photos, covering Michael and his room from every imaginable police photography-school angle. That done, he placed a box of tissues on the table. My initial natural reaction was indeed salty. Michael was lying away from the door, the belt broken close to his neck. The room was oddly tidy. Having been there for three days, he had hardly even unpacked, with most of his things still in his suitcases. The Michael I knew could make a room look lived in very quickly indeed. Poignantly facing up out of his Filofax on the bedside table was one of the photos Mandy and I had sent him of Zoe's second birthday party, three months before.

Before heading home I went to see Mum's lawyer, Joanne Kelly, at her office, as Michael's platinum and gold records and MTV awards and such, were to be divided up between the beneficiaries.

There were only twenty-odd pieces there, and I wondered where the rest were. Somebody had given his platinum record for *Kick* the boot, and instead of something that I would have been proud to put up, like the photo Mum had taken of it in Hong Kong, it arrived as a frameless, bent piece of cardboard.

I had driven down with a friend, Katy, and on the way back up to Byron I fell asleep at the wheel and we both woke up screaming as the car tilted down an embankment and tore up fifty metres of roadside fence pots and barbed wire. The car was basically a write-off, though after the initial shock we found it started again, and clunked into the next nearest town where we found a motel and slept. Katy had insurance, and a temporary vehicle was found, things unpacked and repacked, and she drove us safely back home.

Rachel was back in Byron and arranged another healing for me with her friend Dean, a local shamanic healer who used Aboriginal and North American Indian techniques. Naked, in a tepee, Dean wafted me all over with an eagle feather, scrubbed me with a horse-hair brush, then with a hot coal from the fire placed in a copper holder, gave me some deep tissue work. It was excruciating and I could only imagine that this is how it may feel like to give birth. It was quite a long session too, lasting over three hours, and in the end we were both exhausted. Slowly, with the help of friends and my own undertakings, I was staying cleaner. All these little things that I tried—rolfing, reiki, meditation, healings and therapy—were adding up to a deeper sense of wellbeing, and it really did feel like I was finally on the road to recovery. The trick though, of course, is not to fall asleep at the wheel.

banjo

I had been waiting for an opportune time to spread the rest of our one-third share of Michael's ashes, and in early November 1999 I flew into Nepal. My first impressions of Katmandu were nasal, aural and visual. The roads are busy, narrow and bumpy with people everywhere, poetically weaving their way to a cacophony of horns, whistles and bicycle bells. It goes on like this until around midnight, only to start again at sunrise with the same sound and fury. I spent the next few days meandering about, exploring the side streets and beautiful architecture.

The Nepalese are very friendly, especially the children, who are always running up to greet with a 'Namaste', and a smile or a laugh. It amazes me how they can play all day, seemingly never bored. They run with plastic bags on strings which fill with air becoming kites, play hacky-sack with a used steel wool pad, or shoot marbles in the dirt. Then there's always picking flowers to float and race down rivers and drains, steer an old bike tyre down the street with a stick, or play in the sprinkle of water spouting through the small hole in a garden hose. Some western kids won't even go to the sandpit unless they have the latest Barbie or Transformer.

After I had adjusted to Nepali time, the climate and the altitude, I went trekking, a few days here, a few there. In Nagarkot you rise before the sun, to watch it slowly reveal a 180° view of the distant Himalayan peaks, including Mount Everest. I sat there turning a degree every couple of minutes until lunch, when the cloud layer thickened and obscured the view. Afternoons I walked amongst the light-dappled pine forests, eagles looping overhead. I felt at peace here.

After a couple of weeks of trekking about I went to Bodhnath, on the outskirts of Katmandu. Bodhnath hosts Nepal's largest Tibetan community, and its white-domed stupa is revered by Tibetan Buddhists. Its four levels represent earth, water, fire and ether, and legend has it that it holds a bone from Siddhartha Gautama, the Buddha. Every sunrise and sunset the community walks clockwise around the base, spinning prayer wheels to a symphony of cymbals, chimes, bells, horns, drums, and the odd conch shell. It is peaceful to watch and relaxing to join in.

At sunset on the second anniversary of Michael's death, I went down to the stupa with a small urn containing the rest of his ashes. Michael had been in my thoughts a lot. All good memories, none of the peripheral nonsense usually associated with him after his death, but about him being a nice person and a good brother to me. First I prayed to Buddha, and walked around the base with everyone else. Then starting from the top, I dispersed some of his ashes to the north, walked around and down a level, ashes to the east, down again, to the south, down again, and lastly to the west, with thoughts of Michael firmly in my mind, followed by a final prayer. With the sun peeking over the hills like a huge red disc and Buddha's rays filtering out through the fluffy clouds, it all felt very fitting, and like I had done the right thing. At least some of him was resting in peace.

Mum and Tina had their own ideas for their 'share' of Michael. For some reason they believed that if he were still alive he would presently be living in Los Angeles, and that he would like to be resting there, even after Dad had built a lovely memorial in Sydney. So they built their own shrine in the Forest Lawn Memorial Park in the Hollywood Hills, and interred their share of him there. So my brother has at least two gravesites.

I found my way back to Thailand, and went down to Ko Pha Ngan to get myself settled before the new millennium. The December full-moon party there was crazy, with twenty thousand day-glo tripsters dancing their boogaloo all night long. They began arriving early afternoon and as soon as they hit the island they started consuming, like hungry locusts, devouring nutrients and discarding the remnants. Most braincells are lost on the beach and you don't need to ingest anything. The lights mish with the lasers which mash with the noise from a dozen bars booming different tunes and vying for customers, creating a complete sensory overload. Some spots can seriously do your head in. Just after sunrise the tide came in and swallowed up the beach. I heard later that a couple of people had drowned, and three were still missing.

Just before Christmas I bumped into a friend called Pippa. She was with some Aussie mates, and invited me to do the Christmas dinner thing with them. They had bought a pig, dug a pit, made a fire from coconut husks, and assembled a spit. That, with the chickens, prawns, tom yum, salads, rice, yams, rambutans, mangosteens, beer, good Aussie wine, punch and joints, made for a great night. Though I did get queasy after a friend blew up his finger with a firecracker, and in Sam Peckinpah slow-motion style, sprayed blood all over my face.

A few days later I headed over to Koh Samui to go to the bank, as it was my closest ATM. I hired a bike and thought I would go and visit Pippa at her new pad there, as she and her crew had splashed out and got themselves a nice villa for New Year.

I got there just after lunch. There was no-one in, so I made myself at home. It was a very nice place indeed, and I decided to miss my boat back and stay the night, hang out with my friends. I waited, drank, read, had hot showers and then after dark started to wonder where they were. I went up to the master bedroom to make sure I had the right place. I did, but none of their stuff was there. All the rooms were empty. They had obviously checked out.

I went into Chaweng for dinner, and then to the Cotton Club for drinks, and maybe had a few too many, because on the way back to my new-found bachelor pad I had an accident. I don't remember much, except that I was riding fast on my hired motorbike in just shirt and shorts, barefoot and helmet-less, when I looked up and saw the road ahead narrow dramatically for a bridge. I don't remember locking up or hitting anything, or flying off the bridge—but I did.

It turns out they had just widened the road around the island, but had neglected to widen the bridges. Someone found me, and I woke up in shock in hospital twenty minutes later, not wanting to stay and be a bother. A quick pseudo fix-up would be fine—I had places to go.

Of course when you have insurance you don't need it, and when you don't you do. It was lucky I had just been to the bank. They fixed me up as much as my wallet allowed, then called my parents' wallets for more. I was actually pretty banged up, and spent the next couple of days sleeping with a drip for sustenance, or in the operating room. I had eight stitches under my chin, the same on my left elbow, and around the knuckles on my left hand. My little finger was a worry—it looked deformed, gnarled and ganky. I didn't even like looking at it, though I needed to monitor any progress or deterioration. I also had stitches in my scalp, and was grazed on the left side, my waist, right forearm and both feet.

The worst part was I missed the biggest party in the world of the year, decade, century, millennium. Crappy New Year. The only consolation was I got to watch celebrations all over the world on CNN. That, and the morphine they gave me every three hours. Three days later, after having my dressings changed, I was discharged again with a bag of antibiotics and a bigger bag of morphine. I put on my ripped and bloodied clothes and got the ferry back to Ko Pha Ngan.

It was good to be back in a place I knew and see my friends again, even if they told me I looked like death. Mind you, I did kind of fit in with all the other millennium casualties hobbling around. You could see the festivities had taken their toll. I was told that Chicken corner, a popular crossroads, had looked like Omaha Beach on D-day, and by midnight all the nursing stations were besieged by the sick or wounded, and kept busy all night and the following day.

Every day I had to go to hospital and get my dressings changed, and every day my hand looked worse, as there was infection setting in, and one of the pins they had inserted into my finger had fallen out. My years of travelling told me that if you get seriously injured in a third world country, the best option is a flight home ASAP.

When I arrived in Brisbane, for once Customs didn't hassle me, and actually helped me with my bags. I didn't declare the big bag of morphine I had with me as it would have been an inconvenience. Besides, is it still illegal if Customs carry your bags through?

Alex picked me up from the airport, and because I was in pain we went to score some relief. I rang Mum and Dad to let them know I had got in safely, then we went down to the Valley to see a GP and get my dressings changed yet again. The doctor was quite concerned, and thought that I needed to get to the hospital pronto and see an orthopaedic surgeon. I rang Mum again and she came up from the Gold Coast and drove me to the hospital back in Southport.

It really bugged me that I came home looking worse than when I left, and with a slight morphine habit. Unintentional too. My trip away had been good for me and I had used heroin only once in the two months, while passing through Penang. I had enjoyed being clean and made a decision to head back to Thailand as soon as I could. Not many addicts can go to Thailand and get clean, but the further away from my suppliers I was, the better. I was getting more and more clean time up, like flight hours for a pilot.

I was admitted into hospital and went into surgery almost straight away. The diagnosis was not good. My infection had worsened and there was a 50/50 chance they might have to amputate my little finger. My doctor told me it would probably be useless to me any-way, a burden. I tended to disagree, as I liked all my digits, even if they were going to be stiff or disfigured. I told him if it bothered me later I'd consider amputation then.

The next couple of weeks I rested and self-medicated, supple-menting their morphine with mine, until Mum caught me self-medicating one afternoon and told the matron, who confiscated my medicine. After I was discharged and given my morphine back, I went to stay with Mum and Ross in their new place at Main Beach. But Mum and I were still not getting on, and by now I was supplementing my prescription morphine with smack. This involved daily train trips up to Brisbane to score. Then one day, after my physio appointment, she and Ross turned up at the hospital with my luggage, a letter explaining that I had to leave, and the bus fare to Byron. Love your work Mum.

Six weeks after limping away, I was back on Ko Pha Ngan. Over the next few weeks my health returned, and I felt good. Time passed quickly, and before I knew it, it was time to do a visa run, and I headed up to Bangkok.

I went out drinking with friends one night on Kao Sarn Road, and my next memory is waking in another hospital, having a CAT scan. Two friends had taken me there around five in the morning, before going on to the airport to catch a flight back to England and their absence made it hard for me to piece together what had happened. It turned out I had been hit from behind by someone, and my skull fractured, causing blood to leak into my brain, blocking my ear and making me feel dizzy.

Over the next few days I saw various neurosurgeons and an ear, nose and throat specialist, and as my ear had stopped bleeding, they scraped out the dried blood. Still slightly wobbly, and furnished with yet another bag of morphine, I was discharged after a week.

I decided to head back into Laos, and in a few days was on the slow boat back down the majestic muddy Mekong. We arrived at Pakbang as the sun, a red globe, due to slashing and burning of the rainforest, went behind the hills.

I spent a week cruising about Luang Prabang. The caves, temples and markets make for a beautiful city. It was changing quickly though, with accommodation already twice the price since my previous visit. I headed south to Si Phan Don (Four Thousand Islands), where the Mekong widens out and turns from turbulent brown to calm green. It is a very peaceful and serene place, and there are certain times of the day when you can do nothing but find shade and perfect the art of loitering. The rest was good for me, as I was still getting dizzy at times.

Back in Bangkok I visited a guy called Lyle in Bang Kwang prison, or the Bangkok Hilton, as it is known. I'd first heard about Lyle through the media. It was a big story, as he'd just been caught with two girls at Bangkok International Airport, trying to smuggle smack out of Thailand into Australia. Each had 35 grams of smack, and each had been given forty-five years.

The noticeboards in various hostels and internet cafes around Kao Sarn Road are full of pleas from lonely prisoners wanting a visit and someone to talk to, to break up the monotony. So having heard horror stories and read a couple of books by inmates, I decided to pay a visit to this notorious place myself.

Bang Kwang Prison is a half-hour ferry ride from Kao Sarn Road, up the dirty Chao Praya River. Then there's a short walk from the jetty to the administration block where you show your passport and tell them the name of the prisoner you want to see. They give you a small slip of paper, which you in turn pass on to a guard who asks you to leave mobile phones or cameras with him. After some more scrutiny they unlock the heavy metal gate, and you walk out into a long open courtyard with a rose garden in the middle. You walk past a small shop where the locals stand chatting away, across to a courtyard where a guard motions you to find a spot on the long cement bench which runs the length of the courtyard. There is a small shelf in front of you about two feet wide, then thick bars covered in chicken wire, a two-metre gap which guards patrol, more bars and chicken wire, a shelf and a long cement bench on the far side for the inmates. In order to talk, you have to shout, and everyone hears. Except they don't, as they're all shouting too. Bizarre to say the least.

Lyle finally arrived, manacled and shackled. I yelled my name and introduced myself, and he did the same. Lyle told me he had been an addict for a while, though for the last year or so he'd been on methadone. One day back in Australia he met another guy from the clinic, who after some chatting offered him a job to do a run with two girls. The trip would be paid for, they would get some cash, and a bit of what they brought home. Oh, and it was supposed to be safe. Being broke, Lyle thought it a good option, and signed on.

Things had gone to plan, or so they seemed, and after a week in Bangkok they left their hotel. Six hours before the flight someone tipped off the Australian Federal Police, who in turn informed Thai Customs. The police only knew about the girls, however, not Lyle. They were walking through Departure together when the girls were pulled up at Customs. The Customs officers asked Lyle if he was with them, and, fatally, Lyle said, 'Yes'. Sayonara City. If he'd said 'No' it might have been a very different story.

The Thai authorities blew it all out of proportion, and it became big news at home. Lyle was told he would need US$500,000 to get off with at least a reduced sentence, but he didn't have anything like that. If he had, he wouldn't have been there in the first place. He went to court and got his forty-five years—like waking up to the exact same day 16 436 times.

After an hour of yelling, my visit was up and I asked him if he needed anything. He asked for food and cigarettes which I bought at the shop there, and he asked me to contact his sister and say he was fine and thank her for her parcels. Not even the locals would eat the food they got inside, so he was surviving on the $40 he received from the Australian Government each month, care pack-ages from his family, and the generosity of visitors. Food or anything of value was locked in a metal trunk in his room. Lyle was in league with two other inmates, and one of them had to be in sight of the box all day every day, or everything in it quickly disappeared.

I liked Lyle. It seemed to me that he was just caught up in the wrong thing at the wrong time, and from what he openly told me, he had been. Apart from that, he always had a cool head, which was probably the only way of surviving. He'd been clean for a while now, not daring to use as nearly all the addicts inside were HIV positive, or about to become so.

Checking my email one day, I got the news from a friend that Astra had given birth to a 9 lb 10 oz, very healthy little boy, Banjo, after a six-hour labour. I rang Astra, she was well, Banjo was well, it was all good. It was exciting news and I couldn't wait to tell friends. Dad was a fantastic grandfather who was excited as well, however to this day Mum is yet to acknowledge him. He is now four years of age.

When I got back to Byron I went to see Astra and meet Banjo. She was well and he was, well, gorgeous. He looked like Buddha. I was honoured to meet him.

paula franco pete

Early one Sunday morning in September, I got a call from Dad with the terrible news that Paula had died, and immediately thought of Tiger. I was surprised but not shocked. I phoned Paula's friend Belinda Brewin, who tearfully explained the circumstances to me. When Tiger had asked Belinda, 'Where's Mummy?' she was told that she had gone to visit Daddy. With beautiful childish naivety, Tiger queried, 'Why didn't she take me?'.

It reminded me of when Troy Planet's three-year-old daughter Epiphany once asked, 'Who created the world?'. 'God did.' 'Well, who created God?'. Some questions are just too interesting, or in Tiger's case too poignant to answer.

The following week I was hounded by various English papers for dirt. It's not as though by her death they would suddenly break tradition and decide to print anything vaguely nice. Thankfully, friends helped divert them in every direction away from my house. Later, I succumbed and signed a $10,000 contact with *News Of The World*. As all I had to say was nice, they had nothing to print and didn't pay me.

Tiger was being looked after by Bob, which initially seemed ironic, however I was in no state to do much about it, apart from vowing to go over and see her one day when the time was right. It upset me that I hadn't got my life together sooner, for me, my kids, or Michael's.

Mum and I had been getting on okay again. She and Tina had secured a publishing deal to write a book on Michael's life. Every time I inquired about how the writing was going she told me it wasn't easy, though Tina was helping her and it was coming along. When I phoned Mum to tell her about Paula, she was rather cold about it. 'I knew that would happen,' she said, and was more concerned for Tiger. I asked if there was anything that she should now change in her book regarding Paula, and she replied it made no difference at all and she wouldn't be changing a thing. A couple of weeks later she went to London to join Tina doing publicity for the book, telling me she'd call when she got back.

While she was away I phoned her publishers and asked them to send me a copy of their book, *The Real Michael Hutchence—Just A Man*, which arrived a few days later. Not that anyone's counting, but I am mentioned over four hundred times in a 335-page book that is not about me. And hardly ever mentioned in a nice way either, as one might expect family to write, let alone publish.

The two of them obviously didn't know 'the real Michael Hutchence' well enough to divulge only his dirty laundry. Basically everyone got a caning, Michael, me, Dad, Paula, Helena, Kylie—apart from Mum and Tina of course. And what really hurt was that there were people out there buying it and believing their spiteful crap. I hoped that their advance had been enough to buy them a new conscience.

Mum had been back in Australia for two weeks before I found out through a friend that she'd returned. She hadn't rung me after she discovered I'd been sent a copy. I've hardly spoken ten words to her or Tina since reading it. I called Dad and suggested that due to the state of his health he had better not read it. I don't think he ever did.

When Tina, with the help of Mum, started what might have turned into a bitter custody battle for Tiger, I had no idea what their motives were. I wrote a letter to the Family Division of the High Court in England, stating that I believed that Tiger was in the best possible place for her to be, with Bob Geldof. I voiced my fear that a young girl who had recently lost both parents would go catatonic if removed from the only other world and family she knew, her three half-sisters.

I hadn't seen Franco for over ten years when I bumped into him at the Beach Hotel on Melbourne Cup Day. He was in Byron doing the family thing, and had rented a holiday unit for his mother, sister and brothers, whom I had met previously. Franco had recently married Sharna, a young model. He told me he had done well in life, starting as a photographer's assistant in Sydney and working his way up the ladder to New York where he now lived and worked, shooting fashion for *Elle* and *Vogue*. Their life was five-star hotels, first-class flights and Michelin restaurants—not to mention 'the beautiful people' (though he often did).

When Franco and Sharna turned up later that day with a huge rock in his pocket, I wondered where it all gone wrong, as this was not the guy I knew. Believe me, he'd had plenty of chances to partake in the past, and had previously given drugs the big swerve. Especially after seeing first-hand the causes, effects, and aftermath of wasted lives.

They were up in Byron for a few days so we hung out, shot the breeze, and the rock. Franco had shared an apartment with Helena in Paris so had known Michael as well. I've always liked catching up with people who knew Michael. Performing aside, Michael was a very smart, witty and generous person. I liked introducing friends to him so they could gauge that for themselves.

When Franco and Sharna turned up at the flat I was renting in Bangalow a week later with more dope, I was surprised. Though less surprised at how long it didn't last us. It's a bent wisdom that buying more dope than usual will make it last longer—it never has, never does and never will. He had rented a room at the Great Northern Hotel—hardly the five-star digs they had boasted of. They had been there a couple of nights but were sleeping badly because of the bands playing downstairs, so I suggested they come and stay up at my place in the hills where they could listen to frogs and crickets instead.

I had been cleanish for a couple of months, but my guests were climbing the walls, tilting my big picture. That weekend we went to Nimbin to score. Nimbin is probably Australia's only open drug market. Usually you don't even need to leave the car to score, but with a heroin drought in full swing, scoring was a hassle. Any dealer with wares was instantly swamped, and if you weren't one of the first customers, then tough, maybe tomorrow. Maybe. That day we had no luck at all.

As my flat was small and cluttered, I had given Franco and Sharna my bedroom, and I slept on the couch in the living room. I woke up early on Monday morning. Franco was awake too, and sitting up in bed. I asked him how he had slept, already knowing his answer. I told him I'd have a quick shower, make a couple of calls, and then we had to go into Byron as I'd made a doctor's appointment for him to try and get something to alleviate his withdrawal pains.

After my shower and phone call, I went downstairs to get dressed. Sharna was now awake and wanted to know if I had seen Franco. I said I'd spoken to him five minutes ago, and that maybe he'd gone out for a walk. Dressed, I went back upstairs to make another call.

At first my brain did not register the high-pitched scream that emanated from somewhere outside. It was only when that shriek turned into my name being howled that I clicked, dropped the phone and ran downstairs. Sharna was outside, looking up at the corner of the house and screaming hysterically.

Somehow I already knew what to expect before I saw it. Franco had got the garden hose and tossed it over a beam, tied a knot around his neck and was hanging there motionless. I ran up to him, grabbing him around the waist to lift him and try to take some of the weight off as the knot was too tight and I couldn't undo it. I yelled to Dave in the upstairs flat to rush down with a knife and he ran down with a big kitchen knife. I cut the hose while taking Franco's weight in my arms, and gently laid him down on the grass.

Telling Dave to call an ambulance I started mouth-to-mouth and CPR. To be honest, though, when I first ran up to him I knew it was too late and that he had slipped away already. Sharna was still screaming when the ambulance and police arrived. Too late. Too fucking late. One minute Franco and I are chatting, then not even ten minutes later I'm cutting down his lifeless body.

I will not bother speculating on why he did it there and then, apart from the fact that people in that kind of state just do not care.

They don't think of how death's ripples will affect those who find them, or the loved ones left behind.

Sharna told me later how they had talked of suicide as an option to end their addiction, and had forged a pact to do it together that day. But Franco had woken first, and may have thought that doing what he did would stop Sharna from doing it, as well as making getting clean easier for her. It is virtually impossible for a using couple to get clean together.

Initially, it didn't make a difference, but when I saw her at the funeral down in Sydney a week later, she was clean, and planning on staying that way. So, was Franco's suicide—an act generally considered to be selfish—actually selfless in this case? Had his death in fact saved her life?

I remember how the day before, on the trip to Nimbin, he had quizzed me about Michael's death—the circumstances, how he'd done it, who had found him. I didn't think anything of it at the time, but recalling it later was chilling.

The entire episode, naturally, got me thinking, and once more I curbed my desire to use. Byron seemed new to me, and it was, in a way. I stopped seeing old acquaintances and made new friends, shifting worlds.

On Melbourne Cup Day, 2000, I bumped into Mandy with Zoe and Sophia at the Beach Hotel. Somehow that day, Sophia went missing. Losing a young child, even if only for a minute, must be one of the most terrifying experiences a parent can go through. We frantically looked around, then charged about the very crowded pub looking for her for the next ten minutes, until she was found wandering in the car park out the back.

Mandy and I were at odds, and neither of us handled the situation very well. Alcohol-fuelled, this turned into an argument which soon involved the pub's security.

Mandy left, and two security guys unjustifiably told me it was time to go. Locking my hands behind my back, they frog-marched me through the crowd, across the road to the park, where they held me down with a knee in my back before finally letting me go.

I was banned from the Beach Hotel. Over time, I made various attempts in different disguises to get back in. I tried a bandage around my head while in a wheelchair. I bought a Neanderthal wig, moustache and beard from a toy shop and wore a kaftan while carrying a large book and playing with rosary beads. The girls behind the bar would recognise me and giggle as I ordered.

A week after New Year's Eve, late one Thursday night, the phone rang and it was Michala. We had met the year before in Laos. She was twenty-six years old, and had the bluest eyes for such a brown-skinned girl. She was, of all things, a drug and alcohol counsellor.

She was visiting Byron from New York, where she'd recently married a bigwig banker. Michala asked what I was doing on Saturday, and I told her that I had nothing planned. She asked me if I wanted to come to Thailand, her shout. Nothing sexual, she'd just enjoyed meeting me and thought she'd like to travel with me. She was leaving the following night, and would leave a ticket for me at Brisbane Airport on Saturday morning. We would email when I got to Bangkok to arrange to meet up.

Two nights later I was back on Kao Sarn Road. The first person I bumped into was Pete, whom Mandy and I used to share a house with in Byron. We grabbed a beer, and after the small talk Pete told me the reason he was there. Having been clinically depressed for over a decade now, Pete had decided to stop the anguish, max out his credit cards and kill himself. I told him jokingly that it was going to cost his family a small fortune to get his body back home, then proceeded to try to talk him out of doing it. He said he had tried to kill himself ten years before in Italy, but when the time came he couldn't go through with it. I hoped it would be the same story this time.

Michala and I had swapped emails, and she showed up not long after, and the three of us went out for dinner. We were leaving the next day for the islands and, in the meantime, Pete swore he'd be okay and promised to hook up when we returned a few weeks later.

The Thailand/Laos I saw on that trip was nothing like the Thailand/Laos I had seen before, backpacker style. Michala had her husband's credit card, so we flew everywhere and stayed in five-star hotels whilst taking the concierge's advice on the nicest restaurants and bars. Bangkok, Ko Pha Ngan, Chiang Mai, Luang Prabang, Van Vieng and Vientiane, all accessed at their most opulent. Van Vieng had changed yet again, this time with a crackdown on the opium dens—not that we didn't source one.

Before flying back into Bangkok, I emailed Pete and we met up and went to a Japanese restaurant. He was in good spirits, and said he was thinking of going to Korea to teach English with the $1000 diploma he'd just bought on Kao Sarn Road. He promised me he would call when he returned to Byron, whenever that may be.

A week later I was back in Bangalow when I got a call from a friend telling me Pete had killed himself. At first I thought, 'Pete who?' Then it clicked. He had flown in a few days after me, not telling a soul. Back in Byron, he'd rented a car and bought some hose-pipe, which he later taped to the exhaust. He'd driven up Old Bangalow Road to a lookout over Cape Byron. A beautiful place to do it if you're going to, were my first thoughts. He had started the engine and said his last goodbye to the place he called home, and to life on earth.

Pete had been thoughtful enough to leave three notes explaining his actions. One to the unfortunate person who would find him, another to his family, and the last to his friends. The note to friends was read at his wake, and it was so honest and true that it affected us all. Pete explained that he was forty, had not accomplished the things he had dreamed of earlier in life, and without wanting to hurt anyone at all, just did not want to live any more. He only wanted release from the pain and torment he suffered. I believe anyone who knew him understood and even respected his decision. Everyone, that is, except the owner of the car rental agency who had the gall to give Pete's grieving family an invoice at the wake, explaining it was for the petrol he had used, the battery he had flattened, and to get a new driver's seat as the old one was covered in blood which had leached from his body due to carbon monoxide poisoning. We ripped up the invoice and told the dickhead to leave quickly.

Rest in peace now Pete.

There was a gig I really wanted to go to at the Beach Hotel, and I decided to go in drag, in a Chinese-fringed red wig, and a long red evening dress. I don't mind saying so myself, but I looked good, fuckable even. It was a fun night. I danced up the front, got pinched on the arse, and even got two phone numbers off a couple of guys who bought me drinks. When the house lights came up, one of the security guys started pushing me and calling me a fucking poofter. We got outside, and in front of witnesses he pushed me backwards so that I fell over, hurting my hand and wrist.

The *Gold Coast Bulletin* heard about the incident and sent a reporter down to try to interview me. The *Sydney Morning Herald* and *The Age* in Melbourne picked up the story and splashed it over their social pages, calling me a very cross dresser. The *Herald*'s Column Eight thought I should be nominated for *Ralph* cover girl of the year—then mistook sightings of me for Barbara Cartland.

Then the TV show *Today Tonight* took an interest. They wanted to pay me to get wired up and do a re-enactment. The fee would be enough for me to get a ticket to London and see Tiger, something I'd wanted to do for a while, so I agreed. A few days later, back in drag with a wireless microphone on me, I again tried to enter the pub, this time being stopped at the front.

After the story went to air I was banned from the pub for life. It's a pity, as I liked the place—they just have idiots for security. I went to see Delvene Delaney, the wife of the owner John Cornell, whom I'd known for twenty years-plus as Mum used to do the make-up for *The Young Doctors*, which she was in.

Delvene told me to talk to the publican who told me to talk to security, who were the guys who disliked me in the first place. It doesn't matter: Tom Mooney, the owner of the other two pubs in town, is quite happy to have me spend my money there.

I used the TV money to get to England, stopping off in Bali and Thailand on the way. Bali still holds a special place for me, perhaps from my childhood memories and maybe because it is one of the few countries I have frequented and never ever used in.

In Thailand I got the good news that Lyle was out. He had finally received a pardon on the King's birthday after serving six years, and immediately flew home. He still hasn't seen Bangkok.

On my stopover I got bitten by a mosquito and contracted dengue fever, which I would not recommend to anyone. Sore bones, restless sleep, no appetite, not very social, no energy. That's how I left Thailand and arrived in London. It was strangely similar to severe heroin withdrawal.

The night after I arrived I phoned Bob Geldof, who was expecting me, as Dad had faxed him that I was coming over, and we made a plan to meet up on the weekend.

The timing was right, perfect even. I was straight, and had been that way inclined for over a year and a half now. Bob would have a chance to meet the real me. Any other time he probably would not have wanted to know me or have a bar of me. We made arrangements to meet on the weekend at Tiger's ballet class.

I was really quite nervous, though that all dissipated soon after meeting. Tiger was gorgeous and I couldn't help the tears welling up in my eyes as we watched her dancing around with the other girls. For a six-year-old, she already showed real talent, possibly inherited from her parents, maybe all her own.

Not wanting to disturb the class, Bob, his partner Jeanne and I went down to a coffee shop to chat. They are a very nice couple and we seemed to get on fine. I told them all about myself, my problems, how I had slowly yet surely overcome them and what I was trying to do with my life now, staying straight and trying to get a publishing deal for my book.

Not long after we were joined by Tiger and her nanny, Monique, who was very nice and loved and cared for her as one would hope. We went back to the house and Tiger had great interest in showing me her art, and the photographs of cousins Zoe, Sophia and Banjo that she had on her walls.

Bob called Dad that evening and Dad told me later that Bob said he thought I was a very nice guy. Something he most definitely would not have thought a few years earlier.

Over the next few weeks Tiger and I got together, mainly at her house after school. Before coming to England I had the firm belief that she was in the best place she could be, and seeing her in her home surroundings only reinforced it. It was nice to see, and a relief from any previous concerns I may have had.

No matter what the trauma of her early childhood, Tiger was growing up a normal six-year-old girl, doing what normal six-year-old girls should be doing. She knew that I was her dad's brother, though we didn't mention Michael at all, or Paula. I was more concerned with building a strong foundation for the future, as her uncle, and with Bob and Jeanne.

Apart from Twiglets—a delicious and nutritious English snack, like Vegemite on Vita-Wheat—England is of course horrifically expensive, so when I got invited to a birthday party in Ibiza I decided it would be warmer and cheaper than hanging around London, and booked a flight with a friend, Elaine. All I want to say is that I was relieved to leave Ibiza two weeks later and head back to Blighty, which says something. Relieved to eat and sleep again, something we did little of while there. We couch-surfed the whole time, and every night was party night. When we landed in Ibiza, everyone cheered to be there, though that was nothing like the cheering that erupted when the plane touched down back in Gatwick. I know, Gatwick—now that really says something.

Back in London it was starting to get cold, something I am not used to. Not having had a proper winter for so long makes me notice the slightest temperature difference. I decided I had done what I went to do, making a connection with Tiger and Bob, and made plans to head home. The only problem was that flights were booked solid, and I could only get myself wait-listed to leave in a month's time.

That weekend, Bali was devastated by the bombs at Paddy's and the Sari Club. Not normally places I would go to, though I did happen to go to the Sari for a drink when I was in Bali just a month before. It was a shocking wake-up call for all, that even on the island of the Gods one must not become complacent about what and where is a safe place. The only consolation is that if there is any island in the world that can heal itself, Bali is it.

The next day I rang Garuda, and, as I thought, there were seats available now. I flew out that week. While at the airport I rang Tiger to say goodbye, and it brought tears to my ears when her last words were, 'I love you Uncle Rhett'.

dad

On my stopover in Bangkok I got an email from Dad saying that he was going into hospital. Spots had been found on his lungs, which had proven to be cancer. He'd stopped smoking twenty-six years before, but the damage had obviously been done. Dad hadn't been very well before I left for England, and I'd asked him if I should be going at all, but he was adamant that I go. He said he would be okay, and that he wanted me to meet Bob and see Tiger, so I went.

After putting my bags down in Sydney I went straight over to St Vincent's Hospital. I just knew by looking at Dad that he wasn't well, but I tried to keep as brave a face as he did. It was good to see him and on the whole he seemed alright with his equation. Susie came in every chance she had. I stayed with her at first, but with both of us needing some space to deal with that was going on, I moved to Potts Point with a family friend, James.

Good move bad move. The Cross got me curious as I walked through it daily on my way to visit Dad. And I dabbled here and there, nothing too much, a justifiable amount to help me deal with Dad. I had been off smack for a year and a half, maybe a crazy year and a half, but a good one, and a half. So why I now thought of it as an option I have no idea, as I had to keep it completely under wraps. I didn't want Dad to know, or Susie, or anybody for that matter.

I visited Dad every day, and though he maintained a dignified outlook, he wasn't getting any better. It was interesting, after the suddenness of Michael's death, to be able to talk, share, analyse consider, contemplate, and learn of death through Dad.

After a month he was transferred to a hospice in Woollahra. Mandy had called to say she was coming down with the girls after Christmas, and I had told her that if she wanted to see Dad she had better come sooner. They came down the next day; just in time really.

I had been to see Dad that morning, and had only just returned from the hospital when the phone rang. It was Dad's doctor who told me he thought I had better get back to the hospital.

Upon arriving I heard Dad had passed away. Rest in peace mate. Susie told me he had looked up at a watercolour painting of a marina and said, 'That's France, isn't it?' It was. He had then turned to Susie and said, 'I just want to thank you for the most lovely sixteen years', and passed away. Heartbreaking. The dad I loved was gone, the only concession being I had been lucky enough to spend all my years with him. He was a true gentleman, one of a disappearing breed.

Susie kindly gave me his watch, an Omega Seamaster, the first of the series, which he had bought in Singapore in 1948.

Over the next few days arrangements were made for Dad's funeral. We chose St Columba's Church in Lane Cove for a number of reasons. Both of Dad's parents had their farewells there, and Dad and Mum had married there too.

At some stage Mum had phoned Susie and asked her to ask me if she could come to the funeral. Mum and Dad had buried the hatchet for the umpteenth time a week after Dad went into St Vincent's. Mum had called and sent regards and apologised for various previous incidents, wanting to make her peace. And Dad said it seemed she had. Until only a week later, when obviously still angry over something, she had called Dad and had a shouting match, which sadly turned out to be their last words.

Yes, I could believe Mum could have said something like that, but not to him then. Dad didn't need any extra stress. I hadn't spoken to her since reading her book, though, I thought that if she wanted to pay her last respects to Dad and make her final, final, peace with him, she was welcome to do so.

Dad's ceremony was touching. Jenny Morris sang 'Moon River', after which I said a few words. It was Arthur Grogan, an old friend since the war, who evoked the most emotion, with his words to a true mate who would be deeply missed. I was trying to keep it together for my children's sake, though when Arthur started crying I couldn't stop myself.

After the ceremony we mingled outside with everyone, as the paparazzi snapped away across the road. Mum came up to me and thanked me for allowing her to come, then said she had to go. I asked if she was going to the wake, and she said she had to catch a flight back up to the Gold Coast, and left. I didn't notice at the time, but it was pointed out to me numerous times later that she was wearing red. A strange colour choice, perhaps, for a funeral.

It was nice to catch up with Dad's friends from over the years at the wake at the Greenwood Tavern, which, interestingly, used to house his old school. Garry Gary Beers, who had returned alone to Australia during the current INXS tour, was there. The band had sent a lovely card and flowers. Michele Bennett came with Jenny and Greg Perano. Austen Tayshus quietly slipped in and out to pay respect to a gentleman he had admired. Dad was very well respected and admired by many, a dignified man.

After many a quick hello and goodbye, the family climbed back into the limos and went to the Northern Suburbs Memorial Garden and Crematorium. As with Michael's service, I had decided I didn't want to be stoned for the funeral. When it was over I went into the toilets and had my take-away. I had been using every other day, and if I didn't stop soon I'd be unable to climb out of my deepening rut. I decided to make that my last shot.

At the wake I asked Susie if I could take some of Dad's ashes to Bali for a ceremony, and she agreed. The rest of him was to be interred into the side of Michael's memorial. It is now the Hutchence memorial, and I imagine one day I'll rest there too.

Two weeks later, with a very slight habit, I flew back to Bali.

Bali had also been special to Dad. It was in 1948, just after the war, when Dad was twenty-four years old, that he got a job working for Qantas in Surabaya in Java. The stories he told me about that time were extraordinary and funny, and I often wondered what it would have been like to travel back then. Dad had lied about his age to get into the RAAF, then had to continue the fibs for his job with Qantas. When his two-week holiday came up, he opted for Bali, an interesting choice at the time, and flew into Denpasar in one of the old DC3s, which was probably new at the time.

He didn't speak much Indonesian, and was met at the airport by a driver who didn't speak any English. But the driver knew of some people who spoke English in Sanur, a Belgian artist called Adrien Jean Le Mayeur, who had a Balinese wife, Ni Pollak. Pollak had been a famous Legong dancer. They had met and married when she was fifteen years old, and stayed happily together until his death ten years later in 1958.

The two weeks that Dad spent with them he recalled as some of the nicest times in his life. Everything just fitted together in such a way that he even queried his whole outlook, and contemplated different scenarios for living. Basically, he almost made a life-changing decision, and could easily have stayed on that island forever.

Le Mayeur left his house to the government, and it is now a museum, showing his residence and works from that period. As they didn't have any photos of Le Mayeur at work painting back in the late 1940s, I took some of Dad's photos over, and they now hang in the museum.

When Dad and I had gone to Bali the Christmas after Michael died, it was truly wonderful to be there with him and have him point out where he had stayed, slept and enjoyed life, fifty years before.

With the help of my friend Rachel, who was honoured that I asked her, I started organising things for Dad's funeral ceremony, and she approached Ibu Flower, a high priestess of Seminyak, to conduct it. It took place on the beach at Sanur in front of the Le Mayeur museum, against a dazzling sunset and a clear night sky with full moon rising beside the volcano. Everyone said a special prayer and gave offerings of fruit, food, flowers, money and a hip flask of whisky, and I said goodbye to a Dad I loved and respected.

It meant a lot to me that I was and had been clean for some time, apart from my recent relapse, which I'm sure he didn't know about. So for some time now I hadn't had to explain things or tell him that I was alright. He knew it just by talking to me. I'm sure it made his final days more peaceful.

As I sat and wrote in Bali, I thought about how much I loved it there. It holds my last image of Mum, Dad, Michael and me together as a real family. Two weeks on the beach doing family things. I guess I wanted it to go on forever. In some ways it has and I feel just as at home in Bali as I do in Australia.

However, for one of the first times ever, I was perturbed in paradise. And it was all about my ending. When I think of an autobiography, I think of a dead person's life story, which was the cause of my discontent. I decided to try and type out some thoughts on what I believed my future held and the way it might unfold, and just end the story, not the life.

For some unknown reason, I've always held the belief that if I told everyone in the world that I used, I would have to stop. And though I might as well now list my occupation as KNOWN ADDICT, I would prefer to write SURVIVOR. Not many people come out of sixteen years of heavy addiction, so I suppose it's for a reason. Finding that reason will hopefully be revealed on the next part of my journey. And though I have probably hurt and disappointed many people along the way, I really didn't mean to and am sorry. I doubt that any of my future lives will have heavy addiction as a lesson.

Why I chose that lifestyle, and it was my decision, was to mask myself from the reality of my hurt. Now that I have healed, with that mask off, even though I feel exposed and vulnerable again, I think I can live with it. Basically I was just lucky. Many aren't. And it isn't over. Hopefully my desire to stay clean, coupled with what I've learnt along the way, will keep me on the right path, so I can reclaim some of the time that was taken from me. Those days soo long, those years soo fast.

And if cats have nine lives, this Leo/Tiger must only have a few left, if that. Somehow, telling you everything you have read up until now makes me feel like I've lost another one already! Whacky or what?

so . . . ?

Most friends and many strangers, at the oddest times, either offer their own well thought-out scenarios or ask me 'So…what happened to Michael?' and I reply, 'Bad schooling, bad childhood'. If they don't get the joke, I explain further, depending on my mood and who's asking. If I feel good I may even offer all the information I've gathered over the years, which amounts to my answer being their question.

Three things. Either Michael was killed by someone, Michael was killed by Michael, or it was a sexual release gone accidentally horribly wrong.

I think the first possibility is highly unlikely but not utterly out of the question. Michael's balcony door was open. His room was on the top floor, so the balcony could have been accessible from the roof. Someone could have entered, hit Michael, held him at gunpoint and set the scene up to look like suicide. Okay, perhaps one for the conspiracy theorists, but not a totally impossible scenario.

As for the other two possibilities, which I admit are much more likely, over time one can only go on the evidence at hand. The Coroner's report, the toxicology report, the autopsy, the police inventory, police photos, telephone records, and police statements from Mum and Dad, Kym and Andrew, Bob and Paula, Michele Bennett, Martha Troup, the maid, the woman staying in the room next door, the ambulance officers, police officers and others, all paint a big picture. Part black and white, part conflicting, part missing, all frustrating, and unfinished. Various statements provide various insights into various times, yet a few hours are missing and only two beings will ever know what really went down in those final hours: Michael and God. And neither is telling.

On 6 February 1998, Derek Hand, the NSW Coroner handed down the verdict of suicide, and dispensed with any further inquest.

The verdict of suicide never quite sat with me from the beginning. It's something I don't think Michael had in him or was capable of— but then maybe it is just because I am his brother and loved him that I have found it hard to believe he would really take his own life.

I only ever had one conversation with Michael regarding suicide. It was when we were staying at Palm Beach, just before Christmas in 1996. I mentioned to Michael one morning that I hoped that Rebecca and Phoebe, children of some mutual friends of ours, would be alright this Christmas. Michael asked what I meant. The previous Christmas, the family in question had been having their Christmas lunch. Things were good, the whole clan was there. Then, between mains and dessert, young Phoebe went into a bedroom and found her uncle hanging lifeless from the ceiling. A major 'Fuck you' to everyone. All Michael could say was, 'Selfish cunt'. Which is something I know Michael definitely wasn't.

Derek Hand was satisfied, however, that due to relationship difficulties coupled with the effects of various substances, Michael, in a severely distressed state, intended to and did take his own life. Which I believe is what many people, my parents included, wanted to believe. They're too old-school to even entertain any other possibility, such as a sexual episode gone wrong.

We weren't impressed that somebody leaked the findings to the press before the family was even notified. And Derek Hand was right, to some eyes, as what he states can be seen to have happened as he explains it. But my need to know, determination and interest have uncovered a few things that plainly stick out as, shall we say, strange. All together now, 'Strange'. Okay, let's see if I can get this out, deconstruct it, unpack it as the jargon goes. This we know for sure. Well, I do anyway.

On Saturday, 22 November 1997, Dad had woken at six in the morning, and for some paternal reason felt concerned for Michael, even though at dinner the night before Michael hadn't seemed at all out of sorts. He had even danced into the foyer of the Ritz Carlton when Dad and Susie dropped him off. Despite his concern, Dad decided against ringing Michael that early for fear of waking him and making him angry.

At around eleven that morning Dad tried to call Michael, but the phone rang out. He then called John Martin, the INXS tour manager, asking if he had heard from Michael as he could get no answer. John said he hadn't. When John got off the phone he noticed a message under the door, from 'Mr River'. It said simply, 'Mr River is not going to rehearsals today'.

Even though the rehearsal was the last one before the tour started, and quite important, John thought Michael was just tired, and took the other members of the band to rehearsals, planning on letting Michael sleep and coming back and picking him up later. I don't know if Michael phoned reception to send the message, or if he wrote and delivered it himself to room 528, several doors down from his own. I have never seen the note, so don't know if Michael wrote it.

Rebecca Golfin, a banquet waitress, discovered Michael at 11.55 am. She knocked, then used her master key to unlock the door, but still couldn't open it due to some obstruction. When she finally pushed it enough to see what the problem was, she saw Michael and noticed he wasn't moving. He was hunched up against the door and wall, naked, kneeling with his arms on his legs, hands level with his knees, with his head bent down. She ran to a nearby room and phoned security downstairs. Stewart McGregor, the duty manager, immediately called for an ambulance.

At 12.13 pm two ambulance officers arrived at the Ritz Carlton, taking just four minutes to respond to the call. An employee told one of the officers, 'We have Michael Hutchence upstairs, and he has hung himself'.

The ambulance officers went upstairs, pushed their way inside, and deciding it was too late to help, lay him down and covered him with the bed cover before calling the Rose Bay police. Michael had tied a knot on the door anti-slamming device, which protruded perpendicularly from the wall above the door, and then slipped the looped belt around his neck. At some stage, due to his body weight, the belt had broken at the buckle, which was on his Adam's apple, and he had fallen to the floor. In moving Michael's body and covering him with the bedcover, the ambulance officers had in effect already disturbed what may have been a crime scene.

Senior Constable Crowther arrived at 12.20 pm with probationary Constable Beveridge. Beveridge asked, 'Who is it?' and was told, 'It's Mr River'. Beveridge then inquired, 'Who's Mr River?' and was told, 'You'll know when you see him'.

In the room they found a dictaphone near the bed. The police listened to the tape. They said the recording sounded similar to a party, then a voice like Michael's came on. The recording was bad, however, the police said, and what he was saying couldn't quite be heard. I have never heard this tape, which is a great pity as I, or another family member, might have been able to distinguish what was being said. But the tape was to go the way of many of Michael's things, into the possession of Colin Diamond. The police inventory (see Appendix 1) also lists a 'half finished note', but again none of us has even seen it.

Before phoning for backup and forensics, one of officers removed a silver ring from Michael's finger which was simply inscribed with 'FORGET ME NOT'. They were soon joined by a detective and a Senior Constable from the East Sydney Crime Unit, Warren Stocks, who removed an A$10 note, a US$1 note, and some coins from the pocket of Michael's discarded jeans. After many photographs, his body was conveyed to the Glebe morgue.

At 2 pm Detective Inspector Peter Duclos and Sergeant John Gerrard of Rose Bay Police knocked on Dad's door in Bellevue Hill and broke his heart. Dad had been called half an hour before by a journalist who had asked if he had any comment. Dad thought he was referring to the current tour. The hack hung up.

Not long after, at the band rehearsals, John Martin saw Dave Edwards, the INXS tour director, who told him and the band that he had just received a call from a girl at Mercury Records saying that Michael was dead. At 8 pm John returned to the Ritz Carlton, paid Michael's bill, and asked for a copy of his phone records. He then told the duty manager that now that Michael's bill was paid, the information on his telephone bill was not to be given to anyone but the police.

So how did Michael get to be in this situation? What could have snapped him? Were things that bad? He was such a 'rise above it' sort of guy. Let's rewind.

On November fourth, at their house in London, Michael and Paula had an amicable discussion with Bob Geldof. They were trying to seek his consent to bring Peaches, aged eight, and Pixie, aged seven, out to Australia with baby Tiger. They had wanted the girls from 18 November, would fly them back home to England for Christmas with Bob, then bring them back to Australia a couple of weeks later for around three months. After debating various aspects, Bob agreed to their proposal. Initially he had objected to the girls missing twelve weeks of school, and of course it would all have to be run past the children's head teacher, and their psychiatrist.

Michael and Paula were ecstatic. Away from the United Kingdom, they would be able to spend time with the children without press harassment, or at least a lot less of it. Plus Paula could pursue some enticing career opportunities in Australia. They immediately started making arrangements for travel, accommodation, tutoring and all the other details.

The day after their discussion, however, Bob wrote them a letter in which he outlined objections to the plan, though offering various alternatives, none out of the ordinary. If that wasn't acceptable, they could all meet with the girls' headmaster to consider things further.

An entire week later, on 12 November, Paula received Bob's letter, hand delivered to her house. Why it took so long to pass between them remains a mystery. After another meeting attempting to sway Bob, who continued voicing his concerns and objections, Paula instructed her solicitor, Anthony Burton, to commence proceedings in the High Court in an attempt to gain the right to proceed as originally agreed. The matter was listed for hearing on 21 November.

Bob's concerns increased when he received Paula's statement and application on 18 November. In it, Paula outlined a TV documentary proposal based on her settling in Australia, which Bob feared was really an attempt at permanent relocation for their children. The same day at 11 pm, Michael flew into Sydney, checked into the Ritz Carlton and, tired, fell asleep.

Michael's phone records of the two lines in room 524 reveal a lot, mainly because they are factual and honest slices of his life in that room.

The following day, the 19th, Michael made only two calls. His first was to Erin, his new love in LA, at 10.37 am, and he called Dad at home that afternoon. When I called Michael later that night he sounded good, if tired, and happy to be catching up.

On Thursday 20 November, he rang Erin twice, first at 9.52 am, and spoke for 13 minutes, and then that evening, when they spoke for another 22 minutes. They were his only calls, apart from two quick local calls. Michael and I had our last words that night, at around 11 pm, with me downstairs on the house phone.

One of the local calls was to his long-time friend Greg Perano. The two had met when Greg was playing 'industrial percussion' with Hunters and Collectors in the early eighties. Michael had liked the band so much that he saw four shows in a row, and even tried to get them signed to the same record label that INXS was with at the time, Deluxe. Greg was going out with Michele Bennett then. Seven months later she was going out with Michael.

After seeing the Hunters and Collectors video for 'Talking To A Stranger', Michael rang Greg to ask for the number of the director, who turned out to be a young Swinburne film school graduate called Richard Lowenstein. Richard went on to direct numerous videos for INXS, some of them award-winning, and the four of them—Greg, Michele, Richard and Michael—became the closest of friends. Over the years, apart from family, they were the people in Australia that Michael stayed in most constant touch with. Sometimes on tour, not really knowing who his true friends were and being surrounded by flunkies, hangers-on and INXS-ories, Michael would call up Greg, Richard or Michele for comfort, advice or reality checks.

Greg says he spoke to Michael twice at the Ritz Carlton. Michael called him first, and Greg says his demeanour reminded him of the time the previous year when the opium was found under the bed in London. Michael had seemed fully preoccupied with Paula and the girls coming out for Christmas. He'd called Greg to get the phone number of a mutual friend of ours, who was into heroin. It was not the first time either. Michael had called Greg on a previous occasion trying to get the number so that he could score.

Early Friday morning, Michael rang Paula for the first time, and they spoke for nearly half an hour. I don't know if it was their first conversation since his arrival in Sydney, however, as she might have called him. There's no hotel record of his incoming calls.

Not long after speaking with Paula, he rang Mum. This was when he asked her to pass on apologies to Mandy and me for not seeing us. Then he called Erin again for ten minutes, before ringing Michele Bennett to arrange to have breakfast with her the following morning, and Dad, regarding having dinner with him and Susie later that evening. After band rehearsals he went back to the Ritz Carlton and rang Dad again. Then at 7 pm he rang Erin yet again, talking to her for another five minutes. It was to be their last conversation.

Just before Michael was due to join Dad for dinner, he got a call from Greg Perano. They made plans to meet up with Michele for breakfast the following morning. But when Greg rang as planned at around 10 am on Saturday to confirm the arrangement, the phone just rang out. It is interesting to me that if Michael had premeditated his death, why make plans to meet two of his closest friends?

On 26 November, four days after Michael died, Kym Wilson, seemingly the last woman to see Michael alive, made her statement to police. In it she states that she had known Michael for seven years. They would see each other if Michael was in the country, but didn't communicate when he was overseas.

She had contacted Michael through his manager Gary Grant, on 20 November, inviting Michael to come to the Basement, the famous jazz club, for a benefit for a small theatre company with which she was involved. Gary told her where Michael was staying, and his pseudonym, hence the message Kym left for him, 'Mr River, if the current is flowing right, it should lead you to the Basement from about 8 pm till late. Love very much to see you. Hugs and kisses, love Kym'. This is the same night Michael was supposed to come to Troy Planet's performance at the Kirk Gallery, and had instead fallen asleep.

As Michael hadn't made it to Kym's benefit either, she received two voice mails on Friday evening. The first was 'Sorry I didn't make it last night. I got tired and crashed out. Love to see you tonight. Give me a call', while the second was, 'I am going out for dinner with my father and I'll be leaving about 7.30 pm. Try and call me before then or leave a message'.

Kym tried to call, but as Michael had already left, she left another message at the hotel for him, 'Mr River, please call me after 10.30 pm tonight. I'd love to see your beautiful face again. Lots of love Kym'.

After the play finished, she called Michael, and he said, 'What are you doing, let's do something'. Kym asked, 'Would it be alright if I brought my boyfriend Andrew with me?' and he said 'Yep, come over to the hotel, I'll meet you in the bar. If I'm not in the bar I'll be in my room'. 'Okay, see you soon.'

Kym and Andrew arrived at the Ritz Carlton around 11 pm and found him in the bar, sitting in an alcove with a girl on either side of him. 'Darling how are you? This is Andrew.' Michael stood up and Kym said, 'Do you mind if I give my friend a hug? I haven't seen him for a long time.' The girls made room, then said they had to go back and finish their desserts in the ballroom, and left. Michael told Kym and Andrew that he had never met the girls before and had been waiting by himself when they had come over and said, 'Oh, you're all on your own'. Michael had joked that that was the idea.

Michael was already drinking, so Kym suggested they order some drinks, and Michael said, 'No, let's go up to my room, we'll get them up there'. Then, jokingly, he said, 'Let's see if we can get out of here without paying for this drink'. They made it to the lifts before a staff member came over and asked Mr River to sign his bill.

Inside his room, Michael offered drinks, and they started catching up. Michael said he wanted to be in the room as he was expecting a call from Paula.

After about an hour the phone rang, and it was Martha Troup calling from the United States. Michael was happy to hear that someone wanted him for a film, and that Harvey Weinstein from Miramax had made favourable comments about him. At a meeting in New York earlier that year, Michael Douglas had told Michael that he thought he could 'sell a bit of popcorn'. Michael was very affectionate to Martha at the end of the call.

At some stage that night Michael and Kym made arrangements to meet when he was back in Sydney at the end of the tour, and Michael gave her the dates when he would be back. He told Kym and Andrew that this would definitely be his last tour with INXS, and he'd blow the tour off if anything drastic happened in England, so he could be with Paula. In her statement Kym said she asked Michael if the reason she was there was to support him when he found out the news from Paula, and Michael said yes.

About 2 am, Kym was half asleep on the bed when Michael held up two small empty resealable plastic bags. 'Come on Kymmie, you're not going to go to sleep now.' Kym asked what it was and Michael replied, 'Leftovers'. He ripped the packets open and gave them to her. Kym placed them individually in her mouth and felt a slight tingling sensation and said, 'Well, this will do a lot'.

Later someone rang and told Michael that no judge was available to hear Paula's action in the court in London. Michael still seemed alright at the bad news, even though it was what he had been fearing.

At about 4.40 am, with Kym very tired and Andrew falling asleep on the bed, Michael said, 'You guys go'. Kym asked if he was sure. 'Yeah, look at your boy, he's falling asleep.' Kym says Michael seemed fine, although she was concerned and said, 'We are only two minutes away. Andrew will leave his mobile on and you call me with good or bad news'. Then Andrew wrote down his number in Michael's address book.

'Let's have breakfast tomorrow,' Michael said. 'Oh no, I'm going to have breakfast with Michele. Let's go out tomorrow night.'

Kym said, 'Okay, we'll talk tomorrow'. They all hugged and Kym and Andrew left.

Kym's boyfriend, Andrew Rayment, a barrister, made his statement the day after Kym. It was now getting on for a week since Michael died. He had known Kym for about twelve years, and they had been dating for three months.

He first met Michael at the Ritz Carlton, in the bar, then they proceeded up to his room. Andrew states that the room was pretty messy and there were papers all over the desk and clothes on the couch and the chair near the desk. They had some drinks and started talking, with Michael dominating the conversation. Michael mentioned how he had just tried out for a part in a Quentin Tarantino film, *From Dusk to Dawn, Part II*. He received a call from Martha later that night telling him that he hadn't got the part, but was in fact being given a bigger role in another film.

There had been a great deal of conversation in the room, including about Michael's relationship with Paula, and how her children regarded Michael as their father. Michael had said even though Tiger was their only biological daughter, he was very happy the other children called him 'dad'. Michael said he loved all the children very much, that Peaches was very clever and Tiger was gifted. He also talked of his new house in Chelsea, and how the bathroom was all glass but could be made opaque.

Andrew described Michael's demeanour at this time as being energetic, and he appeared generally to be in an elevated mood, though, becoming pensive while he discussed the court proceedings. Andrew also mentioned that Michael spoke of quitting the band and cancelling the tour if the court battle went wrong. Due to Andrew's occupation as a lawyer, Michael seemed comfortable discussing legal matters, and they spoke about the court matter at length.

At some point they decided to have some daiquiris. Michael rang downstairs to order, but the bar was closed. Michael then rang back and asked for a blender, strawberries, Bacardi, lemon juice, lime juice and ice. The staff then decided to make the drinks themselves, and brought them up.

Andrew also mentions that Michael called Nick Cave while they were there.

It is interesting to me that Andrew states that during the night he received a mobile call from a friend who needed to borrow money. The friend was drinking at the Kendra, just around the corner, so they arranged to meet outside the Ritz Carlton. Kym and Andrew then left Michael for about fifteen minutes while they saw Andrew's friend, before returning to the room. Michael obviously wanted them to be there with him while he awaited news from London so did they both have to go and give $200 to Andrew's friend? Why didn't Kym stay behind? Was Andrew worried about leaving her and Michael alone? Or was it as simple as Kym having to go to an ATM to take out the money for Andrew to lend to his friend?

As for the drugs, Andrew recalled Michael said something like, 'Here you are, suck on this', then handed Kym two small empty plastic bags which seemed to have a white powdery residue inside. Kym later told Andrew that she had placed them both in her mouth. 'What is it?' Kym said, to which Michael had replied, 'Leftovers'. Andrew said he wasn't paying any attention to this comment, and attempted to ignore it. The last thing he states is that during the time they were in Michael's room, neither Kym nor he consumed any illegal substance.

In the early hours of Saturday morning, as per Kym's statement, Michael had indeed received a call with the bad news about the court action. It had come from Paula. Michael also spoke with her lawyer, Anthony Burton. Paula had refused to believe it when the official solicitor, through counsel, expressed their opposition to the removal of the children from school. Friday afternoon, with no time to hear Paula's application, no time to find a judge, she applied for and received an adjournment, to be heard on 17 December. The President of the Family Division made an order preventing Paula from removing the children without the court's permission. The girls would not be coming out as planned.

Michael then started the last of his known phone calls. The first was to Nick Cave, at 4.15 am. At 5.18 am Michael rang Bob Geldof on his mobile in London. Here is Bob's account from his police statement.

'Bob.'

'Who's that?'

'It's Michael man. Are you happy?' (Sarcastically.)

Bob said he chose to ignore it, then replied:

'I'm OK. Listen, can you call back in 10 minutes, I'm on the other line.'

'Ah man, can you call me?'

'I can't. I don't have your number.'

'Hold on, I'll give it to you.'

'I'm in the car and I don't have a pen.'

(Sigh of exasperation) 'OK, I'll call back.'

Next Michael rang Paula, at 5.31 am, and they talked for about five minutes. Paula told me later that Michael had said to her during that call that he was going to ring up Bob and beg him to let the girls come out. Straight afterwards, at 5.38 am, he rang Geldof for the second and last time. Bob was waiting outside Embankment tube station in London for his daughter Fifi's school bus when the call came. (Fifi is Bob's eldest daughter, and it was never proposed that she would come on the trip to Australia with the other girls.)

The two men talked and argued for nearly twenty minutes. Bob says that in the past two and a half years they had spoken only eight times, and this was their longest conversation.

Bob said the dad part of him, despite his own personal academic record, felt that it was better for them to finish their school year.

Michael responded, 'I'm their father, little man', a term Bob says Michael often used on the phone to him, 'when are you going to realise that?'

Bob said he kept an even tone, and said, 'I can understand your feeling that and I know they want to go on holidays, I'd love to go on holidays, but why [didn't] they just wait three weeks…'

'But it's only three weeks man.'

'That's exactly the point Michael why can't you just wait?'

Bob said at this stage he put the view of the children's psychiatrist that school was their one stable environment.

'It's only three weeks', Michael repeated.

Bob said he responded that the children mustn't start to think of school as elective, and that the headmaster had written a letter complaining about their many absences. He then suggested that if no alternative plan could be worked out, they might all meet with the headmaster to discuss things.

He said they went on discuss the past three years, and that he said to Michael that they could probably never be friends, which was unfortunate, and that Michael then began interrupting with things like, 'She's not your fucking wife!'

'I understand that.'

Soon after Michael said, 'You tried to take my own fucking daughter from me.'

'What are you talking about?'

'Don't lie to me man. I've got all the legal documents here.'

'Michael, I can assure you I have absolutely no interest in taking Tiger or anyone else from you. Don't be ridiculous. She's a cute kid but what would I want to take her for?'

'I have it all here.'

'Look, I tell you what, I'll sit down anywhere at any time with you and Andrew Young [Michael's lawyer] and we will go through it page by page. Just the three of us, OK?'

According to Bob, the misunderstanding over Tiger had occurred when his girlfriend Jeanne Marine had offered to mind the toddler for a couple of hours after Paula had attempted suicide. When subsequently told about Jeanne's offer, Paula interpreted it and relayed it to Michael as an attempt to 'snatch' Tiger.

After this, Bob said Michael's voice dropped to an 'in the know' type quiet, and was laced with irony, bitterness and threat. He made a number of allegations concerning Bob's personal behaviour and business arrangements.

'Michael, are you threatening me?'

'Yes I am.'

'This is a threatening phone call?'

Bob described Michael's voice as 'silky' at this point.

'Yes I am threatening you, you coward. I'm going to set the dogs [press] on you.'

Bob said he was outside his car now, pacing up and down waiting for Fifi's bus to come. He said there were people standing around waiting at the bus stop, some saying hello to him and others nodding. He said there was no shouting or remonstrating from him.

Michael went on to say, 'Please man. Please, look I'm asking, I'm begging, it's only three weeks.'

Bob said Michael's tone at this point was 'genuine and normal. No side, no agenda, heartfelt but not heartbroken'.

'Please Michael please don't ask me to do something that I just can't. I can't do it within myself. I don't think it's right. Besides it's the court who won't let them go now. Even if I said yes, they won't go. You brought the court action, not me.'

Bob said Fifi's bus arrived then, and she came up and hugged him.

'Fifi's home now Michael I got to go.'

Bob said, 'Hi love' to Fifi, then turned his attention back to the phone, but Michael had gone.

Bob told the police that compared to previous conversations with Michael it had been relatively constructive, which was why he hadn't bothered to report the threatening part of it. He also says he felt there was an audience in Michael's room, but that could be put down to the quality of the international line rather than anything else. Though at times 'druggy or silky or threatening or enraged', he did not think Michael's voice sounded depressive.

After picking up Fifi he went to a TV studio where he appeared on a Children In Need telethon. Then he went to see a friend, an acquaintance of Michael's who was familiar with the situation, and recounted parts of the conversation. At no time did he mention to the friend that the call from Michael had been 'weird' or different.

He said he went home about midnight and was woken up at 4 am with the horrible news of Michael's death.

I believe Bob's account of the call. I spoke with him on the phone a month after Michael's death while I was in Bali, and what he told me then is mirrored in his statement to the police, which I have been quoting above. I also believe his account shows Michael under enormous stress, exasperated, desperate.

The phone argument is confirmed by Gail Coward, who was next door in room 523. At around 5 am she was woken by a loud voice in the room next door yelling, 'She's not your wife, she's your ex-wife', and various expletives.

At 6.09 am Michael rang Michele Bennett, leaving a message on her machine to return his call. There were no more calls from Michael's room after that until 9.42 am, and one can presume that Michael slept.

At approximately 9.30 am, Gail Coward heard a loud thump come from the next room, as if somebody had fallen out of bed. She then heard a male voice groan or say something like 'Owhh'.

This may explain the cut above Michael's eye. There was a napkin on his desk with a small amount of blood on it next to an open bandaid packet and empty wrappers, and used bandaids in the bathroom rubbish bin.

At 9.42 am he rang Martha Troup in New York and left a message via voice mail, the often-quoted, 'Martha, Michael here. I fucking had enough'. Phone records reveal he was on the phone for a minute and a half, though what else he said, if anything, isn't recorded. She rang the hotel back immediately, but the phone rang out. At 9.51 am he rang Martha back, this time talking to her home message machine for a minute.

His voice sounded deep and slow, which alarmed Martha enough for her to call the tour manager, John Martin, about her concerns. Even though John says he just thought Michael was tired and needed to sleep, if he got the call in time, in many ways it might have been a lost chance to save Michael.

Martha states she had known Michael for twelve years, and in that time he confided everything to her. Lately she had also been helping him set up a deal for Paula with an Australian TV station to make a six-part series. She says Michael was nervous about the

Australian tour and was having self-doubts. He had wanted to pursue a solo career in music and film. Martha had never worried about suicide, but she had a fear he might lose it mentally. He had also been concerned about the amount of money he had been spending in the courts, which she says was a huge issue.

At 9.54 am, Michael made his last call, to Michele Bennett's mobile. Michele answered. 'I heard your call. Maybe we should get together later in the day, rather than breakfast'.

'No, I want to see you', Michael said.

'Don't you think you should get some sleep?'

'I've been asleep.'

'Why don't we have dinner instead then?' At this point Michael started to cry and Michele could tell he was upset.

'I need you.'

'Look, I'll have a shower and come straight down. I'm in Randwick, fifteen minutes away, so I'll see you soon'.

'Alright.'

During this part of the conversation, Michele states, he was continually crying, and didn't sound drunk, just tired. Michele then suggested to Michael that he should notify somebody that he was not going to rehearsal and get some sleep.

At 10.15 am Michele arrived at the Ritz Carlton. After ringing his room and knocking on his door and getting no response, she wrote a note and had the hotel slip it under his door.

Hi M
10.15 am
You have obviously crashed. I must have taken too long. Call me on the mobile if you have the time before rehearsals. I'm in and around Double Bay. Call me anyway I am worried about you.
Love MB x

When Michele got home around 1 pm, she received a call from Jenny Morris who asked her if she had had breakfast with Michael. Michele told her that she had gone over and knocked, but he was asleep. Jenny then told her that she had heard Michael was dead.

Michele is one of the sweetest, nicest girls I've ever met, and I cannot imagine what she would have gone through upon finding out that she made the effort and it was maybe all too late. Michael had been asleep alright when she knocked—forever—the terrible reality of it merely obscured by a closed door.

There are a number of factors to go over. It is interesting to me that Andrew stated that Michael made a lot of telephone calls while he and Kym were in the room—that he rang Martha twice, Nick Cave, and Paula. Nick was called at 4.15 am, Paula at 5.31 am, and Martha not until 9.42 am then 9.51 am. Maybe Andrew was mistaken as they left at around 4.50 am, as he states, or at 4.40 am, as Kym states, arriving home at about 5.10 am. He could have been referring to the time when Martha called Michael, which he thought was about an hour after they had been in the room. Both think they arrived at around 11 pm and stayed in the bar for not long at all, Andrew saying about a minute, before heading up to Michael's room, which would put Martha's call at around midnight, quite early in the piece.

Albert Vega, the last staff member to see Michael, when he chased them to the lifts to sign the bar bill, puts the time at 11.50 pm. They must have stayed downstairs in the bar longer than Andrew recalled. Maybe Andrew thought Michael made a call to Paula instead of receiving one. They must have been there for the call to Nick at 4.15 am, otherwise how would Andrew know about it and why would he mention it?

Interesting too, is Michael's belt. Two of the things that Kym says in her statement concern his belt. She states that when they arrived in the room there were clothes on the chair, so she moved them and sat on a large chair. Andrew was sitting on a chair at the desk. Later she states she remembered when she was moving clothes off a chair that she saw a leather belt with a silver buckle that reminded her of a Country Road belt of which she had the women's version. Which is basically what she had told me the day after Michael died, apart from the Country Road bit.

'When we arrived,' she said in her statement, 'we ordered daiquiris. Michael was sitting on the bed and we sat at the desk near the window. So that we weren't yelling across the room, I moved to the chair (couch) near the bed. I had to move clothes off the chair and put them on the floor, and I saw the belt.'

While making his statement, Andrew was shown a photograph by Inspector Duclos of a belt attached to the rear of a door. Andrew thought the belt was similar to one he had seen on a pair of dark trousers. He had first noticed the trousers when he had moved them off a chair that he sat on near the desk. Intriguingly, Kym says she was the one who moved the trousers with the belt. Michael had only one belt with him, the one he used. Perhaps they both moved the trousers.

Basically I have a belief that things may have happened a little differently that night in the room. Not too differently, just in another way. I dismiss the idea of any drug-fuelled orgies, as some English papers reported. Even if that were the truth, would it have made things easier for those grieving, by having a clearer under-standing? To find out that Michael spent his last night doing crack with five lady boys and two hookers and bonking a chicken would not help explain his absence now.

Though I could be one hundred per cent wrong, I believe that more drugs were involved. Not a lot, maybe a gram or two.

Both Kym and Andrew may have suffered negative publicity if they had been associated with the consumption of illegal drugs. Already, their mere association with the event is slightly notorious.

So do I go on and spell it out? Many of us have done a couple of grams with a few friends on a Friday night, and the last thing one would suspect would be what transpired on that one. I will outline my concerns and questions, you will supply the outcomes and answers. If there are any.

What happened to the two ripped empty plastic bags? Neither of them was found in the room. And if Kym or Andrew had flushed them while there, or known how they were disposed of, why would they even mention that there was any powdery sub-stance involved that night? After all, the evidence would be gone.

That is, apart from what may be detected in a blood sample, but that too would be untraceable after four or five days. The question one is left with is did Michael flush those bags away after they left, and were Kym and Andrew left with the scary scenario of not knowing what had happened to them, and so choosing their words with enormous care when giving their statements to the police, such as giving 'leftovers' as enough of an explanation of what was inside, or in Andrew's case saying you weren't paying attention to powdery substances in plastic bags being presented before you, and attempting to ignore them?

I do find it odd that the last two people known to be with Michael took four and five days after the event to make their police statements. And that their statements were made a day apart. Why take so long?

Then there is the matter of the 'lucky dollar' that Michael wanted Kym to have, and which she gave me the following evening. (And which I sadly lost years later on a bus in Laos.) The only other money found in the room was in the pocket of the jeans he was wearing. If Michael signed for everything at the hotel, what was a dollar note doing out, and how had it come into conversation?

Four times in her statement Kym mentions that she and Andrew were tired and half asleep. Andrew mentions five times being tired and almost falling asleep. Then both state that when back at home, in Andrew's single bed, they fell straight asleep.

One would assume that in the presence of a 'star', upon first meet, greet, and get to know, as it was for Andrew, one would be excited, alert, and not falling asleep. Yet he was at constant pains to tell us how tired he was. Is this a case of the lady (and gentleman) doth protest too much, methinks? Please don't get me wrong—I am not trying to insinuate any diabolical scenarios or blame anything on anybody, especially Kym and Andrew. I honestly believe that they had nothing to do with Michael's death. But being his only full sibling has me searching for answers, and the truth.

New South Wales Health's Division of Analytical Laboratories' toxicology report indicates the presence of alcohol, and illegal and prescription drugs, in Michael's blood, urine, and bile.

The screening for drugs in his blood detects the presence of alcohol (0.116 per 100 ml of blood), cocaine (0.05mg/l), diazepam (Valium) (0.1 mg/l), nordiazepam (0.1 mg/l), fluoxetine (Prozac) (0.1mg/l). Other than the blood–alcohol level, which is more than two-thirds of the level at which 50 per cent of people would be grossly intoxicated, the levels of the drugs are in the official 'therapeutic range'.

However, there has been considerable debate about the effects of central nervous system-depressant drugs such as Prozac. Combined with alcohol and cocaine it may form a deadly combination. There are many tragic stories on the Internet about people with no previous suicidal tendencies who have taken their own lives under their combined influence.

In Michael's urine there was cocaine detected at 1.6mg/l. Does this indicate recent consumption of more than just 'leftovers'? I have a pharmacological opinion that the concentration shows that he took cocaine that night. The opinion also informed me that cocaine may become more toxic when combined with alcohol, and that it can make the side effects of CNS-depressant drugs more powerful.

The Coroner's report reveals little. He puts the time of death as between 9.54 am and 11.55 am on 22 November 1997. He mentions old frontal and temporal contusions (possibly from the incident in Copenhagen), and the healing burn between the left second and third fingers. It was 12 mm in diameter, with a separate round 5 mm area. There was a small laceration on his left eyebrow and another abrasion and bruise on his left hip, which may have been sustained during hanging. The tongue did not protrude, the hands were not clenched, and there were no scratch marks on the neck. There was a small amount of blood on the lips from the cut on the left eyebrow, and two fragments of white paint on the lips too. A small amount of semen was found. The Coroner believed the belt broke during attempts to enter the room.

After Michael died, some items went missing from his room. One of the first detectives on the case told Michele that he had seen a CD, an undeveloped roll of film, Michael's digital camera and some lyrics on notepaper, half finished and dated 20 November 1997. None of these items was ever recovered or even listed as his personal items in the police inventory. I asked Martha if she knew if Michael would have had those things with him at the time, and she said that Erin would know, as she was the one who had packed his suitcase in LA before he left for Sydney. Martha never got back to me about it, and the detective in question was dismissed from the case early on after he gave out Michele's name and address to the press although she had asked to remain anonymous.

The missing items surfaced for a day or so after Michael's death, with the word being they were offered for sale for $100,000 to the first bidder. The detectives tried to follow up the lead, but to no avail. The items, like most of what Michael owned during his life, disappeared after his death.

So too the luggage he had with him at the Ritz Carlton. First it was taken to Rose Bay police station, and then Colin Diamond picked it up so he could get the Vivienne Westwood suit that Michael would be dressed in for his funeral. In point of fact, the suit was not in Michael's luggage at all. It came from his stage wardrobe, which was probably at the ABC studios at Gore Hill, where the band was rehearsing. I also wonder what happened to the rest of Michael's stage wardrobe.

Colin later gave the luggage he took from the police station to Paula, who took it back to London. The family members never even saw it. All we saw or received was the police inventory (see Appendix 1), Michael's everything on three pages.

We didn't even find out what happened to the luggage until Dad went to Rose Bay Police Station to try to pick up Michael's possessions the weekend after the funeral, and was shocked to find Colin had already picked it up, and even more upset when the insensitive policeman said 'You might want this though', and tossed over the counter a plastic bag containing the broken belt Michael had used.

When I look at the police inventory, one thing in particular sticks out for me. Plastic Bag 1 contained items collected from the bedside table and desk, and Plastic Bag 2 contained the bathroom contents and anything else that was left about. Apart from the odd shirt or pair of jeans, most of Michael's clothing remained unpacked in his two suitcases. (And, contrary to media reports at the time, the floor was not strewn with prescription drugs.)

What catches my eye most is an X ring-bolt screw, purchased from Laurel Hardware, in Plastic Bag 1, especially when I think of how Martha had once mentioned to me that Michael had said at the Chateau Marmont, 'Martha, I'm going to get into trouble'. It bugged me why Michael would be carrying a ring-bolt screw with him. So much so that I went back to the Glebe Morgue to see the photos again to see where it was.

Unfortunately, the photos revealed little, in that I couldn't see the ring-bolt screw anywhere. Perhaps it had been covered or obscured by something. However, it may explain the two tiny pock marks Mandy and I noticed in the ceiling just outside the bathroom door, within arm's reach of where Michael was found. Other than the door-closing mechanism, there was nothing else in the room that could have been used to tie anything onto. If he had, however, managed to get the ring-bolt screwed in, it would have been very noticeable—and yes, 'Martha, I'm going to get into trouble'.

The other key figure in this whole affair is Erin, the girl Michael had been seeing on the American leg of the INXS tour. Michael's phone records at the Ritz Carlton indicate numerous calls to her in Los Angeles. I know her name to be Erin, though my Mum and Tina refer to her in their book as Blair (perhaps to try to hide her identity). And to add to the mystery, one of the phone messages in Michael's room says 'Please ring Jessica', with the return phone number being the one I know to be Erin's.

Whatever her name is, I believe she holds some of the missing details. She was one of the last people to speak with him on the phone, and given that they were involved with each other he must have let on how he was feeling. Mum and Tina have kept in touch with Erin/Blair/Jessica over the years, however for some reason have always refused to give me any more details such as her real name or her current phone number. Whatever their reasons are, it seems they don't want me to contact her.

I've also heard from various sources that during the American leg of the tour, Michael had been seeing two girls, supposedly high-class callgirls who were into S&M and drugs, mainly heroin. Over this time Michael had become rather fond of one of them to the point where he was even planning on leaving Paula for her. I believe he wanted to get Paula to Australia, get her settled with a job on television, and then it would be easier to make the break with her so that he could be with his new love interest.

My understanding is that Erin travelled with Michael on most of the American leg and was being introduced to others as a reporter doing an article on him or the band.

So...? What do I think happened? For years I thought it was an instance of auto-erotica asphyxiation, but now I'm coming to the view of a man strained to bursting point, who makes a bad decision on the spur of the moment.

The most frustrating thing is that the evidence is inconclusive, seeming to stack up for each explanation.

The ring-bolt screw found in his room, ceiling pock marks consistent with him perhaps trying to screw it in, his inclination for sexual adventure, the ring-bolt episode at the Chateau Marmont with 'Martha I'm going to get into trouble', the fact that Michael was found naked and the presence of semen, could all possibly indicate a sexual release gone wrong.

But on the other hand the presence of the chemical cocktail in his blood, his anguish at the outcome of Paula's court proceedings in London, the argument with Bob Geldof, crying to Michele Bennett, the note 'Mr River is not going to rehearsal today', his involvement with Erin in Los Angeles which in itself was casting a heavy cloud over his future with Paula and Tiger, and the 'I've fucking had enough' call to Martha, all point to a man clearly in a highly agitated state. Plus he'd just fallen out of bed and bumped his head after only three hours sleep. Given that combination of factors, entertaining the thought of suicide might not be so inexplicable.

We should also take Michael's stated money problems into account. He had complained about having them for some time. Martha Troup had also mentioned he was worried about money. Unencumbered properties had been mortgaged. There were Paula's mounting legal bills, which he was meeting. Plus there was his agreement with Colin Diamond, which was about to expire, though whether this was more of a problem for Michael or Colin, I can't say. But one would have thought they would have been negotiating to renew it.

There's also the matter of the band. For many years he had wanted to pursue a solo career, as this unposted letter to Michele way back in the 1980s, during one of the band's first European tours, indicates.

Dear Michele,

I'm on the coach going back to Paris. We've been to Brussels tonight. It's a great city. We had a top 20 single there!? We played with Hall & Oates again, but it must have been one of the best shows we have done in Europe. It's very hard here for us, it's so slow on the charts etc. As with everything, I've never felt so insignificant as in Europe. I can't speak the language. We don't play enough. And I might as well be in Siberia as far as my own feelings are concerned.

You know already how I've been feeling about the band. It's so hard to abandon my own ideals concerning INXS. As I go back to first form with Andrew and we have all grown up together. But now I am starting to desperately need my own space from everyone in fact. Some days I just can't see anything good in anybody in the band.

It's all become so competitive that I have become a very squashed person. I used to be everyone's Svengali like friend. Someone with respect. Now I have little respect. My creativity has been cut off because why should I work so hard for people that treat me like a joke? Either that or it's pure competitive jealousy which is just as bad of course.

Maybe it's my problem. All I know is that nobody in the band listens to me anymore. This next album is my last if it doesn't happen big everywhere. I want us to have a good quality lifestyle. I know you and I would use any wealth to it's best use. I'm so sick of gracefully letting off 5 people all the time for their ignorant small mind pretentious attitudes. My God I'm so nice to them. Why do I let people get away with so much before I get angry? I suppose I'm toooo nice to them. The problem is that any time I make realistic comment on anybody I get a barrage of 'well aren't you hip, or clever. or a cunt' etc., etc. It's pathetic really because I don't think I'm any better than anyone I just want some understanding from this band—not petty middle class individual against the world shit. Anyway I thought how I'd just let you know how I'm truly feeling these days.

So…? What actually happened was that Michael, a beautiful man, left us. Having lived a very very full life already, if Michael did decide to take a bow, well I have to respect that too. In many ways Michael was just an ordinary person who had an extraordinary life.

What I learned from the whole episode is the brevity of life, and how abruptly it can come to an end, and how important it is to tell family and friends that I love them. You never know when a bus is going to fall out of the sky and kill you.

Mr River is not going to rehearsal.

The rest is mystery.

a matter of trust

Michael's missing millions are really worthy of their own book, though the complex weave of structures that were set up for asset protection and tax minimisation would only leave the most eager legal team or investigative journalists more frustrated, still confused and scratching their heads. Time has covered well-worn tracks and I fear it's too late now for any real justice to prevail. And though it is less physically and mentally taxing to try to explain in one sentence, I will state what I know and believe, and try to give it some justice after all, if only for Michael's sake. If Michael left us with one terrible legacy, it was in regards to his estate. Oh, the tangled web we unweave.

Basically, in layman's terms, Michael entered into an asset protection and tax avoidance scheme operated through trust funds. Participants would turn over their assets in the form of cash or documents which would be exported to Hong Kong, then whizzed around the world via the tax havens of the Cayman Islands, the British Virgin Islands, Liberia, Monaco and the like. The assets would then be lent back to their original owners. Thus the status of the former assets would change to debts, saving big on tax, marital payouts to estranged spouses and so on. So Michael got his financial affairs in order, and while he was alive it worked well and in his favour, or so it seemed to him at least.

Got it? Good—'cause this is where it starts to get tricky.

Michael's last will and testament is clearly black and white, though the copy that was originally faxed to me, like his estate, has now faded to obscurity. It was drawn up and signed in the week following the London opium kerfuffle when Michael and Tiger, Mandy and Zoe, Colin Diamond and Tony Woodhall had flown up to the Gold Coast and stayed at the Isle of Capri house.

Not one beneficiary has ever sighted the original will. Instead we were informed by the executors that if we wished to see it we were welcome to come to Hong Kong and make an application at the Probate Registry where it's being held.

There are a number of points of interest in the document.

Given the assumption that one is supposed to be of sound mind and body while making one's will, Michael's seems flawed from the start. Why Michael would suddenly decide to revise and rewrite his will, when only a few days before opium had been discovered at the house in London, is astounding. The Michael whom Mandy and I observed over that period was someone clearly agitated, pre-occupied, and engrossed in what was going on back in London.

Mandy told me later that Michael had seemed fully under Colin's thumb while they were at the house, with Colin constantly telling Michael what to do and what not to do. Colin had seemed up-beat, working at his office during the day and coming home in the evening to cook dinner. Then one evening Colin mentioned that as they didn't get together that often, they should make use of their time and get Michael's affairs in order and started drawing up a new will.

Michael went into Diamond's office at Nobby Beach on 3 October 1996, and signed his life away, with Colin and his brother Stephen, also a lawyer, serving as the witnesses. Towards the end of the week, Michael was acting like a caged animal, clearly and loudly expressing his anger at being told what to do and when and how to do it. One can only take so much advice.

In his will, Michael appoints Colin Thomas Diamond and Andrew Morrison Paul (Michael's Hong Kong accountant), as joint trustees and executors. This came as a complete surprise to Andrew Paul, who had no idea of his duties until contacted by Mum to get a copy of Michael's will. I have no idea why Andrew was not notified of being co-executor until after Michael's death if Colin knew all along. Michael also appointed Colin, during his life and after Colin's death whomever Colin's will appointed, to be the guardian or guardians of Tiger during her minority.

Michael first bequeaths US$250,000 to Amnesty International, then another US$250,000 to Greenpeace

Australia, as token gestures. He'd done charity work with them before, and liked their causes. The remainder of his estate was to be broken up amongst the other beneficiaries, with Tiger getting 50 per cent, then 10 per cent for Mum, Dad, Tina, Paula and myself. Clear enough.

With Amnesty and Greenpeace getting the first US$500,000, Michael must have thought he had some serious money at the time, otherwise it would jeopardise the amount that the other beneficiaries might receive—and especially, his own daughter.

Odd too that three of his family beneficiaries have their names documented incorrectly. Mum is referred to as 'Anne', which Michael should have noticed was a mistake as we'd often joked that her real name was Agnes. Tina is called 'Christina Ellen', when her real name is Christina Elaine. Then Michael managed to let his daughter's middle name be misspelt as Heavenly 'Hirani' Tiger Lily instead of 'Hiraani'. In his previous 1992 will, which also named Mum and Tina as beneficiaries, as well as myself and Dad (who was also appointed co-executor along with Colin Diamond), there were no mistakes.

Like many wills, Michael's will then states that Colin and Andrew, along with the powers vested in trustees by law, have additional powers, such as the right to postpone the sale of any of the estate as long as they see fit; the right to hire or lease any part or parts of the estate for any period under any terms; the right to invest any monies in any investments; and the right to use the monies in their absolute discretion, as they see fit, in order to exercise any of the powers vested in themselves. As is normal, the trustees had absolute power over Michael's estate, which was a constant source of frustration for us members of the family.

The disagreements started very early, three days after Michael's death, actually, when Colin informed the funeral director, Rodney Claxton of Walter Carter Funerals, that Michael had specifically stated in his will that he wished to be cremated. Colin even signed a statuary declaration to that effect, giving Michael's address as 13–17 La Spezia Court, Isle of Capri, Queensland. It was witnessed by Stephen, again, who acted as a Justice of the

Peace, so it must have all seemed kosher. The statutory declaration in fact stated that all near relatives had been informed of the cremation, no near relatives had expressed any objection to the cremation, and that Michael had left written instructions for the method of the disposal of his remains, being cremation.

Colin also informed Rodney Claxton that Michael's ashes were to be picked up by him only. Control freak, isn't he. Colin told Dad he did this to stop Paula taking the ashes home, even though I think a de facto is normally the last in line to receive any ashes, especially if there are any close relatives still alive. If the fight in the limousine on the way home from the cremation hadn't helped split up the family already, the ensuing tug of war over Michael's mortal remains would certainly seal that fate. And without the family standing united, fighting and bickering ensued and soon most beneficiaries were only talking through their lawyers, or the media, in tit-for-tat slagging matches.

What happened in the months and years after Michael's death was extraordinary. Upon inquiring about what the family thought to be Michael's assets, we were told by the executors that he didn't own any. All the properties had in fact never been owned by Michael. Instead, they were owned by various companies in the form of discretionary trusts. And these trusts are tight as a guppy's butt. We were told that Michael's estate had nothing to do with Michael's trusts and Michael's trusts had nothing to do with Michael's estate. Oh, and he died technically bankrupt, with Andrew Paul claiming Michael's net assets at the time of his death to be $1,200,000 with yet-to-be quantified liabilities and legal expenses. Listed under liabilities is the Liberian-based Pokfield Ltd, with the amount of debt 'yet to be quantified'. Andrew Paul then directed any trust inquiries to be handled by Tony James Alford, an accountant of Colin's from Southport, who was as actively associated with Michael's accounting in Australia as Andrew was in Hong Kong.

I guess I had better try to explain these trusts and their workings. Basically, the trusts are set up to hold assets, which are then managed and controlled by a trustee who is appointed by the person making the trust. The trustee then administers the trust's assets in accordance with the wishes outlined in the trust deeds. Named beneficiaries may be entitled to the annual proceeds that the trustee is obliged to distribute, but not to the trust's assets themselves, as the trustee now owns them. The trustee does, however, have a strict duty overseen by the Court of Equity: they must always consider and act in the interest of the beneficiaries.

Mum and Tina retained a lawyer, Joanne Kelly of Murphy & Moloney, to act on their behalf, barely two weeks after Michael died. This was done initially because of the furore over the ashes, and because they were getting nowhere with Colin, who had not contacted them as promised, except to make five appointments that he didn't keep.

Stephen Diamond did, however, write to Mum, barely a week after Michael died, to let her know that he had been named as the Australian solicitor, so Joanne Kelly now had to go through him. Colin certainly kept it all in the family. Stephen's letter went on to state that 'Colin has personally disbursed over $60,000 from his own personal funds to attend to the funeral and associated expenses'. Then, as the only member of the family 'who has any real prospects of paying' for the funeral was Mum, would she reimburse Colin. I have no idea where Colin's $60,000 went, however, as Walter Carter Funerals continued making legal threats with regards to its unpaid bill. Colin then instructed the Hong Kong lawyers to inform Walter Carter that it could 'stand in line with the other unsecured creditors'.

After returning from Bali, Dad retained the services of David Jackson, from Bray, Jackson and Co, to act on his behalf. Instead of taking sides, Dad sat on the fence gathering info, partly secure in the knowledge that Colin had assured him that he and Tiger would be 'looked after'. Words Colin told Dad before Michael's will was released, and a number of times after. These are the same two words that Colin had told Mandy at the reception at the Mezzaluna restaurant after Tiger's christening. He had pulled Mandy to one side to tell her that Michael would have wanted her and Zoe to be 'looked after'.

Paula, and indirectly Tiger, had her own camp. Her best friend Belinda Brewin was the partner of Andrew Young, who was an associate of Colin. So in having the most contact with Colin, she remained fairly noncommittal to any cause except Tiger's, or 'our 60 per cent' as she called it.

I was the only beneficiary without a lawyer. I figured it was only going to cost me money I didn't have, and as I was gathering enough information through Mum, Dad and various other sources, every now and then I'd fire off a 'twenty perfectly normal discrepancy questions' fax to Andrew, only to receive ten unacceptable answers. After a while I stopped inquiring so much when I was informed that expenses were being incurred on the limited (and diminishing) resources of the estate to answer the various matters I was raising. Well…excuse me.

In May 1998, after an article by the *Sydney Morning Herald* entitled 'Michael's Missing Millions', and hearing of the impending litigation against the estate, Colin renounced his estate duties, making Andrew Paul the sole executor of Michael's estate. Being named as a co-executor in the previous will, Dad offered his services as a joint executor, but was refused by Mr Paul.

In July 1998, Colin and Andrew Young, with his 'roving brief', gave their first and only interview with regards to Michael's missing millions, in the first and only issue of *AXS* magazine (in which Colin and his associate list themselves as editors), explaining, well, not very much at all. As Colin said, 'None of your business. That's the point; it's private. Don't you guys get it? It's PRIVATE'.

Colin goes on to say that he relinquished his role, 'because the lawyers in Australia felt there was a potential conflict of interest if I remained executor of the will or a director of a trustee company'. Colin also said he had 'resigned as a director of any relevant trust company'. One would think that Colin must have foreseen that there might be a potential conflict of interest in being appointed Michael's executor, as he was already a director of various companies.

When Colin was asked who was paying his fees, he responded, 'I'm not getting paid and won't be. There's not even a remuneration clause in the will. I'm doing this as a service to Michael. I'm not only not being paid, in fact I'm out of pocket'.

Odd then that he should also say that as far as he was concerned, 'I owe it to Michael to retain a long-term interest in his affairs and to ensure Michael's instructions are carried out, most importantly, to the best of my ability that Tiger is looked after'. Six months is not a very long time Colin. Now out of the 'missing' picture, Colin still continued to pull strings, even if only as one of Tiger's guardians.

On 25 November 1998, exactly one year after Colin had signed the statuary declaration stating Michael's address to be 13–17 La Spezia Court, Isle of Capri, Queensland, the last will and testament was proved and registered in the High Court of Hong Kong, with probate granted to Andrew Paul, to pay the 'just debts' and the legacies of Michael Kelland Hutchence, late of 18 Redburn St, Chelsea, London SW3, England. This was originally Paula's house, though after leaving Bob, she had signed it over to him and he now paid the mortgage. The Australian Securities and Investments Commission had Michael's address, up until his death, as 18 Tai Tam Road, Hong Kong.

The Hong Kong Inland Revenue Department declared the principal value of Michael's estate to be HK$883,992, with $625,123 of that being the insurance value of the container that Michael had in storage. Take away the storage charges and what he owed to Visa and American Express, and the net principal value of Michael's estate dropped to HK$543,284.

Around the same time, Dad told me that he had received a letter from Diamond's solicitors, Walsh and Partners of Bundall, Queensland, saying in no uncertain terms that Colin wanted nothing more to do with him. Every time Dad tried to pin him down for further talks, Colin was too busy to respond to the faxes Dad sent, even the ones regarding Tiger, of whom he was supposed to be guardian.

In early 1999, Mum and Tina, through Joanne Kelly, started proceedings which turned into a writ being lodged with the Queensland Supreme Court, seeking to have the monies and assets Michael had placed in the various trusts made part of his estate.

Andrew Paul, meanwhile, appointed Colin Cohen of the Hong Kong firm of Boase Cohen & Collins, to handle his affairs. Colin Cohen appointed the Australian legal firm, Hopwood Ganim, to serve as attorneys in the impending Queensland proceedings, who in turn lodged a successful application for Andrew Paul to defend the challenge and have all his legal costs paid by Michael's estate.

In June 1999, at the expense of the estate, Colin Cohen flew business class into Sydney and checked into The Observatory, an up-market hotel in the Rocks. He was there to hold a without-prejudice meeting with beneficiaries and their relevant lawyers to see if an overall settlement could be reached without further expenses being incurred before going to court. Like, say, flying to Sydney for a chat.

I attended the meetings armed only with a long list of very relevant questions regarding discrepancies and typos in Michael's estate documents and trusts. It was a complete waste of time and money as far as I was concerned, as Colin had not one answer for me. He had two, 'I don't know', and 'I can't answer that'. The only thing to come out of that meeting was that Colin brought over Michael's gold records and awards from the Hong Kong container.

By September 1999, Amnesty International had joined Mum and Tina as plaintiffs, to try to recover the missing assets. The defendants were, ahem, Colin Diamond, Andrew Paul, and the various structures which purportedly owned the Queensland properties (the Isle of Capri house, a bowling alley in Nerang, and a large block of land in the heart of Southport); the house in the south of France; 48 Smith Terrace, Chelsea; V2 Music Group Ltd; and the ownership of Michael's IP (Intellectual Property) rights, or royalties, as a solo artist or with INXS.

And you don't get to go to the Supreme Court for nothing, for lack of evidence. Over time and with hard work, Joanne had managed to accumulate quite a substantial case. However, these things cost money and lots of it. For instance, Joanne being a New South Wales lawyer was not allowed to practise in Queensland, so even more lawyers were needed, whom she could only brief. So the lawyers needed lawyers.

Before any litigation was to proceed, mediation was held in May 2000, before the Queensland action was settled. Mum and Tina, having spent over $500,000 of their own money (or Ross's anyway) on legal fees, were basically told that the defendants love going to court, till the cows come home, it's what they do, being lawyers and all. It was going to continue to cost a fortune for Mum, Tina and the estate to pursue their claims and they would probably have to sell their house to finance everything. Mum and Tina were then advised to settle in mediation if they couldn't afford to stay in court for a minimum of six months. If, however, the plaintiffs were to release, discharge and hold harmless the defendants of all claims of any nature whatsoever relating to or arising out of the assets, affairs or estate of Michael Hutchence, they would be reimbursed $400,000, by Colin and a crony of his, Tony Alford, and the various structures (excluding Leaguework France). Facing an uncertain outcome and further expenses, they took it.

At the beginning of the negotiations, Mum and Tina had offered to drop all lawsuits against the defendants if they would put everything in Tiger's name. The defendants agreed under the condition that they could still continue to control all the monies. Not surprisingly, Mum wanted someone other than Colin as trustee, and unsurprisingly to me, Colin Diamond refused.

Though the litigation that Mum and Tina brought against the estate was an attempt to demonstrate their belief that these structures were in effect 'shams', it only really succeeded in costing the estate a hell of a lot of money, driving it even more quickly into insolvency. Had they continued with the litigation, it may have had a double-barrelled effect. In having the structures included in the estate, they may not have been as tax-effective, so could have ended up being worth less than thought anyway.

In fact, the Supreme Court proceedings would have been near impossible to resolve. With most of Michael's assets tied up in structures that were established in tax havens, it would be very hard to establish the true value of any assets and find out who were, or are, the major beneficiaries.

This was all taking place during the time when Mum and Dad were still not talking. For the previous year I had been having phone negotiations with Mum and Dad, her bitching in one ear and him in the other, until I finally got them to come to their senses and see as one. But by then it was all too late.

On 15 September 2000, all beneficiaries of Michael's will were faxed a letter with regards to his estate. In it, they asked us to consider, and in Tiger's best interests, to take a compromise. If the compromise was rejected, it would be detrimental to the estate, and mainly Tiger. Andrew Paul stated that the interests of Tiger should be regarded as paramount.

With regards to the value of the estate, the cupboard was bare. The family members had now become residuary beneficiaries, meaning that there would be nothing left for us after the pecuniary beneficiaries Amnesty and Greenpeace were paid, if they were paid at all. Given the likelihood that there would be no distribution among the residuary beneficiaries, Tiger's interest had no value. After all, 50 per cent of nothing is...

We hardly had time to go over the document, as two days after receiving it, Paula died. I've always believed Paula's overdose and subsequent death to be an accident, but she did have a slight death wish, and that news may have been her last straw. After all, 60 per cent of nothing is...

Interesting that Paula's last will and testament, drawn up and witnessed by Andrew Young, is dated 22 December 1997, exactly one month after Michael died. It seems to me that Paula would not have been in the right frame of mind to think clearly about the matter at hand. Oddly, the will gives Paula's address as 48 Smith Terrace, Chelsea, SW3, London. This is the house that Michael was renovating, and he actually never got to live there.

One strange stipulation in her will is that Tiger Lily should have no access to Michael's parents without prior approval of the guardians she appointed, Martha Troup and her husband Bill Liebowitz. Oh, and no need to phone a friend. Guess who the executors and trustees of Paula's last will and testament are? Belinda Brewin, and, you guessed it, Colin Diamond.

With Tiger now an orphan, and her future soon to be decided by the English High Court, most beneficiaries took the compromise, and in March 2001 the Supreme Court of Queensland approved the compromise agreement.

So, what are or were the assets that Mum and Tina sought to have included in Michael's estate?

INTELLECTUAL PROPERTY RIGHTS

As for royalties, things had got a hell of a lot more complicated since June 1980, when INXS had received their first royalty cheque for their just released first single, 'Simple Simon/We Are The Vegetables', which came to the grand total of $35.86.

In 1985 INXS signed over their rights to publishing royalties to a company called Tol Muziek, which was acting as an agent for PFL International (Pacific) Ltd. There were two assignments issued, one relating to publishing IP (Intellectual Property rights) created before November 1985 and the other relating to IP created after that. The General Manager of PFL International (Pacific) Ltd was Michael's financial adviser, a Scottish barrister and international taxation specialist named Gordon William Fisher.

Gordon Fisher was also a former partner of the law firm Allen Allen & Hemsley who suddenly left Australia for Hong Kong in 1986. Fisher was involved in a complex tax minimisation scheme that collapsed in 1989 and was subsequently investigated by the Australian Federal Police. Charges were never laid. Gordon has never returned to Australia, not even for his divorce or his daughter's wedding.

In May 1986 Michael, then a resident of Australia, entered into a contract with Narestock Ltd, owned then and until early 1999 by Gordon, and his associate, another Scot, Andrew Paul, in which Michael assigned to Narestock all of his existing and yet unassigned IP rights and their royalties. Narestock also had the power to exploit the 'Narestock Rights' for profit.

With the amount of money coming in, in order to keep as much of it as possible, it was time for Michael to do something. The year before, Michael had invested $15,000 trying to write off some tax as a film industry incentive deduction. This only worked in your favour if the film flopped. The film was *Crocodile Dundee*, which went on to gross millions, causing more of a concern than was intended. Michael then invested in *Les Patterson Saves The World*, which did serve its desired purpose.

Michael, following financial advice from his Australian accountant, Sandy Arnold, and Gordon, moved to Hong Kong, and by December 1986 had entered in to an employment contract with PFL International (Pacific) (Gordon Fisher, director), trading as Rimpac Entertainment and Promotion, as their Director of Entertainment and Promotion. This was done to help him obtain a Hong Kong residency permit.

The move excluded Michael from paying any more Australian taxes. As long as he was seen by the Australian Taxation Office as a non-resident, and appeared to use Hong Kong as his home base he would be alright—that is, drop in on the way to and from overseas assignments, spend parts of breaks there, and don't spend more than six months a year in Australia, making his trips 'home' primarily for work and holidays. And as an added bonus, as Colin had once told me with regards to Michael paying Hong Kong tax, 'If you don't generate the money in Hong Kong, you don't pay any tax'.

In January 1987 Michael entered into two further contracts with Narestock; one a contract for services, the other a Deed of Restrictive Covenant. Pursuant to these contracts, Michael agreed that all future intellectual property rights arising from his efforts, including rights to individual works (for example, the *Max Q* album) during the seven-year term of the contract were to belong to Narestock, in its capacity as the trustee of the 'Expatriate Trust'. The sole beneficiary of the 'Expatriate Trust' was Yip Fung Trading Company Ltd, then owned and controlled by Gordon Fisher and Andrew Paul. The company was the sole beneficiary of the 'Expatriate Trust' in its capacity as the trustee of the 'Vocals Trust'.

The 'Vocals Trust' was, in effect, the ultimate holding vehicle for Michael. Michael was not a beneficiary of the 'Vocals Trust' but the 'protector' of it. This was on Gordon's advice, because Michael wished to be in a position whereby his assets would be protected from and against third parties. In a letter that Gordon Fisher wrote to Boase Cohen & Collins explaining the structure surrounding the intellectual property rights, Gordon said that the asset protection trust secured Michael against what Michael had called, according to Gordon: '(a) his "thieving relatives"; (b) his "girlfriends"; and (c) in the event he married, his wife.' This was all achieved without Michael having to hold, in his own name, whether legally or beneficially, either the excess income generated by the rights, or the rights themselves. Michael had placed complete faith in Gordon and Andrew.

As Narestock Ltd was a UK incorporated company, tax laws at the time said that if it was controlled and managed outside the United Kingdom, it was not subject to UK tax. However the 1988 Finance Act changed all that. All future UK incorporated companies would now be tax resident and companies set up before then had five years to reorganise their affairs. Something had to be done before March 1993 for the new fiscal laws, and also regarding the expiration of the 1987 seven-year contracts.

Things had changed in 1988, though, when Gordon Fisher, after having fallen out with Michael, the rest of the band and its management, and facing legal action over other dealings, suddenly left Hong Kong. He took up residence in Monaco, sharing an office with a chartered accountant, Norman Leighton. Gordon was to stay there until 1991, when he just as suddenly left Monaco and returned to Hong Kong.

In 1992, when the contracts were approaching their expiry date, negotiations were entered into with Michael for an extension. Enter Colin Diamond, a previous associate of Gordon's, and Andrew Paul. When Colin complained that he too had been left in the lurch by Gordon's very sudden departure, Michael, who had taken a liking to Colin, decided to help him out. After both made guarantees to Michael of discontinuing all business relationships with Gordon, Colin and Andrew started reorganising and taking over Michael's affairs. And though Gordon no longer worked with

Michael, he continued relationships with his previous associates, Colin, and Andrew.

With regard to the coming UK fiscal laws, Colin decided it would be best to insert another company between Narestock and Michael, by assigning the 'Narestock Rights' to a UK non-resident company, but keeping Narestock as the legal owner. To the outside world it would seem as if little had changed, however, as any income generated no longer belonged to Narestock, it was therefore not liable to the UK taxation system. The company was Chardonnay Investments Limited, yet another trust company. Chardonnay, acting as an agent for and on behalf of Narestock, was given the authority to license the 'Narestock Rights'. Michael entered into the extension contract with Chardonnay and also established the '1992 Michael Hutchence Discretionary Trust', with Chardonnay Investments acting as Trustee. These contracts were for a period of five years, due to expire in December 1997— the week after Michael's death.

In September 1995, with Michael having left Hong Kong and now living more in the United Kingdom, he entered into another agreement with Narestock, through Chardonnay, in which he agreed to provide services to Narestock, through Chardonnay, for his solo album, then titled *Neo-Junkie Philanderer*. This was done because Colin and Andrew were concerned that, as production of the solo album was to take place in the United Kingdom, Michael might be subject to UK tax laws on all his remuneration under the 1992 contracts. Although Narestock agreed to this specific and separate contract, as Narestock already owned all the intellectual property rights, in and to, Michael's individual works, it was in fact unnecessary, apart from the UK tax exposure point.

Gordon Fisher believes there to be some misapprehension that upon the death of Michael the 'Narestock Rights' would revert to Michael's estate and he insists that by the terms of all contracts Michael entered into with Narestock, whether directly or through Chardonnay, Narestock is the owner, for all time, of the 'Narestock Rights'. Until his death, Michael had received royalties and advances totalling more than US$5 million.

AUSTRALIAN PROPERTY

PARADISE LANES

The Marine Parade bowling alley, Paradise Lanes, which Michael purchased with Colin Diamond, was owned by Nexcess Pty Ltd, as the
trustee of the Broadwater Trust, which was set up in January 1994.

When Dad discovered—through newspaper reports—that he
was listed as a major beneficiary, he told me that he asked Tony
Alford about obtaining copies of any trust documents. Dad said that
Mr Alford told him he was not entitled to any copies as they were
private. Dad later found out he was entitled to copies of the trusts,
which he eventually obtained from the government authority in
Brisbane using a credit card over the phone.

I believe, from what I was told, that there were four beneficiaries
of the trust, two of whom were Tiger and Dad. Dad was removed
as a beneficiary of the trust sometime before March 1999.

ISLE OF CAPRI

Though Michael told me, family members, and many others that he
owned the house at 13–17 La Spezia Court, Isle of Capri, it turned
out that Michael did not own the million dollar waterfront mansion
with its five bedrooms, marble-tiled living area, gazebo, spa, sauna
and private swimming pool. It was in fact purchased by another
trustee company called Sin-Can-Can Pty Ltd.

Colin gave this as Michael's Australian address in the statutory
declaration he wrote, then Tony informed us that 'No part of the
purchase was made by Michael'. Again, at the time of Michael's death, I
understand that Dad was listed as a primary beneficiary along with Tiger
and two others, and once more without reason or notification Dad was
struck off some time before March 1999. It is not clear to me when
Tiger became a beneficiary, as the trust was set up before she was born.

Ironically, 'Sin ken ken' is Balinese for 'No worries'.

THE BENTLEY

Included in the Isle of Capri purchase price was the lovely 1994
Bentley Turbo that Michael and Paula drove down to Byron for

Zoe's naming ceremony. The Bentley had previously been owned by the late Gold Coast hotelier, Stan Elson.

SOUTHPORT

The large commercial development site situated on the corner of Nerang, Garden and Bay streets, Southport, was also under dispute. McLaughlins Solicitors of Southbank, acting on behalf of Nextcircle, contested the claim that any money was advanced by Michael for the purchase of the property. However, without money to support the case, it would be hard to prove that the funds provided by Michael to Byron Ltd were for the purpose of assisting in the purchase of the property so there was little point in pursuing the subject.

THE HARLEY-DAVIDSON

Michael's pride and joy was a Harley-Davidson motorbike, which was looked after by a friend who did occasional security work for Michael. From what I was told, this friend wrote to the estate regarding expenses he was owed for storing the bike in his garage, licence fees/registration, maintenance, and for the parts and accessories that he had bought to fix and upgrade the bike. In lieu of his costs, he apparently asked if he could keep the bike. My understanding was that it would cost more than the bike's value in legal fees to challenge the expenses claim, so it was easier to just let him have the bike. We reluctantly accepted its fate.

In May 2002, I went online and did a search on e-Bay, for anything of Michael's, as I sometimes do, yet what I found that day I didn't expect—Michael's Harley-Davidson up for auction for the mere asking price of £40,000 (considerably more than the estate's original valuation). When it hadn't received any bids after a month, the price was lowered and, not long after, it sold for $56,000 to an entrepreneur who planned to use it as the centre-piece in his new Sydney restaurant.

FRENCH PROPERTY

LA VIELLE FERME DE GUERCHES

The ownership of the villa in France that Michael had lived in since 1991, and of the motor vehicles he garaged there, was under dispute as well. I believed the villa to be Michael's, as did the rest of the family, as he told us it was. Greg Perano even told me that Michael had proudly shown him the title deed while he was staying there.

However, the executors advised Mum that Michael did not purchase, and at the time of his death, did not own a villa in the south of France. Then, in the July 1998 *AXS* interview, Andrew Young insisted that, 'The property in France is owned by a French company and you'll discover they've owned it for over a decade'. So, we were off to a good start.

In a letter from Terry Morris to Boase Cohen & Collins, Mr Morris stated that the property in Roquefort Les Pins was bought in March 1991 by a French company, Leaguework France SARL, which was owned by Leaguework (UK) Limited. Mr Morris is unaware who funded the purchase though he recalls that the ownership plan was devised by Gordon Fisher to avoid French property tax under a UK/French treaty.

In December 1998, Leaguework France sold the villa to Adam Clayton, the bass player from U2.

PERSONAL EFFECTS FROM FRANCE

The five-page inventory of Michael's personal effects and chattels was not made available to beneficiaries until nearly two years after his death, though the date on the inventory states that it was made two days after he died. In it is listed everything in the living room, dining room, studio, kitchen, basement and five bedrooms of the fully furnished house.

From what I understand, three guitars and ten oil paintings were removed from the villa. Apart from the Michael Saker painting that I gave Michael for his thirtieth birthday, which I asked Linda, the house's caretaker, to put aside and send to me with a box of tin toys that I'd left there, and that Mum asked to be returned, everything went with the house, I suppose.

THE ASTON MARTIN DB5

Beep beep and beep beep, no. 'Michael never owned an Aston Martin. He had use of one while in France', Andrew Young stated in the *AXS* interview. I was with Michael in Los Angeles the day he bought his four-wheeled pride and joy. After we literally had a very quick test drive, he purchased it for US$152,000, which I thought was slightly expensive. 'It's worth every penny', he told me, as the aluminium-bodied Superleggera was fully optioned. He planned to send it to his new place in France and being a left-hand drive, it was perfect.

It took more than a year to be shipped over to England, and after registration (UK EGF 354B), it was driven down to the house in the south of France. While I was staying there, I was under strict instructions not to drive it. Michael joked that I wasn't even allowed to look at it or point at it. He considered the car to be his, and certainly treated it as his own.

I believe that the Aston Martin went to Adam Clayton with the house.

THE MERCEDES 300 GD

I don't know who ended up with Michael's Mercedes but I some-times wonder what became of 'Pepé'.

THE PEUGEOT 205 CABRIOLET

Asset statements show a US$10,420 Peugeot in France to be Michael's. *Sacre bleu*, Michael actually owned a car in France.

THE DUCATI

I believe the Ducati 916 Desmoquattro was purchased by Paula as her 1995 Christmas present to Michael, but I don't know where it ended up after Michael's death.

UNITED KINGDOM PROPERTY

48 SMITH TERRACE, CHELSEA

Again, the true ownership of the London terrace was under dispute. And once again, the family was under the impression that it belonged to Michael, and the executors were adamant that it did not. Nothing new there. This was the house Paula was living in when Michael died and she used it as her address in the will she signed only one month later.

Michael was very proud of the house that he never got to live in. He had enlisted Marc Newson, the famous Australian designer, to help with the interior and started extensive renovations not long after the purchase. Michael was excited about the work being done and relished telling me how they had completely knocked down the back wall and replaced it with windows that could be frosted over at the touch of a button, how he could see the stars from the upstairs bedroom, and that there were no joins to be seen in the woodwork. He even planned on installing a lap pool in the basement.

To ascertain the value of the property we got an independent appraisal based on an external examination as we were not allowed inside the house. That being the case, Chestertons Residential gave the informal valuation at £775,000–825,000, mainly based on what similar nearby houses had recently sold for.

It came as quite a shock to discover that the £370,000 house, after over £350,000 worth of refurbishments, was privately sold, as opposed to an auction or tender, during litigation (March 1999), for only £450,000.

CHEROKEE JEEP

Michael's English runabout was sold for £18,785 and the proceeds quickly eaten up in legal fees.

INDONESIAN PROPERTY

LOMBOK

Lombok is an island off Bali, Indonesia, and I first heard of Michael's involvement through Mandy after she had helped him look after Tiger at the Isle of Capri house. Michael had mentioned to her that he had invested in an island off Lombok, Gili Tawan, to build a studio and residence for the family to holiday in, and Colin had shown them a video of the ongoing construction and said it was the only island with natural water. Mandy said it looked beautiful. I'd love to get to the bottom of Michael's Indonesian investment, if anyone can help me. End of story?

HONG KONG PROPERTY

PERSONAL EFFECTS

Beneficiaries were informed that any personal effects of value would be auctioned, and if any beneficiary wished to purchase these items, we could do so once a valuation had been obtained. Then after nearly two years of negotiations and storage fees to Crown Worldwide Storage, Michael's container was finally sent to Sydney in August 1999 for the family to disperse what Colin Cohen called 'items of little or no value'. We were then allowed to got through and choose things we would like to keep and every-one involved was quite amicable. That container held the only things that we ever received from Michael's estate.

The paintings in the container, which we were originally told were of no value, turned out to be: a Norman Lindsay, a Brett Whiteley, a Charles Condor monoprint, a Russell Drysdale, and three Donald Friend's. The auction of the artworks in Sydney at Christie's realised $56,600. After insurance, auctioneer's commission, illustration expenses, bank transfer charges and freight from Hong Kong, the estate received $47,659, which was quickly gobbled up in legal fees. I guess they were of no value after all.

Michael's Alberto Vargas, *Legacy Girl*, and a John Lennon poem *The Poet's Page Alphabet* from 1969, stored in LA, took the same off ramp. I don't know why they called them assets.

SOLO ALBUM

Michael's solo album *Michael Hutchence,* with the working title of *Neo Junkie Philanderer* was finally released in June 1999 on Sir Richard Branson's V2 label. Michael had been working on the album for two years before his death. Initially he had been working with producer Tim Simenon from Bomb the Bass. However, after recording over a dozen songs, one of which, 'The Passenger', was released on the *Batman Forever* soundtrack, Michael thought that things were not going in the direction he had wanted, so he started writing in his 46.47 per cent of his French house with ex-Gang of Four bass player, Andy Gill. The sixteen tracks would later be produced by Danny Saber, whose resume included The Rolling Stones, U2, and David Bowie, with thirteen of them making it onto his album.

The problem was that the album was released while Michael's estate was still in litigation. It's a shame really, as Michael's solo album was worthy of proper recognition. Personally I think it deserved more than the reception it got. Brotherly love aside, I find it cannot be placed into any eighties or nineties category, and remains a significant testimony to what Michael wanted the world to remember him by, apart from the INXS tracks that he co-wrote. No-one will ever know if the running order was the way Michael envisioned, whether all the tracks would have made the final cut, or if production would have turned out the way it did. I would like to think that Michael would have been happy with the final outcome.

DISCRETIONARY TRUST

As the 1992 Michael Hutchence Discretionary Trust seems to turn up a bit, let's look into it. The Deed of Settlement between Michael and Chardonnay Investments Ltd was known as the 1992 Michael Hutchence Discretionary Trust and identifies Chardonnay as the trustee. Discretionary trusts, named because of the absolute discretion vested in the trustee, are even more legally, though not necessarily ethically or morally, binding. I have no idea who the beneficiaries of the Chardonnay trust are now, but I doubt very much whether Dad, Mum, Tina, myself, or even Amnesty are still listed.

In May 1999 Colin's ex-wife, Robyn Diamond, went public and gave an interview to *The Sunday Telegraph* to end the pretence of supporting her ex-husband. Robyn had met him when he was a struggling twenty-three year old solicitor on the Gold Coast. Their lives changed, however, when Colin met Michael in Hong Kong four years later.

And they changed again in 1999, after Robyn was appalled to learn that Colin was allegedly having an affair with her twenty-five year old daughter from her first marriage, Evie, whom Colin had helped raise since she was eight. Evie had been working as Colin's personal assistant the previous year, and has been travelling with him since then.

In the article, Robyn is quoted as saying, 'The greatest irony of Colin's low profile is that he's desperate to be famous. He always wanted to be a pop star, but he can't sing for quids. Colin used to tell me he could sing better than Michael.'

The last time I spoke to the 'hard to pin down' Colin was in July 2003, completely by chance in Bali. I was with Gus Till, a good friend of Michael's and mine, who had previously worked with Michael playing keyboards on the *Max Q* album. We'd just arrived at Ku De Ta, a world-class restaurant and bar in Seminyak, when I walked past a table where Colin was seated having lunch with three women, including Evie.

At first I didn't realise it was him, and he of course made no attempt to acknowledge me, until I said, 'Colin?', to which he nodded. I said hello, told him I was surprised to see him here and asked if he'd join us at the bar after his meal so we could catch up.

I was indeed surprised to see him as Gus and I had only just been talking about him, and Michael's estate, or the lack thereof. Gus knew of Michael's business affairs very well, as one night while staying with him at the house in France, Michael had explained the whole complex arrangement to him…how he had signed over his assets, and how after his royalty cheques were rerouted through various tax havens, that tax-free funds were made available to him via his American Express card.

Colin eventually finished his lunch and came to join us, albeit briefly. I told him that I would like to catch up a bit longer to discuss some things and he told me that would be no problem. Sin ken ken. Colin then invited me over to his hotel, the Ritz Carlton, where we could talk as he was flying out the day after. Thanks mate, see you tomorrow.

Was I surprised when I arrived there to find that they had no-one staying there by that name? No. I wasn't surprised when I rang the other top ten hotels to find they'd never heard of him either. These days he spends his time flying between New Zealand, Indonesia, Hong Kong and Australia.

By December 2001, the accounts stated that Michael's estate had a net value of approximately minus A$7000.

In October 2003, I flew to Hong Kong with my current squeeze, Anmarie, to attend a friend Nichole's fortieth birthday party, and what the heck, I might as well arrange an appointment with Andrew Paul and Colin Cohen while I'm there and see what they have to say. Well, not much at all. They made me feel like I was completely wasting their time during the fifteen minutes that they gave me. Andrew Paul told me he was not being paid and was doing this as a service. I told him, 'Well at least you got to meet a very lovely man'.

In summary, Michael's money has been swallowed up in an impenetrable legal web. And nearly seven years after he died, his estate has still not been finalised. Closure can not be too much longer though.

I guess I was one of the only beneficiaries not to get too upset with regards to the estate. From the start, I didn't think I would be getting any money when it became clear that Michael's tangled financial web would not be unravelled. Anyway, Michael's estate means fuck all to me without Michael in it.

That is, apart from one time I was in Singapore, on my way home from Thailand. I thought I would check my emails, and read on the MSN home page about the estate having been settled. The linked story said that I was to receive $1,000,000 and I let out a suitable 'Wahoo!', much to the surprise and shock of everyone around me. Of course this all turned out to be untrue.

So it seems that certain individuals appear again and again in the scheme of things. These 'specialists' obviously know more of the workings of Michael's estate and trusts than any of the members of his family. Especially the executor Andrew Paul, as he's been the one who was involved with Michael's affairs for the longest, more than ten years.

If Michael's wish had been for his relatives to get sweet fuck all, and for Tiger to be the beneficiary of the structures that were set up, that's fine. However, I believe the executors could have called a meeting with the family to sit us down and explain it all. But they haven't.

Robyn Diamond recalled in her 1999 interview that Colin had called her out of the blue one day to let her know that he had left her $100,000 in his will to run his affairs. 'He said that if he dies, to lock the gates to the farm and don't let any bastard in, then ring Andrew Paul, who'd explain it all to me'. Well I certainly wish he'd explain it to someone.

I wonder if it all worked out how Michael expected?

rewind

Many years ago I wrote a list of things I would like to achieve in my life. From parachuting to scuba diving to riding a Harley-Davidson—forty-odd things I have slowly and surely ticked off. I'm not sure why I thought of it then, however top of the list was WRITE A BOOK.

Why write, why me? Because I do believe that everyone has a book to write, a story to tell, a beginning, a middle, an end. And if they say 'write what you know', then I know about me. A bit about me anyway. Plus, having a memory like a big grey thingy with a long watch-u-call-it helps too.

It's hard to explain the 'why?' to all those years. I just suppose that I was, and am, very lucky to be alive. Over time I lost perspective of what it was and is to be normal, living a daily, day-to-day day.

A typical day. My eyes open, and in my waking thoughts I quickly work out my whereabouts and whether I'm holding. If I'm not, my brain starts plodding through a myriad of information about whether I have any money, either owed to me or coming, that I could juggle to stay afloat.

Then I figure out which dealers are up and their working hours, who has the good stuff, taking into consideration the quality versus hassle factor. Dealers who act like God, keeping you waiting, waiting, waiting, hours or even days, or those who don't wait a second longer than planned, or the ones just too stoned to deal with. If for some reason I don't have a current dealer (busted, not holding, holiday or trying to get clean) I have to ponder which middleman would be best for the least taxing experience. All this in my first waking minute.

I could worry about other things on the way to the dealer, like who I owed money to, and which route I should take to avoid confrontations, to duck and weave. With my eyes down and a slight pep in my step.

At first you think you're getting away with it, fooling everyone, family and friends. Then in no time you don't care any more what anyone thinks. Your long days in Heaven quickly turn to years in Hell. Through it you change and adapt, trying to survive, to feel normal. You lie, cheat, manipulate and cross other lines you never would have crossed before. You learn not to trust anyone, especially yourself. Some don't even learn that.

Horror stories abound, like being severely strung out and having your runny nose drip into your spoon while mixing up. And why is it that after hearing of some 'killer dope' on the streets, you want to go out and get it?

Things have changed now—like the times. I used not to care about life and death, and now I do. For some reason, as if through lack of trying, it is important now for me to be good to myself and others. As if I have slowly matured 'out of it'.

appendix 1

POLICE INVENTORY OF MICHAEL'S HOTEL ROOM.

PLASTIC BAG 1

1 x Black vinyl shoulder bag, Tuesday brand.

1 x Pair of Persol sunglasses in brown leather case.

1 x Salon Lady Jane hairbrush.

1 x Sony micro cassette recorder.

1 x pair of Katherine Hamnett silver framed spectacles in black Chanel glasses case.

1 x American Match brand cigarette lighter.

1 x Australian passport in the name of Michael Kelland Hutchence, containing 1 Canadian employment authorisation in the name of Michael Hutchence.

1 x Manuscript from the Goldstein Company, story *Johnny Nitrate*.

1 x Papyrus brand personal diary in brown leather folder.

1 x Polaroid family photograph.

1 x Airline ticket in the name of Hutchence, Qantas, Sydney.

2 x Blank postcards.

1 x Ring-bolt screw, Laurel Hardware.

1 x American Express Gold Card in the name of Michael Hutchence.

1 x Global key calling card.

1 x Silver gent's wristwatch, IWC brand.

1 x American one dollar note.

2 x American quarter coins.

1 x American dime coin.

1 x American five cent coin.

3 x American one cent coins.

1 x fifty Rupiah coin.

2 x one pound coins.

1 x fifty pence coin.

1 x ten pence coin.

1 x twenty pence coin.

1 x penny coin.

1 x Canadian 25 cent coin.

1 x English new pence.

BLACK PLASTIC BAG 2

1 x Sony portable clock radio.

1 x Brown coloured Brett Whiteley personal diary.

1 x Box containing 2 bottles of herbal cleansing tablets.

1 x Paperback novel titled *Sap Rising*.

1 x *Road and Track* magazine.

1 x Gold plastic travel bag, WH Smith, containing 1 cassette tape entitled *Beast*, 3 cakes of dinosaur soap, 1 tube of poly sporin antibiotic ointment, 1 empty Aquarius brand pill box, 1 Elvis Presley pocket knife 1 x toiletry bag containing 1 tube of gel cleanser, 1 x spray pack containing purple liquid, 1 x box containing Nicotinell Smoking Patches, 1 pair grey underpants, Skinny brand, 1 compact of shoe cleaning foam, 3 x 24 exposure of unused film, 1 tube of Red Earth brand moisturiser, 1 bottle of Gillette antiperspirant, 1 tube of Arm and Hammer brand toothpaste, 1 bottle of Juniper Shampoo, 1 black leather wristband, 1 blue toothbrush, 1 x yellow cigarette lighter, 1 x Sensor razor.

8 x Family photographs.

1 x Cardboard box containing toy tiger.

1 x Vamp Modern personal ashtray.

2 x Mini digital video cassettes.

1 x Sony micro cassette container.

1 x Note on Wyndham Hotels and Resorts paper.

1 x One page unsigned letter on Ritz Carlton note paper.

1 x Yellow ruled writing pad with three loose pages pencilled writing.

1 x INXS rehearsal schedule.
1 x INXS media/promotional schedule

SAMSONITE SUITCASE
1 x Gold and brown tie.
1 x Gold and brown mesh shirt.
1 x Beige striped slacks.
1 x Beige singlet.
1 x Black jeans.
1 x Cream shorts
1 x Blue and white check slacks.
1 x Black velour hooded jumper.
1 x Green knitted T-shirt.
1 x Floral and cream shirt.
1 x Black pinstriped slacks.
1 x Surfboard design T-shirt.
1 x White long sleeved shirt.
1 x Black striped long sleeved shirt.
1 x Yellow coloured flowered casual trousers and shirt (pyjamas)
1 x Black cotton casual shirt.
1 x Navy blue long sleeved casual shirt.
1 x Black and gold cloth (sarong)
1 x Pink cashmere jumper.
1 x Navy blue oriental design casual shirt.
1 x Light blue long sleeve shirt with white trim.
1 x Grey and black casual slacks.
1 x Red white and blue casual shirt.
1 x Beige casual slacks.
1 x Black track suit bottoms.
1 x Black sock.
1 x Pair of Blundstone boots.
1 x Pair of Airwalk brand joggers.
1 x Pair of brown C.O.X. sandals.

BLACK CANVAS TYPE SUITCASE

TOP OUTSIDE POCKET

1 x Compact disc *Apogee*

BOTTOM OUTSIDE POCKET

1 x Compact disc zippered holder containing assorted compact discs.
1 x Envelope containing facsimile to Martha (Troup) re: television series for Paula.
1 x Envelope and letter from Joaan Bengtson Sweden.
1 x Envelope from Le Parker Meridian containing photograph, note and telephone account.
2 x Compact discs.
1 x Small Case Logic compact disc zippered holder containing compact discs.
1 x Novel *Between Thought and Expression, the Lyrics of Lou Reed,* inside, 1 English 5 pound note.
1 x Black sock.
1 x Polaroid photograph.

INSIDE SUITCASE

1 x Beige purse containing, 3 x pairs of underpants and 1 x pair socks.
1 x Black mid length leather jacket.
1 x Nylon mid length waterproof jacket.
1 x Black mid length jacket.
1 x Blue velour mid length jacket.
1 x Pair of Costume Homme black pants.
1 x Pair of John Richmond green suit pants.
1 x Pair of Gucci green pants.
1 x Pair of Levi navy pants.
1 x Mambo blue casual shirt.
1 x Diesel Industry navy jeans.
1 x Maroon and purple gym long sleeve pullover.
1 x Dolce & Gabbana black and white striped casual top.

1 x Cream coloured underpants.

1 x Carol Christian Poell white longs sleeve shirt.

1 x Catalini boxer shorts.

1 x Beige purse containing 1 pair of underpants, 1 x orange tie, 1 black casual shirt sleeveless.

1 x Black La Rocka sports jacket.

1 x Black and blue Body brand T-shirt.

1 x Pair black underpants.

1 x John Richmond Green coloured suit jacket containing 2 x fifty-pound English notes, 1 x photographs, 1 note with the word Michael on it.

1 x Pair cream underpants.

1 x Black T-shirt with oriental motif.

1 x Brown Costume National brand sports jacket.

1 x Grey and blue short sleeve casual shirt.

1 x Blue silk short sleeve shirt.

1 x Salmon long sleeve shirt.

1 x Grey and black T-shirt.

1 x Black vest.

1 x Black long sleeve DKNY mesh pullover.

1 x Brown, gold and beige sarong.

1 x Black beige boxer shorts.

1 x Black John Bartlett long sleeve shirt.

1 x Black Changes Kitchen T-shirt.

1 x Black Calvin Klein singlet.

1 x Gold and purple singlet.

1 x Black Ron Herman casual shirt with oriental motif.

2 x Odd black socks.

1 x Pair black boots.

appendix 2

FOUND NOTE MADE BY MICHAEL IN THE
EARLY DAYS OF THE BAND.

Born in Sydney 1960

Family moved to Hong Kong (1964)

One younger brother Rhett and an older step sister Tina to my mother her first marriage out of three.

Father is and always will be in the rag trade. Claims he'll be a millionaire any day now. And will be By God. Lives in the Philippines at the moment as parents divorced and has set up factory for exporting Italian design cheap labour fashion junk by the container loads. It's actually good stuff! Known to charm the pants off anyone.

Mother is a make-up artist, was always professionally minded and worked on many movies from Hong Kong and Europe. She was a 60s woman gaining her independence (so to speak) and this was not a delight to my father (the beginning of the end).

Parents were cosmo-socialites in the papers gossip columns etc. embarrassing at times but lots of parties and groooovy people around us (claim to fame) meeting Natasha Kinski at 7 or 8 years old with her father Klaus and beautiful mother. All sorts of people and this included musicians and very loud soul music being played all the weekends, I was drawn in by the energy of the creative types and started playing records all the time. Motown was my favourite along with some classical and then to RnB/heavy metal/the Beatles etc. etc. etc.

Started an acoustic band in Hong Kong, and took about a year and half of acting lessons at 12 years old. Did some modelling as well to buy things.

Went to an excellent high school, King George V and was doing very well. Although maths wasn't my forte.

I loved Hong Kong. Its every changing contrasts a fantasy to grow up in, although it didn't prepare me for Australia's middle class sensibilities. The same old thing. No culture, lots of 'g'day mate' and the worst education system (I still can't spell because I hated my teacher, very Freudian.) Actually had my 4th form English project given the boot as teachers would not believe I wrote it, what the hell,

I'll start pleasing myself and so begins my career of writing prose and also a lot of rubbish.

Moved to Sydney again when I was 13. My first day at high school was shock shock!! Got cornered by the heavies and along comes Andrew Farris and a large friend to stop me from putting shit on everyone in my HK accent and stop the bashing too. Quite a funny meeting that. Turned into a long friendship. Andrew and I being the sensitive souls we started making music our prime motive in life and eventually with the help of others recorded a lot of experimental music in garages living rooms etc. Andrew had a few bands but I wasn't in them, just an innocent bystander, then due to 'Divine Intervention' he needed another singer (thought I had potential) and I sang along while they auditioned a drummer. He was no good and we came upon Jon in a sweep of logic. He was in the same house too! So the beginnings of a band were formed. Then Gary was found on a beach somewhere, we needed another guitarist and Tim was found under the breakfast table one morning. Alas my voice was terrible and Kirk joined up to give us lovely back up vocals.

Next I moved to Perth and my move from being a hippoid type searching for an ideal to a subterranean!! (Apologies to Kerouac.)

Met a girl who 'worked' and got in with all that scene. Madams/cops/gangsters/money/dark poetry/general assortment of decadence. Nothing shocks me anymore but I'm searching.

Read a lot of beat writers work. Went to poetry readings—many strange friends loved every second.

Moved back to Sydney with our new songs and hopes high that we wouldn't starve for too long.

We must have been doing something right because one thing leads to another and suddenly the band now INXS was gaining popularity fast. And I was also becoming a 'lead singer'. It sort of crept up on me.

appendix 4

EULOGY BY RHETT HUTCHENCE ON ANNIVERSARY OF MICHAEL'S DEATH

One year ago exactly, I was out buying some new sunglasses, and I came home to find out I'd lost my brother, I do however still have my sunnies. God works in mysterious ways.

For the first few weeks after Michael's untimely death, one line of his many lyrics kept playing in my head. It was from 'Bitter Tears' and the line was 'And I thought I was doing no wrong'.

And to be honest I don't believe he thought he was. Or he realised the full ramifications of his actions. Not that it would have made a difference at the time.

One year, long in grief and short in time. And one where it seems some people's grief has been manifesting in anger, the pain of loss.

In the eternal cycle of life, death, and rebirth, life is constantly presenting us with opportunities to totally let go of what encumbers us, in order for us to fully embrace life with fresh openness, and forgiveness plays a major part.

Unless we have full gratitude for those we have loved how can we expect the fragile bud of rebirth to emerge within us.

It is time to let go, time to forgive.

The past cannot be changed, remember Michael with love and joy, not misery.

We are here on the anniversary of his death. We are here to celebrate his life.

If Michael's death was a tragedy, his life was not. And how does one sum up such a full life.

The beauty is that some of his many talents will surface forever, due to the huge legacy he left us all, in a dozen albums, hundreds of songs, and the performance of thousands of truly memorable shows, all around the globe. Sometimes I feel Michael is everywhere, literally.

Michael, the poet, the lyricist, the natural performer certainly kicked his goal of world domination.

The hardest thing for me to reconcile is the death of Michael Hutchence, the normal human being. The ordinary man with an extraordinary life.

It's Michael, the searcher, the explorer, the healer, the big brother, the kind gentle sensitive loving man that I miss.

Thank God for memories.

It hurts that I won't hear his spoken word, even if it was rousing on me, or feel in my heart the roar of the crowd when he stepped on stage.

I truly feel proud and honoured to have known him and lucky to have spent some of the best years of my life with him, and I cherish those memories.

I would never have wanted it to turn out this way, however Michael's death has been my rebirth. It is the least I can do for him.

How we live and how we die are less than a breath apart.

Rock on mate, I love you.

I'd like to let go with a poem:

Please take a few soft breaths
As we move
From one level to the next
As in growth, or dying
We need to let go
At the edge
To continue further
Trust the process
Let go lightly
Pass on gently